The Three Images of Ethnic War

The Three Images of Ethnic War

Querine Hanlon

The Changing Face of War
James Jay Carafano, Series Editor

PRAEGER SECURITY INTERNATIONAL
Westport, Connecticut • London

Library of Congress Cataloging-in-Publication Data

Hanlon, Querine, 1969-
   The three images of ethnic war / Querine Hanlon.
     p. cm. — (The changing face of war, ISSN 1937-5271)
   Includes bibliographical references and index.
   ISBN 978-0-313-35682-7 (alk. paper)
  1. Ethnic conflict. 2. Ethnic conflict—Case studies. I. Title.
  GN496.H366 2009
  305.8—dc22   2008052699

British Library Cataloguing in Publication Data is available.

Library of Congress Catalog Card Number: 2008052699

ISBN: 978-0-313-35682-7
ISSN: 1937-5271

First published in 2009

Praeger Security International, 88 Post Road West, Westport, CT 06881
An imprint of Greenwood Publishing Group, Inc.
www.praeger.com

Printed in the United States of America

The paper used in this book complies with the
Permanent Paper Standard issued by the National
Information Standards Organization (Z39.48-1984).

10 9 8 7 6 5 4 3 2 1

For
Peter
and for
Grace, Kevin, Joseph, and Caroline

Contents

Acknowledgments

I am deeply grateful for the support and guidance from my colleagues, friends, and family who made this book possible. Dr. Richard Shultz guided my early study of ethnic violence, and his continued support during the writing of this book has been invaluable. I am also grateful for the guidance that Dr. Robert L. Pfaltzgraff and Dr. Sugata Bose provided for the early draft of this book. I owe a debt of gratitude to my colleagues at National Defense University, whose support and encouragement helped make this book possible. Much gratitude also goes to my parents, Evert and Titia Heynneman, for the wonderful education they gave me. Last but certainly not least, I am deeply grateful to my family, my husband Peter, and our four children, Grace, Kevin, Joseph, and Caroline, for their patience and understanding. This book competed for my time, and I am grateful for their enthusiastic support.

1
Chapter A Multilevel Framework

INTRODUCTION

In August 2008, a column of Russian Federation tanks entered the former Soviet Republic of Georgia ostensibly to protect ethnic Ossetians from Georgian ethnic cleansing. Although the Georgians vigorously denied the pretext for the Russian invasion, Georgian forces had entered the separatist province of South Ossetia, after intense shelling of Georgian enclaves by the rival Ossetians.[1] In the days following the Russian invasion, Russian forces penetrated deep into Georgia proper and forcibly evicted the remaining Georgians from Abkhazia, another separatist region in Georgia. The violence prompted an immediate response from the international community. France's president, representing the European Union, brokered a ceasefire aimed at Russian withdrawal, and the United States publicly questioned its strategic relationship with Russia.[2]

At first glance, the violence in Georgia can be seen as a consequence of the westward expansion of U.S. influence and the diminution of Russia's superpower status. These are *systemic* reasons why violence erupted in Georgia. Yet the conflict is also inextricably tied to Tbilisi's desire to consolidate its authority over Georgian territory and to redefine the post-Soviet republic as a *Georgian* state. Thus, the idea of Georgia as belonging to all its inhabitants, as well as the desire to enhance the capacity, authority, and legitimacy of Georgia's government, suggests that there are distinct reasons why groups adopt violent means that belong to the *state* arena. Finally, ethnic war in Georgia is also, at its root, a conflict over competing identities that are interwoven with ties to ethnic homelands, to fears of group survival and swamping by ethnic strangers, and to key decisions by competing ethnic leaderships that trigger political closure and deepen ethnic cleavages. These reasons are linked to aspects of *group* identity.

We see in the Georgian conflict not a single cause of ethnic war but patterns of causes at the three levels of analysis—the group, the state, and the international.

These are the three images of ethnic war. At each image, we find distinct reasons why ethnic groups adopt violent means. How are the causes of ethnic violence at each of these three images related, and how does this relationship further our understanding of why groups adopt violent means?

The central argument of this book is that ethnic violence is a complex and multifaceted phenomenon. The numerous reasons why groups adopt violent means against ethnic strangers or the state controlled by ethnic strangers can only be understood through a multilevel framework that incorporates both the three images of ethnic war and the interrelationships among them.

UNDERSTANDING THE RESURGENCE OF ETHNICITY

Why do ethnic groups adopt violent means? In the 1990s, an upsurge of violence brought this question to the fore. In the Balkans, the Caucasus, Central Asia, and the Middle East, and across Africa, Asia, and Latin America, ethnicity emerged as the principle source of organized violence around the world.[3] Wars in these regions were no longer internal conflicts between substate actors. They challenged state sovereignty and taxed the international community's ability to respond. They also introduced new terms into the ethnic conflict lexicon. In places like Rwanda and Bosnia, "ethnic cleansing" became the new term of art for a centuries-old practice of ethnic homogenization. These strategies were employed not against a nameless foe but against "enemies intimately known."[4] At the other extreme, the global phenomenon of societal violence became the basis for a new paradigm of civilizational conflict in which fundamentally *dissimilar* groups clashed along faultlines.[5] Theories highlighting the themes of both local intimacy and systemic dissimilarity ignored the role of the state despite the fact that many conflicts were triggered by state collapse and were fought by groups that aimed to create *new* states.

The violent conflagration that accompanied Yugoslavia's collapse demonstrated that ethnicity, far from being an anachronism on the verge of disappearance, was the most readily activated and most intense political emotion of the contemporary era.[6] Rather than being a relic of the past, the power of local identity in places like Bosnia and Chechnya was changing the nature of war. This was the position of the "new war" theorists, who saw in Bosnia a harbinger of the future: with the demise of the Westphalian state, interstate conflict would be replaced by local conflagrations between adjacent ethnicities.[7] New war would be fought "*amongst* the people."[8]

By the end of the 1990s, the global magnitude of such conflicts began to diminish. The number of major societal wars declined, and ethnonational wars declined to their lowest level since 1960.[9] Despite these positive trends, ethnic conflict remained a leading threat to international security as the violence in Kosovo, Chechnya, and Iraq demonstrates. In 2005, the most recent year of complete data, the trend shifted, and the number of active conflicts rose sharply.[10] The renewed violence in Georgia, where conflict was essentially "frozen" between 1992 and 1998, suggests that this upward trend continues.

Notwithstanding the attention paid to the systemic implications of the rising power of substate actors and the eroding power of the state, most of the ethnic conflict literature focused on single levels of analysis, and, with few exceptions, most of that effort focused on the ethnic group. Ethnic violence was attributed to individual motivations,[11] modern hatreds and symbolic politics,[12] elite manipulation,[13] or elite demobilization.[14] Gradually the "neglected dimension" of the international system was addressed in studies that emphasized why states intervened in ethnic conflict.[15] These were followed by a spate of studies that focused on subcategories or *types* of ethnic violence, such as the ethnic riot,[16] collective violence,[17] ethnic cleansing,[18] or ethnic terrorism.[19]

Much of the work on ethnic conflict remains divorced from the study of systemic change and the declining authority, capacity, and legitimacy of weak multiethnic states. This book attempts to bridge these gaps. It argues that the phenomenon of ethnic violence must be understood though a multilevel approach—one that addresses the three images of ethnic war and the interrelationships among them.

THREE IMAGES

This book develops a multilevel theory of ethnic violence using Waltz's three levels of analysis to answer the question of why ethnic groups adopt violent means. In *Man, the State and War*, Waltz develops three "images" or levels of analyses based on classical political theory to answer the question, "Where are the major causes of war to be found?" He groups the explanations for the causes of war at three different loci: within man, within the structure of individual states, and within the state system.[20]

At the first level of analysis, it is the nature and behavior of man that is the primary cause of war.[21] Explanations at the individual level focus on humanity's battle between passion and reason. Those who accept a first image explanation of war would argue that "the evilness of men, or their improper behavior, leads to war; individual goodness, if it could be universalized, would mean peace."[22] First image analysts, whether sanguine about the prospects for eradicating violence or not, share the assumption that in order to achieve a more peaceful world, mankind must be changed.

First image explanations of ethnic violence attribute violence to the ethnic group itself, to exclusivist passions and ethnic chauvinisms that spark violence. They focus on the process whereby nations are formed and whereby groups are differentiated from the "other." Here we see explanations that attribute violence to the transcendence of passion over reason, the resurgence of hatred, ancient or not. We also see explanations framed in terms of the strategies of ethnic elites who alternatively manipulate or inspire groups to demand recognition of group worth and status. Those who accept a first image explanation of ethnic violence believe that resolving ethnic war requires changing the ethnic group itself. For classical liberalism, the mechanism of change is education, information, science, progress, and modernity.[23] For realists, it is accepting the reality of ethnic violence and managing its impact. And for globalists, it is the creation of a cosmopolitan identity to replace the particularist identities of the old nation-state system.[24]

At the second image, the locus of war is found in the nature of individual states, the type of national government, or the character of a society. The argument that democracies are more peaceful, and authoritarian states more aggressive, is an example of a state-level argument. Those who accept a second image explanation of war believe that resolving war requires reforming the state itself. But how should the state be reformed? What defines a "good" state? The answers vary widely. For Karl Marx, it was ownership of the means of production, whereas for Woodrow Wilson, it was national self-determination that produced democracies, which were by definition peaceful.[25]

If we accept a second image explanation for ethnic violence, then we must ask the question of what defines a "good" *multiethnic* state? Some have argued that the answer lies in a federal or confederal structure and, until Yugoslavia's collapse, touted her model as a success. Others suggest that democratization is the only solution to ethnic violence in multiethnic states. This belief is reflected in the 2008 recognition of Kosovo. Both first and second image solutions assume the possibility for perfection in the conflicting units.

Finally, at the third level of analysis, the cause of war is found in the anarchical nature of the international system. Without effective overriding international authority, relations among states resemble a zero-sum game: an advance for one state is exactly equal to a loss for another. International organizations, when they function as intended, are only as effective as their membership's commitment to action. "There is a constant possibility of war in a world in which there are two or more states seeking to promote a set of interests and having no agency above them upon which they can rely for protection."[26] Those who accept a third image explanation of war argue that it is the search of imperfect states for security in a condition of anarchy that is the cause of war. That crises will arise is assumed rather than explained by third image analysts.

Third image explanations of ethnic violence focus upon the system itself as a cause of war. The system presents constraints and opportunities that shape a group's decision to adopt a strategy of ethnic violence. For globalists, an increasingly interdependent system has led to the decline of the state, creating an environment in which ethnic violence is not only possible but also likely. For realists, the collapse of the Cold War system eroded systemic constraints on ethnic mobilization that had long denied substate actors the right to a state of their own. Regardless of whether third image analysts believe effective international organization is possible, they see the cause of violence, and thus the solution, as existing at the international level: the system must be constrained or transformed.

PLAN OF THE BOOK

In this book, I employ Waltz's three levels of analysis to answer the question of why groups adopt violent means. Is ethnic violence a function of the group, of the state, or of the international system? Like Waltz, I conclude that there is considerable interdependence among the three images.[27] The answer can only be found in a systematic treatment of the causes of ethnic war at each of the three levels and of the interrelationships among them.

I begin by developing eight models to explain why ethnic groups adopt violent means. Chapter 2 introduces four group-level models, Chapter 3 introduces two state-level models, and Chapter 4 develops two systemic-level models to explain why groups adopt violent means.

Each of these models approaches violence from a different locus of initiative (group, state, or system) and focuses specifically on ethnic *violence* as opposed to ethnic *conflict*. Conflict describes a situation in which two or more parties pursue incompatible goals.[28] It encompasses both sporadic, small-scale violent incidents and sustained, large-scale violent wars. I focus on the latter category. I use the term "ethnic violence" to describe the sustained, large-scale use of violent means by ethnic groups against the "other," or against the state when one ethnic contender "owns" the state.

How then does "ethnic cleansing" differ from mere ethnic violence? I use the term ethnic cleansing to describe violence conducted by groups, not states, that has a specific *territorial* purpose. Ethnic cleansing connotes the forceful removal by an ethnic group of ethnic strangers in a given territory with the purpose of creating a homogenous population in that territory.[29] Ethnic cleansing thus includes both violent (expulsion or extermination) and nonviolent (deportation or forced population exchanges) means. Ethnic homogenization is ethnic cleansing conducted by the state.[30] It similarly includes both violent and nonviolent actions, such as forced religious conversion, assimilation, expulsion, and extermination.[31] It aims to create a homogeneous population within the boundaries of the state. At the extreme end of the spectrum of ethnic violence, we find genocide, which unlike ethnic cleansing and ethnic homogenization, is exclusively violent and can be conducted either by a state or by an ethnic group. It aims to exterminate an ethnic other in its entirety.[32] While the effect of genocide may be to remove ethnic strangers from a given territory, its purpose is not explicitly territorial. I will examine the full range of action encompassed by the term "ethnic violence," specifying particular forms of ethnic violence—cleansing, homogenization, or genocide—where relevant.

In Chapters 5–7, this multilevel framework is applied to three cases of violent ethnic war. Chapter 5 examines Yugoslavia's violent ethnic wars in Croatia, Bosnia, and Kosovo. Chapter 6 applies the framework to the war over Nagorno-Karabakh between ethnic Armenians and Azerbaijanis, and Chapter 7 examines the violence between Kurds and Arabs in Iraq. Chapter 8 explores the interaction of the models across the three images and draws some further conclusions about the nature of ethnic war.

THE MODELS AND PROPOSITIONS

At the first image, the reasons why groups adopt violent means are captured in four models of related propositions (see Table 1.1). The first is the *Homeland Model.* A homeland is a special category of territory. Ethnonationalists choose violent means to reclaim or defend a homeland because homeland ownership is vital to group identity (Proposition 1). Because they are regionally concentrated, ethnonationalists will likely attempt secession (Proposition 1.1), and because homeland claims are rarely unopposed, defense of a homeland will prompt ethnic cleansing (Proposition 1.2).

The second model is the *Ethnochauvinism Model.* Ethnic chauvinism prompts groups to adopt violent means because the group believes it is superior to the ethnic other and has the right to dominate it (Proposition 2). Dominance necessarily involves the segregation, deportation, expulsion, or annihilation of the ethnic other (Proposition 2.1) and raises the likelihood that groups will adopt more extreme forms of ethnic cleansing and even genocide (Proposition 2.2).

The *Group Survival Model* suggests that a threat to group survival will prompt groups to adopt violent means in self-defense (Proposition 3). There are four factors that lead groups to determine that their survival as a distinct ethnic group is threatened: a decrease in the absolute size of the ethnic group (Proposition 3.1), a decrease in group size relative to ethnic strangers (Proposition 3.2), a loss or lack of cultural autonomy (Proposition 3.3), and encroachment by the state or ethnic strangers on group land and resources (Proposition 3.4).

The final model at the group level is the *Ethnic Leadership Model.* In this model, an ethnic leadership determines whether violent means serve group interests and mobilizes group members in support of strategies of ethnic violence (Proposition 4). Charismatic leaders build on the charisma and appeal of the leadership to outmaneuver ethnic competitors in support of violent means (Proposition 4.1), whereas militant leaders promote violent means to co-opt more militant challengers and sideline moderates (Proposition 4.2). Factional leaders promote strategies of ethnic violence not only against the ethnic other but also against ethnic rivals to secure their position within the group (Proposition 4.3).

In Chapter 3, we turn to two models that explain the pivotal role of the state in the outbreak of ethnic violence (see Table 1.2). The state is both an arena and an actor in ethnic conflict. The *Weak State Model* suggests that interrelated authority, capacity, and legitimacy deficits limit the state's ability to respond to ethnic demands (Proposition 5). When a weak state offers concessions but lacks the will or capacity to implement them (Proposition 5.1), or when the state represses ethnic mobilization (Proposition 5.2), groups will adopt violent means to challenge the state's right to rule. In the case of severe repression, groups will temporarily refrain from adopting violent means (Proposition 5.3). However, if a state responds to ethnic mobilization with genuine concessions and the group is willing to settle for less than secession, then the likelihood of ethnic violence will decrease (Proposition 5.4).

Table 1.1 The First Image

Homeland Model	If possession of an ethnonational homeland is viewed as vital to an ethnic group's identity, then the group will adopt violent means either to defend the homeland or to reclaim it (Proposition 1). – Homeland ownership prompts ethnonationalists to secede (Proposition 1.1). – Defense of a homeland prompts ethnic cleansing (Proposition 1.2).
Ethnochauvinism Model	If ethnochauvinism is widely held to define group identity relative to the ethnic other, then there will be a strong tendency for the ethnic group to adopt violent means (Proposition 2). – Ethnochauvinism prompts the segregation, deportation, expulsion, or extermination of ethnic strangers (Proposition 2.1). – Ethnochauvinism raises the likelihood that groups will adopt more extreme forms of ethnic violence (Proposition 2.2).
Group Survival Model	If group members commonly believe that their very survival as a distinct ethnic group is threatened, then there will be a strong tendency for the group to adopt a strategy of ethnic violence in self-defense (Proposition 3). – If an ethnic group experiences a decrease in its absolute size within the same state or region, then the group may conclude that its survival as a distinct ethnic group is threatened (Proposition 3.1). – If an ethnic group experiences a decrease in its group size relative to ethnic strangers within the same state or region, then the group may conclude that its survival as a distinct ethnic group is threatened (Proposition 3.2). – If a group experiences a loss or lack of cultural autonomy, then the group may conclude that its survival as a distinct ethnic group is threatened (Proposition 3.3). – If an ethnic group experiences pressure on group lands and resources by ethnic strangers or the state controlled by ethnic strangers, then the group may conclude that its survival as a distinct ethnic group is threatened (Proposition 3.4).
Ethnic Leadership Model	If an ethnic leadership determines that group goals require violent means and if it acts successfully to mobilize group members in support of those means, then the group will adopt a strategy of interethnic violence (Proposition 4). – A charismatic leader will build a broad base of support among ethnic kindred for the adoption of a strategy of ethnic violence to secure group goals (Proposition 4.1). – A militant leadership will promote the adoption of a strategy of ethnic violence to sideline moderates and consolidate its position (Proposition 4.2). – Factional leaders will adopt violent means both to defeat rival factions and to secure group goals (Proposition 4.3).

Table 1.2 The Second Image

Weak State Model	If a state's authority, capacity, and legitimacy deficits prompt the denial or repression of ethnic group demands, the ethnic group is likely to adopt violent means to challenge the state (Proposition 5).
	– If a state offers concessions but fails to implement them, then the ethnic group will be more likely to adopt or resume violent means (Proposition 5.1).
	– If a state attempts to repress group mobilization and fails effectively to increase the costs of action to the group such that the costs outweigh the benefits, then the ethnic group will adopt violent means (Proposition 5.2).
	– Severe repression will temporarily suspend a group's strategy of violent resistance (Proposition 5.3).
	– If a state responds to ethnic mobilization with genuine concessions, then the group will be less likely to adopt violent means (Proposition 5.4).
Exclusion Model	If an ethnic group is excluded or is threatened with exclusion from the polity, then the ethnic group will be more likely to adopt violent means (Proposition 6).
	– If an ethnic group is threatened with exclusion from a polity, then the ethnic group will adopt violent means to protect its status (Proposition 6.1).
	– If an ethnic group is excluded from a polity, then the ethnic group will adopt violent means during transitions of rule to overturn the prevailing political-societal order (Proposition 6.2).
	– If an ethnic group faces permanent exclusion in a deeply divided society, then the group will adopt violent means to seize the state, or where the group is regionally concentrated, to secede (Proposition 6.3).

In multiethnic states, settlement and stratification patterns shape a state's response to ethnic mobilization. The *Exclusion Model* applies Donald Horowitz's typology of ranked and unranked systems to the choice of violent means. When an unranked ethnic group is excluded or threatened with exclusion from the state, the group may adopt violent means (Proposition 6) to protect its status (Proposition 6.1), to overturn the prevailing political societal order during transitions of rule (Proposition 6.2), or, in the case of permanent exclusion in deeply divided societies, to secede (Proposition 6.3).

Two final models are developed in Chapter 4. These capture the impact of third-party support, intervention, and resources at the systemic level (see Table 1.3). The first, the *External Support Model*, suggests that third-party support for a conflict with ethnic strangers will increase the likelihood that groups will adopt violent means (Proposition 7). Four scenarios describe this interaction.

Table 1.3 The Third Image

External Support Model	If an ethnic group secures external support for its conflict with ethnic strangers, then the ethnic group will be more likely to adopt violent means (Proposition 7).
	– If ethnic competitors secure third-party support, then the ethnic group will seek to offset the advantage, triggering escalation of the conflict and increasing the likelihood of violence (Proposition 7.1).
	– If third-party support deepens existing cleavages, awakens latent identities, or triggers factionalism and within-group conflict, then the likelihood of interethnic violence will increase (Proposition 7.2).
	– When third-party mediation is either biased or exclusionary, or when it selectively denies group aims, then the disadvantaged group will be more likely to adopt or resume violent means (Proposition 7.3).
	– If third parties recognize the secessionist bid of one or more groups while denying it to ethnic competitors, then the ethnic group will adopt a strategy of ethnic violence to claim the rump state or to secede (Proposition 7.4).
	– If third parties recognize the independence of one or more regionally concentrated groups while denying it to regionally dispersed groups, then the excluded groups will be more likely to adopt strategies of ethnic cleansing (Proposition 7.5).
Resource Model	If an ethnic group with grievances against ethnic strangers secures sufficient arms and resources to sustain a strategy of ethnic violence, then the group will be more likely to adopt violent means (Proposition 8).

The first suggests that third-party support will escalate conflict when ethnic competitors compete for alternate sources of third-party support to offset the group's advantage (Proposition 7.1). The second suggests that third-party support will trigger ethnic violence when it deepens existing cleavages, sparks mobilization of previously quiescent ethnicities, or triggers factionalism and within-group conflict (Proposition 7.2). Third-party mediation that favors one contending group over others or that deliberately excludes one group from the settlement process will prompt groups to adopt violent means (Proposition 7.3), whereas the combination of selective recognition of one group's secessionist bid and denial of recognition to ethnic contenders will prompt groups to resume violent means to seize the rump state or to secede (Proposition 7.4). When selective recognition denies state ownership to regionally dispersed groups, the disadvantaged group will adopt measures to cleanse the contested territory (Proposition 7.5).

The other third image model is the *Resource Model*. This model contends that the provision of essential arms and resources for ethnic war from either third-party suppliers (states, arms dealers, or diasporas) or domestic sources (battlefield capture, government armories, or domestic manufacture) will significantly raise the likelihood that a group with grievances against ethnic strangers or the state will adopt violent means (Proposition 8).

These models capture eight distinct reasons why groups adopt violent means. Waltz notes that "the superficial virtue of a single-cause explanation is that it permits a simple, neat solution."[33] In the cases below, it will become apparent that no such neat explanation exists.

THE CASES

In the second part of the book, each of the models at each of the three images of ethnic war is tested against three cases of violent ethnic conflict. These cases were selected for a number of reasons. First, all three conflicts exhibited high levels of ethnic violence rising to the level of interethnic war, including ethnic cleansing, mass rape, torture, chemical weapons attacks, forced population transfer, and even claims of genocide. Furthermore, all of the included cases were well documented and have since been studied in depth by regional experts. In fact, most of the recent work on ethnic violence deals with some or all of these case studies. In addition, all three cases involved multiple ethnic groups with a history of both violent and nonviolent interactions. Two of the conflicts occurred in the midst of state collapse, the third showed the impact of both state power and state weakness at various stages over the decades of conflict studied, and all three cases involved significant and extensive international support. All three cases thus had a degree of sustained ethnic violence sufficient to develop the theory and against which to test the models.

Yugoslavia

Chapter 5 applies the models to three interrelated conflicts in Croatia between Serbs and Croats; subsequently in Bosnia among Serbs, Croats, and Bosnian Muslims; and finally in Kosovo between Serbs and ethnic Albanians (Kosovars). These wars span nearly a decade, although the roots of the conflict go back at least as far as the founding of postwar Yugoslavia. Because of the multiple ethnic groups involved, the extensive violence, and the significant involvement of third parties, this case allows for the testing of the entire framework. The Yugoslav case study also demonstrates a considerable interdependence among the eight models.

Nagorno-Karabakh

The 1988–1994 war between Armenians and Azerbaijanis over Nagorno-Karabakh, an enclave in Azerbaijan with a large Armenian population, was the first serious ethnic conflict that emerged out of the Soviet collapse. It began as a large-scale protest movement in 1988, the first real test of the policies of *glasnost* and *perestroika*; escalated to a full-scale conventional war in 1992; and was finally halted by a tenuous ceasefire in 1994. Although the conflict between Armenians and Azerbaijanis is not ancient, the history of relations between these two groups is longer and more troubled than is the case with Yugoslavia or Iraq. Like Yugoslavia, the war in Nagorno-Karabakh erupted in the midst of state collapse. With the dissolution of the Soviet Union in December 1991, the three-year internal conflict was effectively transformed into a war between two independent, post-Soviet republics. Although a tenuous ceasefire remains in place, sporadic violence continues, making this conflict one of the most potentially dangerous "frozen conflicts" of the post–Cold War period.

Iraqi Kurdistan

Kurdistan, "the land of the Kurds," sits astride a major geopolitical crossroads in the Middle East, straddling the political boundaries of six states. The Kurds are the fourth-largest ethnic group in the Middle East and the largest ethnic group in the world without a state of their own. With the exception of a short-lived Kurdish Republic in Iran and persistent terrorism in Turkey, Kurdish resistance has centered in Iraqi Kurdistan, where the frequency, scale, and duration of violence have been the greatest. As in the case of Yugoslavia and Nagorno-Karabakh, the violence in Iraqi Kurdistan demonstrates the considerable interdependence among the models at the three images of ethnic war.

EXPECTATIONS

In Chapter 8, I return to the initial question framed by Waltz's three images: Where are the sources of violence to be found? A multilevel approach highlights the significant interrelationships among the models across the three levels of analysis.

Homeland claims are claims against the other, but they are also claims against the state. An ethnochauvinist group that is excluded is more likely to employ violent means both to ensure its own inclusion and to dominate the inferior "other." A weak state's response to ethnic mobilization, whether through partial accommodation or repression, adds a state-level threat to group survival. And an ethnic leadership is more likely to defeat moderate challengers and adopt violent means when subjected to state repression or exclusion. The provision of third-party support and resources enables groups to adopt violent means against the ethnic other or the state to secure a homeland, dominate ethnic strangers, ensure the survival of the group, and realize group aims. The perception of bias on the part of mediators erodes support for moderates and increases the likelihood that an ethnic leadership will resume violent means, particularly when a homeland or exclusion is at stake. Finally, selective recognition not only increases the likelihood of violence: it also offers a third image explanation for the more extreme forms of ethnic violence.

A multilevel approach corrects the tendency in much of the literature on ethnic conflict to focus exclusively on a single level of analysis. These single-level explanations, captured in eight distinct models at three levels of analysis, are compelling but incomplete. Ethnic violence is also a function of the interaction of the models across the three images of ethnic war. The myriad reasons why groups adopt violent means can only be understood through a multilevel framework of interrelated models and images.

2
Chapter

A First Image
Theory of Ethnic Violence

INTRODUCTION

First image explanations of violence suggest that humans are the primary cause of war. When we apply Waltz's first image to the study of ethnic violence, our primary actor is the ethnic group. First image explanations of ethnic violence focus on individual members of the ethnic group or on the group as a whole. In this chapter, four models capture the first image reasons why groups adopt violent means. These models draw on individual action, ethnic group emotion, and threats to ethnic identity to define the first image reasons why groups adopt violent means.

THE HOMELAND MODEL

Violent ethnic conflict is frequently fought over territory—not just any territory, but a homeland. A homeland is a special category of territory, the value of which derives not from its wealth of natural resources, proximity to the sea, or strategic value but from its vital place in the identity of the group who claims it. "No matter how barren, no territory is worthless if it is a homeland."[1] Rarely do homeland claims proceed unopposed. Contending groups lay claim to the same territory using both myth and historical fact to prove that they "arrived first" and thus have the right to claim "native status." Kosovar Albanians and Serbs both claim Kosovo as a homeland. As descendants of the ancient Ilyrian people, the Kosovar Albanians claim to have arrived first. For Serbs, however, Kosovo is the birthplace of the Serbian church and the symbol of the Serbs' resistance during centuries of Turkish occupation.

Wars fought over homelands are not only violent: they are frequently intractable. What ethnic leadership will countenance a settlement if, in giving up a portion of its homeland, the leadership risks the very survival of the ethnic group? Data from the *Minorities at Risk* study demonstrate that ethnonational groups are the most violent communal competitors[2] and that ethnonationalist rebellions are "the most protracted and deadly conflicts of the late twentieth century."[3] Clearly there is something about territory, and specifically about ethnonational homelands, that prompts protracted violent conflict.

The first model at the group level posits that ethnonational groups adopt strategies of ethnic violence to defend or reclaim a homeland threatened by ethnic strangers. We use the *Minorities at Risk* category of ethnonational groups to define the ethnic groups most likely to be motivated by homeland claims. Ethnonationalist groups are regionally concentrated ethnic groups that have an historical attachment to a homeland through a history of autonomy or self-rule in that homeland. They view possession of a homeland as vital to the group's identity. Ethnic identities are molded out of historical experiences, mytho-historical legacies, and particular traits that the group believes define it and distinguish it from the ethnic "other." These markers are self-selected by the group and include language, religion, ideas of inheritance, ancestry and descent, place of origin, kinship, and links with an historic homeland. For ethnonationalists, territory is the defining feature of group identity—not just any territory, but a homeland.

A homeland is vital to ethnonational group identity because it both defines the group and ensures its "continued existence as a distinct ethnic group."[4] A homeland is valuable not only for its symbolic value but also for the real benefits that groups derive from possessing it. A homeland may represent a group's golden age—a real or mythical greatness to which the group seeks to return. A homeland claim is frequently intertwined with historical events, whether in the near or distant past. A homeland can also be the site of an historical event deemed crucial to a group's identity, the location of a great cultural center, the site of past glories and critical battles against historic enemies, or the center of a great empire. This historical connection to a homeland need not be recent to resonate with members of the ethnic group.

Owning one's homeland also brings concrete benefits. Homeland ownership means that groups can enact language and education policies to ensure that future generations continue to identify themselves as members of the group. It also protects place names and historic sites and secures land ownership such that land can be passed or sold to members of the group. Finally, homeland ownership ensures that the ethnic group will retain its link to the homeland even if the group declines in size relative to ethnic strangers. Ethnonationalists believe homeland ownership to be essential for their own survival.[5] Homeland ownership guards against the erosion of group identity and protects the existence of the group.

Homeland claims are frequently justified in terms of blood and tenure—how much blood has been spilled protecting or claiming a homeland and how long the group has owned the homeland. Groups will justify their rightful ownership of a homeland based on the number of group members who have been sacrificed defending or reclaiming that homeland. Even if the group no longer constitutes a majority of the population, ethnonationalists argue that blood spilled protecting the homeland entitles them to ownership of the territory, over the claims of "outsiders." Tenure further buttresses the claim, even though ownership may be a distant historical fact. Homeland claims based on tenure are frequently exclusionary: a group that claims "native status" maintains that because it arrived first, the contested territory belongs exclusively to that group. Native status also implies that a group has the moral right to own or rule the homeland, even if the group does not constitute a majority of the population in the contested territory. Blood and tenure claims explain in part why ethnonationalist wars over homelands are so intractable. Neither claim can be resolved through negotiations if what is at stake is the basis of the group's very identity. To negotiate is to deny one's identity; to continue fighting is to protect and affirm it.

Ethnonationalists adopt a strategy of violent interethnic warfare to reclaim or defend an ethnic homeland because failure to do so threatens the very existence of the group. The first proposition for why groups adopt violent means is as follows:

> If possession of an ethnonational homeland is viewed as vital to an ethnic group's identity, then the group will adopt violent means either to defend the homeland or to reclaim it (Proposition 1).

Is violence the only alternative for achieving ethnonationalists' aims? To ignore the loss of the group's homeland to ethnic strangers is to deny the group's identity. To compromise, or to accept alternatives that guarantee less than complete ownership of a homeland, threatens the survival of the group. Ethnic conflict is frequently zero-sum. When the occupation of a homeland is thwarted by the presence of ethnic strangers in that territory, or when ethnic strangers contend for the ownership of a homeland, ethnonational groups may conclude that there is no alternative to violence and no room for compromise.

Homeland ownership also prompts groups to adopt violent means because solutions short of complete ownership fail to protect the group's identity and existence. Ethnonationalist groups are thus rarely willing to settle for autonomy. Because ethnonationalists are regionally concentrated, homeland claims are essentially demands for national self-determination. Autonomy is "a second-best option" when groups determine "that their claims to independent statehood are unlikely to be fulfilled" or when "their ability to survive as an independent state or to provide essential services to their citizens would be limited."[6] Because ethnonationalists are regionally concentrated, and because they are rarely willing to settle for autonomy, homeland ownership will prompt groups to attempt secession. The tendency to choose secession over autonomy is expressed in the following subproposition:

> Homeland ownership prompts ethnonationalists to secede (Proposition 1.1).

Although the dissolution of the Soviet Union and Yugoslavia created conditions wherein secession was achieved with little or no violence, such conditions are the rare exception, rather than the rule. By its nature, a strategy aimed at secession has a very high likelihood of being violent and protracted, pitting the ethnic group against the state—both of which are fighting to survive.

Ethnonationalists are also likely to adopt violent means when homeland ownership is threatened by ethnic strangers or by the state. Because ethnonationalist groups are regionally concentrated, many "own" their homeland. When that ownership is challenged by ethnic strangers through in-migration, higher birthrates, or government resettlement policies, ethnonationalists may adopt strategies of ethnic cleansing. These strategies aim to remove ethnic strangers by expelling or killing them. Because homeland ownership is vital to group identity and survival, the group must protect the homeland. This tendency to adopt a strategy aimed at ethnic homogenization is expressed in the following subproposition:

Defense of a homeland prompts ethnic cleansing (Proposition 1.2).

Homeland ownership ensures ethnonationalist group survival. Groups will adopt violent means not only to reclaim a homeland, but also to defend it. Cleansing that homeland of ethnic strangers, whether by killing or otherwise expelling them, protects homeland ownership and ensures the survival of the group.

Because homeland possession is such a vital component of group identity, ethnonationalists will contemplate a strategy of ethnic violence even when the likelihood of success is low. When groups conflict over the right to exclusive ownership of a homeland, violence is likely to be protracted. When ethnonationalists fail to achieve their objectives because of exhaustion, severe repression, or the loss of third-party support, among other reasons, there is also a strong tendency that conflict will resume. Because homeland ownership is vital to group identity, ethnonationalist groups will repeatedly adopt violent means after previous attempts fail.

THE ETHNOCHAUVINISM MODEL

Ethnic identities define an ethnic group and demarcate the boundaries that separate that group from the ethnic "other." When an ethnic group experiences intensified political and economic competition or sudden shifts in group position or power relative to ethnic strangers, these boundaries become more sharply defined. In the process, the attributes that define the group are brought into greater congruence with each other, and group identity is solidified.[7] This process of boundary demarcation involves "political closure."[8] Political closure occurs when an external threat to the group propels greater cohesion among group members. Competing nonethnic identities of clan, tribe, or class erode as group members come to identity themselves exclusively in ethnic terms. Political closure is frequently driven by fear—fear of imminent group extinction, erosion of group identity, or loss of group dominance over ethnic strangers. When the ethnic other is blamed for the group's predicament, then the other is not only a stranger but also an enemy.

Ethnic chauvinism emerges when political closure centers on notions of group superiority. Group members come to believe that their collective identity—their attributes, symbols, myths, and historical experiences—is not only distinct from, but *superior* to, the ethnic other. Ethnic chauvinism is the "belief that one's own group is *better* than others, and therefore has the right to dominate or displace them."[9] As Hannah Arendt suggests, the chauvinist mystique is about more than superiority: "it claims its people to be unique, individual, incompatible with all others."[10]

Ethnochauvinism frequently draws on a group's history or mythology—what Anthony Smith terms "myths of ethnic chosenness"[11]—to create a narrative of superiority that has wide appeal among group members. These narratives of superiority create a sense among group members that they share both a common history and a common destiny. These narratives extol a group's historical mission or role as the guardians of a faith, territory, or identity, detailing past sacrifice and suffering. Although these narratives may be loosely or closely based on historical fact, what matters most is their meaning for group identity. The group achieved greatness by virtue of its superior attributes, its capacity for suffering and survival, and its achievement of an historic mission.[12] These myths "prove" a group's collective superiority over inferior others and also justify dominance: a group's historic achievements entitle it to primacy over inferior groups.

Narratives of superiority, when they focus on past suffering at the hands of ethnic strangers, are likely to spur efforts to redress past grievances and to avenge the group against "filthy outsiders and fifth columnists."[13] The reexamination of history, particularly of past violence perpetrated by the ethnic other, awakens feelings of national danger and solidifies group identity. As the past melds with the present, the group will mobilize against its "historic" enemy in modern guise to avenge itself, believing that its superiority justifies frequently violent measures aimed at securing the group's dominance over its historic enemy.

Ethnic chauvinism creates an environment that is conducive to violence. When group members are fearful, belief in the group's superiority assuages that fear, and belief in the group's right to dominate the inferior other justifies violent action. When a collective sense of superiority and rightful dominance is widely held, it justifies violent means of dominating the ethnic other. A second source of ethnic violence is thus reflected in the following proposition:

> If ethnochauvinism is widely held to define group identity relative to the ethnic other, then there will be a strong tendency for the ethnic group to adopt violent means (Proposition 2).

Ethnochauvinism not only justifies violence: it also defines the objective for which violent means are employed. Securing a group's dominance over ethnic strangers necessarily entails the segregation, deportation, expulsion, or extermination of ethnic strangers—objectives that are rarely achievable without violence.

The following subproposition addresses the goals for which ethnochauvinists adopt violent means:

> Ethnochauvinism prompts the segregation, deportation, expulsion, or extermination of ethnic strangers (Proposition 2.1).

Ethnochauvinism also increases the likelihood that groups will adopt more extreme forms of ethnic violence. Ethnochauvinism "denies theoretically the very possibility of a common mankind long before it is used to destroy the humanity of man."[14] As the targeted group is dehumanized, the moral and ethical constraints on killing erode. Ethnic neighbors are no longer merely inferior: they are subhuman. Dehumanization of the enemy thus combines with feelings of superiority and with belief in the right to dominate, which together engender widening support for a strategy aimed at the physical destruction of an entire ethnic group. This tendency to extreme violence is reflected in the following subproposition:

> Ethnochauvinism raises the likelihood that groups will adopt more extreme forms of ethnic violence (Proposition 2.2).

Is there no hope for moderates to challenge chauvinist policies? Chauvinism narrows the available options for moderate constituencies to promote an alternate conception of the group that does not center on its superiority and right to dominate the ethnic other. Ethnic chauvinism can be elite-led or mass-led. Chauvinist elites restrict group identity, such that alternate narratives have little resonance among fearful populations, leaving moderate elites with few options to meet group demands for dominance. The stark contrast between the superior group and the inferior other destroys any room for accommodation and compromise. To negotiate with the inferior stranger, particularly if that group is viewed as an historic enemy, presents moderate elites with the risk of being characterized, at best, as naïve sympathizers and, at worst, as traitors.

Mass-led chauvinism similarly restricts the options available to more moderate elements of the population. If ethnic chauvinism gains a wide following among the population of ethnic kindred, then more moderate factions may be intimidated or neutralized. Mass-led chauvinism may force a more moderate leadership to adopt increasingly militant policies to retain power. Whether elite- or mass-led, ethnic chauvinism destroys any room for negotiation and compromise and narrows the options available to moderates to counter the militant strategies engendered by ethnic chauvinism.

THE GROUP SURVIVAL MODEL

The outbreak of violent interethnic conflict can be traced to a real belief among members that their survival as a distinct ethnic group is threatened by the policies or actions of ethnic strangers. Just as the basic human response to a threat is to fight for self-preservation, so too will an ethnic group mobilize rapidly in self-defense when it experiences a serious threat to its survival as a distinct ethnic group.

Defensive group mobilization in response to a clear and present threat will produce a more rapid and aggressive collective response than will offensive group mobilization to exploit opportunities for uncertain future benefits.[15] A clear threat to group survival will lead groups to mobilize in self-defense and to adopt a strategy of interethnic violence against the ethnic strangers deemed responsible for the group's precarious position. A third proposition to explain ethnic violence is as follows:

> If group members commonly believe that their very survival as a distinct ethnic group is threatened, then there will be a strong tendency for the group to adopt violent means in self-defense (Proposition 3).

For our purposes, a threat to group survival is defined more broadly than a physical threat to individual group members. A threat to group survival is one that imperils the group's continued existence *as a separate and distinct ethnic group*. Four factors lead groups to determine that their survival is at risk: namely, the absolute decline of group size, the relative decline of group size, the loss or lack of cultural autonomy, and pressure on group lands and resources. Although they frequently operate in tandem, each of these factors provides sufficient cause for group mobilization and the adoption of violent means.

The first factor that leads groups to determine that their survival as a distinct ethnic group is at risk is a decrease in the *absolute* size of an ethnic group through declining birth rates, out-migration, forced resettlement and assimilation policies, deportation, expulsion, and massacre. As the size of the group diminishes, group members may fear that their continued survival as a distinct ethnic group is threatened. This first factor is laid out in the following subproposition:

> If an ethnic group experiences a decrease in its absolute size within the same state or region, then the group may conclude that its survival as a distinct ethnic group is threatened (Proposition 3.1).

As the absolute size of the group declines, ethnic groups come to fear that a demographically dominant population of ethnic strangers may dominate the group or subject it to social, political, economic, or religious discrimination.[16] Less immediate but equally threatening is the fear of eroding group boundaries and eventual assimilation. As their size declines, groups fear the potential loss of group status, particularly if that status is tied to the possession of a homeland, as is the case with ethnonationalists. Without adequate numbers to possess this territory or to ensure the group's continued distinct identity, it will mobilize in self-defense.

The second related factor is the fear of domination and demographic imbalance created by a decline in a group's size *relative* to ethnic strangers. These fears are precipitated by the in-migration of ethnic strangers, demographic pressures caused by higher birthrates among ethnic strangers, and government settlement and forced assimilation policies. In each instance, the absolute size of the group may not be declining, but the size of the group relative to ethnic strangers is declining. A second subproposition relating to group survival is as follows:

> If an ethnic group experiences a decrease in its group size relative to eth-
> nic strangers within the same state or region, then the group may con-
> clude that its survival as a distinct ethnic group is threatened
> (Proposition 3.2).

The decline in group size relative to ethnic strangers creates fear and appre-hension. These shifts frequently occur in significant numbers due to government supported in-migration, resettlement, and assimilation schemes. When the threatened group is regionally concentrated, such measures frequently provoke a separatist response.[17]

A third factor that leads groups to conclude that their continued survival is threatened is the loss or lack of cultural autonomy. Cultural autonomy relates to "the rights and symbolic dignity"[18] accorded to an ethnic group's language, cul-ture, history, and religious practices. The loss of group members or the decline of an ethnic group's position relative to ethnic strangers is often tied to declining or absent cultural autonomy, particularly when forced assimilation policies lead individuals to stop identifying themselves as members of the ethnic group. The central issue, however, is whether the group is granted the cultural freedom to ensure that members, particularly younger generations, continue to identify themselves as members of the ethnic group. Thus, a third subproposition relating to ethnic violence is as follows:

> If a group experiences a loss or lack of cultural autonomy, then the group
> may conclude that its survival as a distinct ethnic group is threatened
> (Proposition 3.3).

Conflict over cultural autonomy is based on any combination of issues. These include whether an ethnic group has the right to pursue openly its culture; whether it can educate its children in the group's language (and to what level); whether it can use the group's language in state institutions or in the regional administration of a homeland in which the group predominates; whether its language has official status in the region or state; whether cultural institutions are allowed to flourish; whether group members may publish in their language; whether they may teach the group's history to their children; and whether state or regional policies encour-age the legitimization of the group's culture or whether they ensure or promote assimilation with the culture and practices of ethnic strangers.

When public policy fails to legitimize, dignify, and reward ethnic pluralism, when it encourages cultural and social assimilation of minorities into the dominant community of ethnic strangers, and when it enforces legal or de facto inequality in status and treatment,[19] groups readily conclude that their survival is threatened. A group's culture is a vital element of group identity. A group that is unable to pass this identity on to its children or finds that its past ability to do so is threatened will mobilize to secure these rights and to strengthen group boundaries against ethnic strangers, and where regionally concentrated, will seek to secede from a state controlled by ethnic strangers.

A fourth factor that leads groups to determine that their survival as a distinct ethnic group is at risk is pressure on group lands and resources, what Ted Robert Gurr terms "ecological stress." According to Gurr, "ecological stress . . . is the single strongest correlate of separatism among most of the regionally concentrated minorities."[20] The destruction of villages or the confiscation of land under the guise of land reform creates ecological stress. Groups may face restrictions on their ability to buy land or access critical resources such as water. Regional boundaries may be redrawn to exclude valuable resources, such as oil fields or mines, from the group's homeland or autonomous region. Central authorities may pursue policies aimed at the deliberate neglect of regions where the ethnic group is concentrated. Such regions frequently experience less development relative to the rest of the state in terms of roads, dams, and irrigation projects. When such pressure is serious enough, group members may be forced to migrate out of the region, further reducing the group's size in both absolute and relative terms. What is critical to group survival is the impact such pressure has on a group's way of life. When identity is based on a particular way of life (such as farming or herding) or on particular geographic features (for instance, a desert or mountain), pressure on group lands and resources directly threatens the identity and survival of the group. When such pressure threatens group survival, groups are likely to adopt violent means to defend their way of life. A fourth subproposition is thus adapted from Gurr's *Minorities at Risk* project:

> If an ethnic group experiences pressure on group lands and resources by ethnic strangers or the state controlled by ethnic strangers, then the group may conclude that its survival as a distinct ethnic group is threatened (Proposition 3.4).

Does economic discrimination constitute a threat to group survival? Long-standing discrimination, particularly in resource distribution; rising expectations that fail to reflect existing rates of growth or development; and restricted access to wealth and to employment opportunities may prompt ethnic groups to mobilize in order to demand access, equality, and in many cases, the exclusion of ethnic strangers. However, claims of economic discrimination are likely to indicate an underlying grievance that has more to do with issues that endanger group identity than with economic position. As Walker Connor notes, "economic considerations may be an irritant that reinforces ethnic consciousness." However, when competing with "the emotionalism of ethnic nationalism," these economic factors "come in a poor second."[21]

Horowitz argues that "when ethnic conflict occurs, materialists tend to see it as an epiphenomenon, a manifestation of deeper economic conflicts that lie beneath the surface." Such a view is one that "systematically undervalues ethnicity and misunderstands ethnic conflict even when it perceives it to be present."[22] Claims of economic discrimination are employed to protect a group's relative prosperity equally often as they are used to secure access to resources necessary for a group's collective economic advancement. Economic discrimination, while important to group mobilization, is insufficiently grave to constitute a threat to group survival.

The absolute and relative decline of group size, the loss or lack of cultural autonomy, and pressure on group lands and resources, however, do provide sufficient cause for group mobilization and the choice of violent means. An ethnic group fighting for survival will be willing to take great risks and to suffer enormous losses. The fear of imminent group extinction will prompt groups to justify a wide range of measures to ensure their survival. Ensuring the survival of the group provides a strong motivation for the adoption of violent means in self-defense.

THE ETHNIC LEADERSHIP MODEL

The final group-level model defines the choice of violent means in terms of the decisions and actions taken by an ethnic leadership. An ethnic leadership is central to group mobilization, the decision to adopt violent means, and the implementation of a strategy to secure group goals. How and why ethnic leaders choose a strategy of ethnic violence varies. The ethnic leadership model develops three distinct pathways or scenarios that explain elite-led violence. Each demonstrates that ethnic leadership is necessary for sustained interethnic warfare.

The term "leadership" is used here in its broadest sense. Two categories of ethnic leaders affect the adoption of a strategy of interethnic violence—the political and military leadership, on one hand, and the ethnic intelligentsia on the other. The first group encompasses what is traditionally defined as a group's leadership, including politicians, party members, and bureaucrats as well as straight-line military leaders, paramilitary leaders, and other self-styled ethnic "generals." This group develops and implements a strategy of ethnic violence. The second category of ethnic leadership is the more broadly defined group of ethnic intelligentsia, the so-called "ethnic entrepreneurs"[23] who trigger political closure and mobilize the group against the threat and in support of a strategy of ethnic violence.

The first category of ethnic leaders, the group's political and military leadership, organizes and guides the struggle. This leadership determines if violence serves the interests of the group and of the leadership itself. It decides whether violence is necessary or optimal to defend the group or to improve or advance the group's position. These assessments guide the development of a group's political and military strategy. The ethnic leadership's strategic and operational assessments present one important threshold of violence: unless these assessments support the adoption of a strategy of interethnic war, elite-led ethnic violence is unlikely.

The political and military leadership secures the resources necessary to embark upon a strategy of violence. The group needs not only the arms and financial resources to undertake a strategy of violence, but also requires securing those arms and resources for the duration of the conflict. This key assessment presents a second important threshold to both elite and mass-led violence: without the necessary group resources, it is unlikely that groups can sustain a strategy of ethnic violence.

The political leadership must also secure external support and maintain such relationships to guard against being abandoned midway through the conflict. The External Support Model, discussed in Chapter 4, suggests that such support ultimately determines whether the group will reach its aims. The task of securing this support falls to the ethnic leadership.

Finally, an ethnic leadership must effectively silence or co-opt aspiring leaders who offer competing, nonethnic or anti-ethnic ideological or political strategies. To undermine internal challengers, an ethnic leadership must present all grievances as primarily ethnic as opposed to regional or class-based. To do so successfully requires the assistance of the second group of ethnic leaders, the ethnic historians, language unifiers, and cultural entrepreneurs.

This second category of ethnic leadership includes members of the group's academic and cultural elite, including religious leaders, historians, artists, poets, and writers. This broad group includes the "ethnic entrepreneurs" who define group identity and heighten awareness of group uniqueness; the "language unifiers" who seek to purify the language of foreign elements; and the "cultural entrepreneurs" who create "mytho-historical charters"[24] of group greatness through books, poetry, theater, music, films, and documentaries. Whereas the political and military leadership develops a strategy and organizes and deploys group resources available for the struggle, ethnic entrepreneurs tap a reservoir of group frustration and group pride.

Although ethnic entrepreneurs may not have direct access to the resources necessary for adopting a strategy of violence, their skills and following among members of the ethnic group are crucial to political closure. They vocalize the historically validated and morally justified group mission. They draw upon latent grievances and mold opinion regarding the dire nature of the threat to the group. They can build support for the political and military leadership and for the choice of violent means.

Whether it is the traditional political and military leadership or the ethnic intelligentsia or some combination of the two, this leadership assesses the group's resources and available strategies and drives the decision to adopt violent strategies of ethnic confrontation. The final proposition for understanding ethnic violence at the group level is as follows:

If an ethnic leadership determines that group goals require violent means and if it acts successfully to mobilize group members in support of those means, then the group will adopt a strategy of interethnic violence (Proposition 4).

How and why an ethnic leadership adopts a strategy of ethnic violence varies. Three scenarios suggest distinct ways leadership impacts the outbreak of ethnic violence: the charismatic leader scenario, the militant leader scenario, and the factional leader scenario. Each demonstrates that ethnic leadership is necessary for sustained interethnic warfare.

The *charismatic leader scenario* suggests that the choice of violent means is a function of a charismatic leadership's ability to mobilize support among ethnic kindred, to win over factions that initially oppose the strategy, and to undermine support for ethnic competitors by offering a more persuasively articulated rationale for violence. The charismatic leader is one who draws on his or her charisma and appeal to outmaneuver ethnic competitors. This charisma may derive from the attributes of a great leader or from a genuine commitment to the group's goals and aspirations. This scenario suggests the following subproposition:

A charismatic leader will build a broad base of support among ethnic kindred for the adoption of a strategy of ethnic violence to secure group goals (Proposition 4.1).

The *militant leader scenario* suggests that a strategy of violence is promoted by a militant leadership in an effort to sideline more moderate competitors and secure that leadership's hold on power. In this scenario, committed militant leaders may build a base of support among the population of ethnic kindred by outmaneuvering more moderate contenders. Effective use of the ethnic intelligentsia to prove that the militant leadership's policies serve the group's historic mission will broaden support for militant over moderate competitors. Alternatively, elites may adopt increasingly militant positions as a result of a growing consensus among ethnic kindred that violence is the only means by which to achieve group goals. Moderates may be forced to tap the same mass emotions that militant leaders draw upon in order to protect their flanks. In this instance, elites may adopt a more militant posture for fear of losing their position. According to Joseph Rothschild, "what has happened and is happening in many situations of interethnic violence is not that volatile and emotional ethnic masses slip out of the restraining leash of rational elites but that outbidding and outflanking counter elites seek to tap this mass emotional potential by inciting ethnopolitical radicalization."[25] This scenario suggests the following subproposition:

A militant leadership will promote the adoption of a strategy of ethnic violence to sideline moderates and consolidate its position (Proposition 4.2).

The *factional leader scenario* suggests that a strategy of violence is driven by violent within-group conflict among factional leaders to defeat rivals and assume undisputed leadership of the group. In this scenario, one faction will adopt violent means both to undermine rival factions and to achieve the group's broader objectives. The actions of factional leaders trigger internecine conflict that ultimately undermines broader group goals. Frequently, this scenario produces spiraling violence in which each faction escalates in the hope of finally defeating rival factions, and as the group is weakened by incessant within-group conflict, ethnic strangers or the state controlled by ethnic strangers capitalize on the growing weakness to undermine the group. The factional leader scenario results in significant costs to the group and decreases the likelihood of prevailing against ethnic strangers. The persistence of violence aimed at defeating rival factions will escalate both within-group violence and violence between the group and the ethnic other as each faction attempts to defeat the enemy and claim predominance within the group. This scenario is reflected in the following subproposition:

> Factional leaders will adopt violent means both to defeat rival factions and to secure group goals (Proposition 4.3).

Ethnic group leadership is a critical source of ethnic violence. Whether that leadership comprises the traditional political and military leaders or the ethnic intelligentsia, or both, ethnic leadership plays an important role in defining the threat, mobilizing the group around that threat, and adopting a strategy of ethnic violence. The charismatic leader scenario, the militant leader scenario, and the factional leader scenario suggest three distinct ways leadership impacts the outbreak of ethnic violence. Each demonstrates that ethnic leadership is necessary for sustained interethnic warfare.

CONCLUSION

The interaction of these first image models with those at the second and third images of ethnic war will enhance our understanding of why groups adopt violent means. We will return to this interaction in Chapter 8. There is also likely to be considerable interaction among the four models at the first image alone. A threat to a group homeland, particularly when it comes from a state-owning ethnic contender, is likely to trigger threats to group survival. Similarly, when ethnochauvinist beliefs in group superiority and rightful dominance operate in tandem with a homeland claim, the choice of violent means will likely tend to the extreme. Ethnic leadership interacts with each of the first image models—survival, chauvinism, and homeland claims—to shape how ethnic groups adopt violent means. In the case of the militant and factional leader scenarios, violence will likely escalate and risk the goals for which groups fight. When the goal is homeland ownership, the likelihood that war will protract significantly increases.

The interaction of the four first image models alone demonstrates that ethnic violence is complex and multifaceted. As we move on to the second and third images, we find an even greater degree of complexity. A multilevel framework provides an analytic tool to frame our understanding of why groups adopt violent means. The first image is the first component of this framework. The next two will follow.

3
Chapter

A Second Image
Theory of Ethnic Violence

INTRODUCTION

Second image explanations of war assume that the nature of the state, its regime, or the character of its society is the cause of war. The democratic peace thesis is an example of a second image explanation for war—or the absence of war. It suggests that democracies do not fight other democracies.[1] A corollary, that democracies are less likely to engage in war against non-democracies, however, has not been supported by the evidence. Other second image explanations, such as the more peaceful nature of communist regimes over capitalist ones or the more warlike nature of authoritarian governments, have similarly not held up to scrutiny. Second image explanations of *war between states* offer insight into, but do not provide a sufficient explanation for, the causes of war.

Second image explanations of *interethnic war*, however, are some of the most compelling. The state is the primary arena of ethnic conflict. The nature of the state, its regime, and the character of its society shape how and when ethnic conflict emerges, the escalation and frequency of violence, and the goals for which ethnic wars are fought. Most ethnic conflict occurs in weak states, and most weak states are multiethnic. These two state arenas—the multiethnic state and the weak state—are the key second image environments in which we find the causes of interethnic war. When the state is "owned" by one ethnic group, it also becomes a primary actor in ethnic war. These state arenas suggest two second image models to explain a group's choice of violent means.

THE ARENA OF ETHNIC CONFLICT

We begin by defining how the state serves as an arena of ethnic violence. A state can be defined in two realms: the international and the domestic. The first treats the state as a closed unit, the so-called billiard ball of International Relations

Theory.[2] All states possess juridical statehood and are sovereign actors in the international system. Internal aspects of the state are ignored. The state is defined by its territorial boundaries—even when, within those boundaries, government is weak or nonexistent and society is deeply fractured.[3] The emphasis here is on the interrelationship of sovereign units in the international system, a discussion that belongs to the third image. We will return to the interaction of states as an explanation for ethnic war in Chapter 4.

The second realm is inward-looking. It also treats the state as a unit but defines it in terms of three internal aspects. The first element is the political, defined as the interrelationship between the state's governing institutions and its society. The second element is the physical dimension of the state—the territorial confines that bound government and society. The final element is "a widespread and deeply rooted idea of the state among the population."[4] These three elements—the idea of the state, its territorial dimensions, and its political-societal expression—define the state arena in which ethnic conflict occurs. They also define "the prize to be occupied and exploited by contending ethnic groups."[5] Ethnic groups compete for the right to "own" the state and the right to define the idea of the state. When this right is claimed exclusively by one ethnic group in a multiethnic state, conflict inevitably follows.

Interethnic violence occurs predominantly in two kinds of states, the multiethnic state and the weak state. Some 90 percent of the 191 recognized states worldwide are multiethnic, and two-thirds contain three or more ethnic groups.[6] According to the 2007 Failed State Index, of the 177 states included, 60 met the 12 criteria for state weakness or failure.[7] When these 60 states are cross-referenced with *Minorities at Risk* data, it can be seen that all 60 of the weak states are also multiethnic states.[8] Of those 60 states, 57 have three or more con-centrated ethnic groups. It is apparent from the data that multiethnic states, and particularly weak multiethnic states, are the arenas of interethnic violence. Understanding how these state arenas impact the choice of violent means is thus the place to begin.

The Multiethnic State Arena

Multiethnic states are defined as states with two or more ethnic groups.[9] Not all multiethnic states face ethnic-based challenges, but when ethnic identity is politically salient, groups will mobilize along ethnic lines and make claims against the state that are framed in ethnic terms. Unlike homogenous states in which one ethnic group "owns" the state and national identity is uncontested, multiethnic states face the challenge of accommodating competing claims. Multiethnic states that successfully face this challenge are states in which ownership of the state is defined in the broadest and most inclusive terms.

In multiethnic states, the idea of the state can be expressed in two ways; the first is a broadly inclusive civic idea of the state, and the second is a more sharply exclusive ethnic or national state identity. The first limits the utility of mobilizing along ethnic lines. The second encourages mobilization along ethnic lines and, in sharply exclusive systems, so narrows the range of options as to leave only the ethnic one.

Civic nationalisms base their legitimacy on loyalty to a set of political ideals or institutions. In these states, inclusion is defined in terms of birth or long-term residence within the state.[10] Civic nationalisms are often founded on an ethnic core. Over time, a civic culture and shared historical myths are generated. These become the basis for a more inclusive definition of who "owns" the state.[11] Civic nationalisms do not deny ethnic identities; they simply create a super-identity that incorporates multiple layers of identity below. These identities are rarely fixed. Individuals select from among multiple identities depending on the nature of the claim. Inclusive ideas of citizenship thus mitigate the likelihood that groups will mobilize along ethnic lines and, when they do, increase the likelihood that such challenges will be resolved without the use of violence. Because a civic idea of the state tends to include layers of identities, the rare ethnic-based challenge is likely to be accommodated within that range of available identities.

Multiethnic states that base their legitimacy on ethnic nationalisms use a more exclusive definition of state citizenship. Loyalty to the state becomes synonymous with loyalty to the ethnic group. Legitimacy is founded on the identity markers of one constituent group that by definition excludes all other groups who do not share these same self-selected markers. Because ethnic identities are fixed from birth and multiple layers of identity do not exist, these states lack the fluidity inherent in civic systems. Exclusive ideas of citizenship institutionalize ethnic divisions in society.[12] They preclude the emergence of an overarching identity and increase the likelihood that challenges between the state's "owners" and excluded populations will result in violent confrontation.

In "deeply divided societies," the likelihood of ethnic violence is even greater. Deeply divided societies are "deeply riven along a preponderant ethnic cleavage,"[13] such that ethnic divisions appear permanent and all-encompassing. In such societies, ethnic cleavages cannot be overcome by appeals to a wider, more inclusive identity, as was apparent in post-Tito Yugoslavia. Lines between each of Yugoslavia's ethnic nations and the "other" were tightly drawn, and a Yugoslav identity no longer resonated with Yugoslavia's citizens except in a few isolated multiethnic cities such as Sarajevo. The seeming permanence of ethnic cleavages in deeply divided societies precludes movement toward a more inclusive idea of the state.

A second important aspect of the multiethnic state relates to its political-societal expression in terms of settlement patterns and the stratification of groups within the state. How communities are settled within the state and how they are stratified explains why groups will adopt violence to secede or to claim the state for themselves. It also offers a partial explanation for why groups will adopt strategies aimed at cleansing the ethnic other. Finally, settlement and stratification explain why violence occurs and what direction that violence will take.

Settlement patterns refer to how ethnic groups are dispersed throughout the state. There are a broad range of settlement patterns. Regionally concentrated groups include both majority and minority groups that are settled in a concentrated pattern in a distinct geographic region within the state. Dispersed groups, both minority and majority groups, are scattered throughout the state, living intermingled with the ethnic other. Ethnonational groups are an example of a regionally concentrated group. A regionally concentrated settlement pattern in a multiethnic state where the idea of the state is narrowly defined is a state arena with a high likelihood of ethnic unrest and ethnic violence.

Settlement patterns add to our understanding of how the arena of the state shapes ethnic violence. Regionally concentrated groups are more likely to attempt secession, whereas dispersed groups are more likely to challenge the state to secure group demands and, in the extreme, to claim the state for themselves. Regionally dispersed groups are also more likely to adopt strategies aimed at cleansing the ethnic other in order to shift from a dispersed to a concentrated settlement pattern to buttress claims for autonomy, if not secession.

Stratification refers to how ethnic groups are ordered in society. In his seminal book, *Ethnic Groups in Conflict*, Donald Horowitz develops a typology of ranked and unranked groups that persuasively shows how significant group structure is in understanding ethnic violence.[14] Ethnic groups can be said to be ranked when ethnic origins coincide with social class: one group is subordinate and the other superordinate. In a ranked system, the concept of an independent elite among the subordinate group is a "logical impossibility."[15]

In unranked systems, class and ethnic origins do not coincide. Ethnic groups stand in parallel relation to each other. These groups constitute "incipient whole societies," insular national groups whose membership crosses social, economic, and educational classes. Rather than a logical impossibility, an independent elite is a definitional requirement of an unranked system.

The structure of relations between ethnic groups provides an explanation both for why ethnic conflict occurs and the direction in which it occurs: ranked systems produce class-based conflict aimed at social revolution, and unranked systems produce conflict that resembles war in the international system.[16] Structure also explains why ranked groups are concerned with domination or subordination, whereas unranked groups are most concerned with exclusion. In ranked systems, the stratification of society into subordinate and superordinate ethnic groups means that group mobilization and violence will be sparked by the domination of one group over the other. In unranked systems the parallel stratification of groups means that mobilization and violence are driven by the threat of exclusion. When one group excludes the other, it is not only the elite or subordinate members of the group that are excluded, but the entire ethnic nation.

When ethnic identities matter in multiethnic states, they frame group interactions and group claims against the state. When the idea of the state is defined in exclusive terms, and when ethnic groups within it are regionally concentrated and unranked, the result is a state arena that has a great likelihood of experiencing ethnic violence.

The Weak State Arena

Weak states are a second key arena of ethnic violence. Weak states are states that suffer from interrelated authority, capacity, and legitimacy deficits. An authority deficit exists when the authority of the state does not extend across the territory defined by its legally recognized boundaries. In this case, the state is consistently weak throughout its territorial domain. An authority deficit also exists when that authority is wielded across only portions of the state and is absent in others, creating islands of government-enforced stability and zones of ungovernability over which the state exercises little or no control. Frequently, these ungoverned spaces serve as safe havens and sanctuaries from which groups challenge the state, filling the vacuum left by declining state authority to offer an alternate social and political authority structure controlled by ethnic kin. Authority is not absent; state authority is. In other cases, a vacuum may be created by external intervention or by affiliated proxy groups seeking to weaken the state. The state is precluded from extending its authority over the whole of its territory. In the extreme case of a collapsed state, government authority effectively ceases to exist throughout the state, creating a vacuum of authority.[17] These scenarios undermine not only state authority, but also its capacity and, more ominously, its legitimacy.

The second dimension of state weakness is *capacity*. Along this dimension, weakness is measured by the state's failure to provide key political goods to some portion of the population. Robert Rotberg identifies a hierarchy of political goods, the most important of which is security, especially human security. The state's prime responsibility—its part of the social contract—is to prevent cross-border infiltrations, eliminate domestic threats, prevent crime, and enable citizens to resolve their differences with the state and fellow citizens without recourse to violence.[18] Failures of capacity are thus closely linked to weakened or absent authority. If the state's authority does not extend across its territory, then it cannot effectively maintain a monopoly over the legitimate use of force.

Security is the gateway for the provision of other political goods, including key social services such as education, public health policies, and medical care; public infrastructures, including basic utilities, communications systems, and transportation networks, as well as a money and banking system; a reliable infrastructure for fiscal extraction; and an effective judicial system. None of these public goods can be provided with any uniformity across the state if a basic level of security cannot be maintained. Authority deficits also limit the state's ability to collect essential revenues, which further undermines its capacity to deliver these goods. The result is a collapse of the social contract: the state fails to uphold its end of the bargain.[19] Deficits in authority and capacity thus undermine the legitimacy of the state.

The third dimension of state weakness is *legitimacy*. Kalevi Holsti defines a legitimacy deficit as a fundamental lack of legitimacy along two dimensions, the vertical and the horizontal.[20] The vertical dimension involves the "right to rule." It is measured by the degree to which populations accept the authority of the state, consent to its rule, and offer their loyalty to the idea of the state and its institutions. When voluntary participation and general acceptance of the right to rule are present, states enjoy a high degree of vertical legitimacy. Where state authority and capacity have eroded, voluntary compliance and general acceptance of the right to rule are undermined, and that state can be defined as suffering from a vertical legitimacy deficit.[21]

Authoritarian states are a special category of weak state—"states that are fundamentally weak but appear strong."[22] Authoritarian regimes rule through fear, coercion and force: participation is not voluntary, and the "right to rule" is not freely extended to the state and its ruling elite. Despite the significant coercive power of authoritarian states such as Iraq and the former Soviet Union, elites were not accorded the "right to rule" voluntarily. This absence of vertical legitimacy explains the rapid collapse of these states when the coercive power of the state was withdrawn.

The horizontal dimension of legitimacy involves the definition of the community that is to be ruled. States that define the political community in broadly inclusive terms, regardless of ethnic or sectarian affiliation, are states that enjoy a high degree of horizontal legitimacy. Horizontal legitimacy is also obtained when a robust minority-rights scheme or real autonomy ensures that minority groups are full participants in the political community of the state. The more inclusive the political community, the more the state can be said to enjoy a high degree of horizontal legitimacy. States that restrict the definition of citizenship to only one ethnic or sectarian group are states that suffer from a horizontal legitimacy deficit. The community is defined in exclusionary terms. One group is seen as "owning" the state; the remaining ethnic groups are relegated to the role of outsiders.

Weak states can thus be defined as states with interrelated authority, capacity, and legitimacy deficits. Because the severity of these deficits varies from state to state, it is useful to view relative strength and weakness along a "continuum of strength."[23] At one end of the spectrum are strong states with well-established regimes for rule that enjoy a high degree of vertical and horizontal legitimacy. At the other end of the spectrum lie the many weak and failed states of the Third World and some of the newly independent states of the former Soviet Union and the former Yugoslavia. These states lack wide acceptance of their elites' right to rule and wide participation in the polity. These states are also frequently exclusionary.

The two state arenas—the multiethnic state and the weak state—are analytically useful as we identify the causes of ethnic violence at the state level. In practice, however, these two arenas frequently overlap. Most weak states are simultaneously multiethnic states in which the idea of the state is defined in sharply exclusive terms. When excluded groups mobilize, their claims and strategies are shaped by settlement and stratification patterns. When weak multiethnic states seek to overcome these deficits, their responses spark interethnic conflict and violence. Two state responses—ethnic group repression and exclusion—have a particularly high likelihood of triggering ethnic war. We will examine each in turn below.

THE WEAK STATE MODEL

State responses to ethnic group mobilization can prevent ethnic violence or trigger interethnic war. How states respond to ethnic group mobilization correlates with where they fall on the continuum. Strong states have the capacity to accommodate ethnic demands through legitimate government institutions and processes. Weak states are constrained by interrelated authority, capacity, and legitimacy deficits. Their range of response options tends to be limited and involve significant trade-offs.

States vary in their strategies of conflict management and may pursue any number of policies aimed at accommodating or repressing communal contenders. At one end of the spectrum are the strategies commonly viewed as the most effective in accommodating ethnic group demands. These include a federal system of government, autonomy, a system of disproportional power for the minority group, voluntary integration (as opposed to assimilation), minority rights, and democratic majority rule. At the other end of the spectrum are the problematic responses. These include institutionalized discrimination (segregation), coercion or domination, population expulsion, and actual or symbolic extermination.[24]

A state with a high degree of vertical legitimacy can accommodate demands for inclusion, and a state with a high degree of horizontal legitimacy can expand the social contract to include new members in its political community. Communal political action in these states is thus likely to be limited in scope and to take the form of protest.[25] At the other end of the continuum we find states with diminished authority, constrained capacity, and either vertical or horizontal legitimacy deficits—or both. These limit the state's ability to accommodate ethnic demands and increase the likelihood that the state will respond with force.

When groups mobilize against a weak state, an authority deficit limits the state's ability to implement autonomy or cultural provisions, or to alter internal boundaries to accommodate homeland claims. A capacity deficit constrains the state's ability to offer political goods to the ethnic contenders. Finally, legitimacy deficits constrain the regime's ability to alter the ruling structures of the state and to widen participation in the state's institutions. Concessions that expand the vertical dimension of legitimacy undermine the regime's tenuous right to rule. Changes to the horizontal dimension of state legitimacy threaten the regime's already narrow base of support. Both alterations jeopardize the regime's hold on power. These interrelated authority, capacity, and legitimacy deficits limit the state's ability to accommodate ethnic demands. They also increase the likelihood that the state will respond with repression. Because the state is weak, serious challenges may well constitute an existential threat to the regime. Both state responses impact an ethnic group's choice of violent means. When the state either denies or represses ethnic group demands, the group is likely to adopt violent means to challenge the regime's right to rule. A fifth proposition for understanding the choice of violent means is as follows:

> If a state's authority, capacity, and legitimacy deficits prompt the denial or repression of ethnic group demands, the ethnic group is likely to adopt violent means to challenge the state (Proposition 5).

Four state responses—partial accommodation, repression, severe repression, and full concession—impact how and when groups adopt violent means. When a weak state attempts to accommodate ethnic demands through limited cultural rights or partial or full autonomy, it is unlikely to have the capacity or authority to implement them. When accommodation threatens the dominance of the state-owning ethnic group or its exclusive ownership of the state, the state is likely to face significant risks if it proceeds with implementation. When these measures threaten the regime's right to rule, the will to accommodate ethnic demands will rapidly disappear. Ethnic groups are thus likely to adopt violent means when the state fails to implement an agreement, or to resume violent means when a cease-fire fails to result in a successful settlement. This suggests the following sub-proposition:

> If a state offers concessions but fails to implement them, then the ethnic group will be more likely to adopt or resume violent means (Proposition 5.1).

Because a weak state suffers from interrelated authority, capacity, and legitimacy deficits, it is more likely to counter group demands with repression. Repression involves fewer trade-offs, is less costly (at least in the short term), and, depending on the severity of the repression, tends to produce rapid results. Repression can "resolve" an ethnic-based challenge quickly without forcing an already weak state to make concessions that could set a dangerous precedent and undermine the idea of the state as belonging to the state's ethnic owners.

Repression involves forcibly denying group demands and forcibly restraining group action such that the group ceases to present a threat to the state. Repression includes segregating the offending group, particularly when the group is regionally concentrated, or, alternatively, dominating the group through various coercive measures aimed at limiting or removing the group's ability to participate in and shape state policy and institutions. More extreme measures may include population expulsion and actual or symbolic extermination. When a weak state represses ethnic-based challengers, it can demonstrate its authority and capacity, and its measures may have the added benefit of serving as a deterrent, particularly if other groups are contemplating claims against the state.

Repression increases the likelihood that groups will respond with violent measures and that group strategies will escalate from sporadic resistance to full-scale interethnic war. The more severe the repression, the greater the likelihood that groups will conclude that they have little to lose by embarking on a full-scale ethnic war for their own survival. If repression fails effectively to increase the costs of action to the group such that the costs outweigh the benefits, groups will respond with violent means. This suggests the following subproposition:

> If a state attempts to repress group mobilization and fails to increase the costs of action to the group effectively, such that the costs outweigh the benefits, then the ethnic group will adopt violent means (Proposition 5.2).

When the state responds with *severe* repression, groups will reassess their strategy of ethnic violence. Severe repression is used to distinguish mere coercion from more extreme forms of state violence, including physical extermination and genocide. In this instance, the threat is so severe that groups reassess the potential benefits against the significant costs of continued violent resistance. When groups are subject to severe repression, they will temporarily suspend violent resistance and reassess their choice of violent means. This suggests the following subproposition:

> Severe repression will temporarily suspend a group's strategy of violent resistance (Proposition 5.3).

Severe repression is a choice strategy when the threat to the state is such that the state's survival is at stake, or when the state has the resources to conduct what is often a lengthy and costly campaign, as the decades of Iraq's repression of the Kurds show. Although repression and coercion may buy the regime temporary respite, such measures further weaken the state. The case of Iraq demonstrates that repression is "ineffective in the long run and in many instances can turn mere autonomists into fully-fledged secessionists overnight."[26] Repression will temporarily strengthen state authority and capacity, but it will destroy both vertical and horizontal legitimacy. Should the state subsequently offer accommodation, as Saddam Hussein did with his offer of an autonomous region for the Kurds, the state's legitimacy deficit will doom its efforts to failure. Once groups have been subjected to increasingly lethal repression, it is unlikely they will accept the states' right to rule or agree to join the social contract and become part of the political community.

Repression comes with substantial hidden and long-term costs. Repression rapidly unifies the targeted ethnic group. The state, in effect, completes the task of the group's ethnic leadership. Its actions serve to mobilize the group, often more rapidly and more extensively than in the absence of an external threat. It also gives ethnic leadership ammunition in its effort to secure external support. Repression, and particularly atrocities, can be used to "prove" that the group is worthy of financial, military, and diplomatic support not only from regional states and international actors but also from diaspora communities.

Repression also favors more militant segments of the targeted ethnic group. When a state controlled by the ethnic other attempts to repress an ethnic group using violent means, its actions prove the claims of more militant factions at the expense of moderates who might have been willing to support less violent strategies. Repression also heals internal divisions. If the targeted group suffers from internal divisions and within-group conflict, state repression may act as a catalyst to bring factions together against the larger external threat of the state. The consequence, for the state, is that repression has created a more unified, and hence more effective, opponent.

Repression furthermore creates legacies of mistrust that are likely to persevere long after active repression has ended. Once repressed, the group is unlikely to contemplate a negotiated settlement for limited cultural rights or partial or full autonomy. These measures require a modicum of trust—some assurance that, once entered, the state will uphold its end of the bargain and the group will not be subject to further repression and coercion. When subsequent efforts are made to find a negotiated settlement, a legacy of repression will cast a long shadow over any efforts at conflict resolution, even when the repressive government has been replaced by a new government or new coalition of ethnic leaders.

Full concession (a genuine effort to address group grievances) reduces the likelihood that groups will adopt violent means. If new rulers seize power and attempt to address these deficits by establishing what is in effect a new social contract—one that widens state ownership and offers full participation for its citizens or meets, at a minimum, demands for group autonomy—groups may reassess their choice of rebellion. This suggests a final subproposition:

> If a state responds to ethnic mobilization with genuine concessions, then the group will be less likely to adopt violent means (Proposition 5.4).

Because the state suffers from interrelated authority, capacity, and legitimacy deficits, renewed or intensified efforts to settle ethnic disputes may trigger renewed repression. As the state makes concessions to one ethnic group, ethnic rivals may mobilize to overturn the agreement. What frequently results is a cycle of accommodation and repression as weak regimes collapse, new governments attempt to resolve competing group claims, and rival groups challenge the state or overthrow it in an effort to secure their own demands. This cycle of accommodation and repression demonstrates the crucial link between state weakness and an ethnic group's choice of violent means.

THE EXCLUSION MODEL

In multiethnic states where ethnic groups are unranked, exclusion offers an alternative response option when ethnic groups mobilize against the state. Whereas repression offers an immediate, albeit short-term solution, exclusion seems to offer a permanent way to resolve ethnic challenges in unranked systems.

Once the offending groups are removed, figuratively or literally, the state's new owners can proceed unchallenged with nation-building.

Exclusion aims not to repress the ethnic challenger, but to redefine the state such that the challenging group is excluded—from participation in state institutions, from its material benefits, and from the idea of the state as belonging to all its constituent groups. At one extreme, exclusion is achieved through the expulsion or mass extermination of the ethnic other; at the other, democratic elections may produce undemocratic results. Whether achieved through violent or nonviolent means, exclusion narrows the idea of the state such that, to borrow Ernest Gellner's phrase, ethnic group and state are congruent.[27]

Exclusion is, at its root, about ownership of the state and all that ownership conveys—both the material benefits and the less tangible, but nonetheless vitally important, recognition of a group's status and prestige. Ownership means that the ethnic group has the right to define the idea of the state as belonging exclusively to ethnic kin, thus giving it the power to deny the ethnic other the right to participate in the polity and to benefit from the state's services and resources. Given what is at stake, exclusion has a high likelihood of triggering a violent response and of sparking a protracted war between contending groups over the right to own the state and to redefine the idea of the state. A sixth proposition to explain a group's choice of violent means is thus as follows:

> If an ethnic group is excluded or is threatened with exclusion from the polity, then the ethnic group will be more likely to adopt violent means (Proposition 6).

Exclusion triggers violence in two ways. When one group attempts to dismantle or destroy the inclusive idea of the state, groups threatened with exclusion will adopt violent means to protect their status. Alternatively, when the state is already founded on an exclusionary idea of ownership, during transitions of rule excluded groups will adopt violent means to overturn the prevailing political-societal order. In so doing, previously excluded groups will claim the right to redefine the idea of the state in ways that exclude the state's previous owners. These are both reflected in the following subpropositions:

> If an ethnic group is threatened with exclusion from a polity, then the ethnic group will adopt violent means to protect its status (Proposition 6.1).

> If an ethnic group is excluded from a polity, then the ethnic group will adopt violent means during transitions of rule to overturn the prevailing political-societal order (Proposition 6.2).

Both scenarios are triggered by unranked group structure. Exclusion leads to interethnic war in multiethnic states where groups are stratified such that each stands in parallel relation to the other. These unranked ethnic systems are conducive to periodic violence that resembles war in the international system.

When faced with exclusion or the threat thereof, unranked groups adopt violent means to protect their status or to claim ownership of the state for themselves and, in so doing, the right to redefine the idea of the state to exclude the ethnic other. Because each unranked group constitutes an incipient whole society, violence is aimed at transforming the system into a ranked one.[28] Each incipient society will mobilize and adopt violence, much like individual states wage war in the international system. Because of what is at stake, these wars tend to be protracted. They are also the most difficult to resolve given the parallel structure of groups within the state; any effort at accommodating competing demands must remove both the incentive and the opportunity for transforming the system into a ranked one.

Whether an unranked system is transformed into a ranked one through violent or nonviolent means, it is equally likely to trigger a violent response. When exclusion is imposed through a violent seizure of power by one group in a multi-ethnic state, that group's ownership is complete. The dominant group controls the state's institutions, including its military and police forces, as well as its legal system, revenue collection, and natural resources. Equally important, the now-dominant group can impose a new idea of the state upon its population, one that is narrowly defined to reflect exclusively the identity of the dominant group. This scenario has a high likelihood of triggering an immediate, violent response.

Transitions from authoritarian to democratic rule may trigger the violent exclusion of ethnic groups in the transitioning state. Democratizing states are states in which democratic institutions and practices are not firmly established. These nascent institutions must contend with competition among groups for power in the new state. When former elites are threatened by their loss of power, their commitment to democratization may waver. When these former elites belong to one of the state's constituent ethnic groups and adopt measures aimed at excluding rival ethnic groups from participation in the newly democratizing state, excluded groups are likely to resist, and to resist violently.

In deeply divided societies, both violent and nonviolent exclusion are likely to trigger a violent response. When one group excludes ethnic competitors following a violent seizure of power, that group's ownership is complete. The newly excluded group is likely to resist its loss of access and status through violent means. When exclusion results from nonviolent and legitimate processes, the response is likely to be violent, although not necessarily immediately so. In democracies and democratizing autocracies, severely divided societies produce ethnic-based party systems[29] where party and group boundaries coincide.[30] Elections take on the character of a census, registering ethnic affiliation rather than choice. Regardless of the issue at stake, groups vote by their identity. When one ethnic group wins by its sheer demographic weight, the ethnic other sees itself as losing all—excluded not only from government, but also from the larger political community.[31] Because elections register ethnic affiliation, that exclusion is likely to be permanent.[32] In federal systems, and particularly in consociational systems, exclusion may result from changes to a carefully crafted balance of power among the state's constituent nations, resulting from the unilateral actions of one ethnic group or because of longer-term demographic shifts. If the state's institutions are weak, a powerful ethnic group may successfully dominate them and use that power to exclude the ethnic other. Because society is deeply divided, excluded groups have few options to redress their loss of power through nonviolent means.

Given the permanent nature of their exclusion, ethnic groups in deeply divided societies are likely to adopt violent means to redress their exclusion from the polity. When the excluded group is dispersed throughout the state, it may attempt to seize the state, whereas a regionally concentrated group is likely to contemplate secession. The seeming permanence of the group's exclusion will lead groups to contemplate violent means when protest fails (and seems likely to fail in perpetuity). We can thus add the following subproposition:

> If an ethnic group faces permanent exclusion in a deeply divided society, then the group will adopt violent means to seize the state, or where the group is regionally concentrated, to secede (Proposition 6.3).

The threat of exclusion will prompt previously included groups to adopt violence to protect their status in the polity, whereas excluded groups are likely to mobilize and adopt violent means during transitions of rule to overturn the prevailing political-societal order and claim the state for themselves. Because exclusion is permanent in deeply divided societies, both nonviolent and violent exclusion will prompt ethnic groups to adopt violent means either to seize the state or to secede.

CONCLUSION

At the second image, an ethnic group's choice of violent means is shaped by the arena of the state and the state's response to ethnic mobilization. Because these arenas frequently overlap, there is considerable interaction between the Weak State and Exclusion Models. An unranked structure will limit a weak state's ability to accommodate ethnic demands, and repression will likely trigger rapid mobilization if it threatens group inclusion. When the repressed group is both unranked and regionally concentrated, repression will likely trigger a secessionist response. When an unranked group is excluded from a weak state and adopts violent means to challenge the state's right to rule, accommodation will likely fail; inclusion threatens the regime's hold on power, whereas repression will intensify the likelihood that groups will either seize the state or secede. The interrelationship of the second image models further demonstrates that the reasons groups adopt violent means are both complex and multifaceted. In the next chapter, we add an additional layer of complexity when we examine the systemic reasons why groups adopt violent means.

4
Chapter

A Third Image
Theory of Ethnic Violence

INTRODUCTION

Third image explanations of war are rooted in the anarchical nature of the international system. Waltz defines the international system as one with many sovereign states; with no system of law enforceable among them; with each state judging its grievances and ambitions according to the dictates of its own reason or desire; and with conflict, sometimes leading to war, bound to occur.[1] Anarchy means that the state, as the primary actor in the international system, must provide for its own security. War is thus likely in a system with no effective global governing body to mitigate disputes, maintain a monopoly on the use of force, or constrain the ability of states to pursue their own interests and provide for their own security.

At the third image, systemic anarchy is the primary cause of war *between states*. Because interstate war is a function of the international system, internal aspects of the state are either discounted or ignored.[2] Yet most ethnic conflict occurs *within states*. Indeed, substate and non-state actors present a growing threat to the post 9/11 security landscape. Even when ethnic conflict is internationalized through state collapse, the intervention of foreign belligerents, or cross-border refugee flows, the origins of conflict are frequently found within the state arena. The exception is when conflict erupts out of a security vacuum created following state collapse. In this instance, anarchy within the collapsed state resembles the anarchy of the international system. Yet state collapse is an extreme case. How can we explain the violent ethnic wars that erupt short of state collapse?

Given that systemic explanations of war ignore internal aspects of the state, it is not surprising that the literature dealing with international aspects of ethnic conflict has focused either on the mechanisms by which ethnic conflict is internationalized,[3] or on a narrow category of secessionist and irredentist ethnic conflicts that have a high likelihood of being internationalized.[4] Internationalization is said to occur through two processes: horizontal escalation (diffusion) and vertical escalation. Horizontal escalation describes a process whereby events in one state directly change the balance of power in a neighboring state.[5] The *example* of ethnic conflict elsewhere—of a successful autonomy agreement or the mobilization of ethnic kindred—emboldens the group to act. Vertical escalation occurs when foreign belligerents *intervene* in an internal ethnic conflict, triggering crises and even interstate war. The behavior of one state creates a crisis for one or more state actors who perceive a threat to vital interests, thus triggering international war.[6]

Diffusion suggests that indirect contact can inspire and inform, triggering mobilization that may eventually lead to violence. It does not, however, suggest a direct causal link between the inspiration to mobilize and violence. In this instance the causes of violence are equally likely to be found at the group and state levels. Similarly, vertical escalation explains why conflict is more likely to be internationalized, but not why conflict erupts between groups. Both approaches define escalation as a consequence of the intervention by foreign belligerents in an internal conflict that causes it to become internationalized. When we study ethnic violence, escalation is better defined as the widening and intensification of violence between groups either within or across state boundaries. An ethnic conflict is said to escalate when it extends in space from the local to the wider regional or international arena; in number from two to three or more conflicting ethnic groups; or in intensity from limited engagements to full-scale war. When third parties intervene in an ethnic conflict, their actions can escalate violence between groups.

Other third image studies of interethnic violence focus on the outcomes of ethnic wars, suggesting that the success of an ethnic group's strategy is determined at the international level, a conclusion supported by our case study research below.[7] Internationalization is said to increase the levels of violence,[8] and the use of a neighboring state for support and sanctuary is said to make conflict more intractable.[9] Yet none of these approaches offers a direct causal explanation at the systemic level for why groups adopt violent means.

It is the purpose of this chapter to identify the causes of ethnic group violence at the systemic level. How do factors *outside* the state cause ethnic groups to adopt strategies of violence that trigger interethnic war between groups, many of which erupt *within* states? Although systemic causes of ethnic group violence are less readily apparent at the third image than they are at the first and second images, there is more to be found at the third image than an explanation for the internationalization of ethnic war.

The purpose of this book is to build a framework of propositions about the causes of violence that spans all three levels of analysis. In this chapter, we will focus on the sources of group violence at the third image. Although states remain the primary actors in the international system, when we study ethnic violence we cannot ignore the role of other systemic actors. The interconnectedness of an increasingly globalized world, the uneven erosion of state sovereignty, and the rise of non-state actors have heightened the impact of the system on internal ethnic conflict and war. When these actors lend material and nonmaterial support to one group, faction, or state controlled by ethnic strangers, ethnic conflict is likely to escalate to ethnic violence.

We begin by examining the international system, the impact of globalization on the nature of communal conflict, and the contention that globalization is a primary systemic cause of communal strife. Globalization has transformed non-state armed groups—but not necessarily ethnic groups—into global actors capable of challenging the state, particularly weak states. This transformation has enabled non-state actors to operate alongside and against states in the international system. How third parties affect the choice of violent means is captured in two models. Both identify systemic causes of ethnic violence that complete our multilevel framework.

SYSTEMIC ACTORS AND ETHNIC WAR

A key feature of the international environment is that it is increasingly globalized. Globalization is an imprecise term. There is little agreement on what globalization is beyond a vague theme of "interconnectedness," a linkage between the global and the local, and an equally vague sense about change. Globalization has been defined as a process, a transformation, even a revolution. The effects of globalization have not been uniformly felt. Globalization brings greater interdependence and propels isolated groups into modernity with all its attendant benefits. Yet the dark side of globalization is its power to obliterate traditional cultures, weaken sovereignty, and further isolate the "haves" from the "have-nots."[10]

The effects of globalization are apparent in the rising power of non-state armed groups as global actors, the uneven erosion of state sovereignty, and the emergence of a new form of communal violence described as "new war" or "war amongst the people."[11] My contention is not that the demise of the state is imminent, as some globalization theorists suggest, but rather that states, particularly weak states, face a new peer competitor in the non-state armed group. The paradox of globalization is that it has strengthened strong states and further weakened weak states, many of which are multiethnic.

Globalization enables non-state armed groups to target weak states and challenge the legitimacy of state rule in a new way. Defined as terrorists, insurgents, militias, and criminal organizations, non-state armed groups are increasingly global actors that operate through networks linking these groups on a global scale. These networks vastly increase the organizational reach and the resource base of such groups. They also vastly increase the nature of the threat to individual states, regions, and the broader international system.

Whereas non-state armed groups have become global actors, ethnic groups are inherently self-limiting. The extent of an ethnic group's geographic reach, and more broadly its appeal, extends only so far as the group itself. Diaspora groups notwithstanding, an ethnic group's appeal rarely extends beyond the regions in which it resides. Thus, we could not conceive of a specifically *ethnic* Kurdish movement having a global appeal in the way that Al-Qaeda's violent Salafi ideology targets Muslim communities across the globe. Although globalization has enabled the transformation of non-state armed groups, it has not transformed the ethnic group in the same way. Except through instrumental linkages with global, non-state actors for arms, resources, and profit, ethnic groups are not global actors.

If globalization has not transformed the ethnic group into a global actor, then perhaps it has activated or eroded the meaning of communal identity. John Ishiyama traces two arguments that create a direct link between globalization and ethnic politics.[12] First, the homogenizing influence of globalization has activated latent ethnic identities and unleashed them onto the world stage. Second, globalization has intensified conflict resulting from a "backlash against globalization's encroachment on ethnic identity."[13] The first argument suggests that globalization triggers ethnic groups to mobilize, but it does not explain why groups adopt violent means. Although the salience of ethnic identities may be heightened when a previously isolated group interacts with the outside world through increased economic and cultural linkages, heightened identity alone is an insufficient explanation for ethnic violence. Globalization may trigger mobilization, but mobilization alone does not explain why groups adopt ethnic violence. Globalization may produce "ethnic awakening," but whether it results in violence "depends heavily on other intervening variables."[14]

The second argument suggests that globalization destroys traditional identities, leading groups to mobilize in order to "stabilize ethnic identity amid the uncertainties of globalization."[15] Here we find a link between globalization and defensive group mobilization that fits within the first image Group Survival Model. If globalization does destroy identity, then groups are likely to mobilize and contemplate violent means as a measure of self-defense. Yet the threat itself is likely manifested in the scenarios defined in the survival model: in- and out-migration of populations, encroachment upon cultural rights, and the destruction of traditional lives and livelihoods. Ethnic violence is thus an indirect consequence of the awakening or the destruction of ethnic identities by the forces of globalization.

Mary Kaldor and others have suggested that globalization has given rise to new forms of communal violence, what she and others term "new wars."[16] New wars are not fought for geopolitical or ideological goals. They are about identity politics and are fought using means that defy the laws of war. Gone are the rules for the treatment of rank-and-file prisoners, the wounded and noncombatants, as well as distinctions between war and crime. Forces intermingle with the civilian populations in what Martin Van Creveld terms "extreme dispersion."[17] New wars are sustained by a globalized economy, which fosters linkages between communal groups and crime in ways that erode the sovereignty of the state.

What Kaldor and others describe is how communal wars have changed. The decline of state sovereignty—and thus the state-centric paradigm—engenders wars that are protracted. These new wars are fought between combatants that are less clearly defined, using means that increase the violence experienced by noncombatants. Rupert Smith's "war amongst the people" is thus an apt description of how traditional lines between combatants and noncombatants have blurred.[18] But does the new war paradigm tell us something new about *why* communal groups adopt violent means?

The new war paradigm suggests that war is a consequence of competing claims between groups and states over the right to rule. Globalization has enabled ethnic groups to challenge state rule more effectively, and ethnic groups actively pursue external support and cultivate linkages with systemic actors beyond the arena of the state to secure their objectives. In identifying the third image causes of ethnic violence, we must consider a system that has expanded to include not only states, but also increasingly powerful non-state actors as well as international organizations. As the capacity of these actors to intervene in communal conflicts has expanded, the sovereignty of many multiethnic, weak states has eroded, as have the constraints on ethnic groups with grievances against the state or ethnic strangers. An ethnic group's ability to sustain interethnic war against ethnic strangers or a state controlled by ethnic strangers is determined largely at the third image. In the two models below, we will examine two critical systemic enablers of ethnic conflict, namely external support and access to the resources necessary to wage war.

THE EXTERNAL SUPPORT MODEL

At the third image, external support for an ethnic group with claims against ethnic strangers increases the likelihood that the ethnic group will adopt violent means. External support is a broad category that encompasses a range of activity from diplomatic support in international fora to direct intervention. External support enhances a group's capacity to resist in both material and nonmaterial ways, yet it carries significant risks, most notably when the achievement of group aims depends entirely on third parties. Research has shown that there is a direct linkage between external support and the achievement of group *aims*.[19] In this model, we examine the link between external support and the choice of violent *means*.

Alexis Heraclides divides external support into two categories, namely tangible support and political-diplomatic support.[20] Tangible support includes material or utilitarian aid, aid by way of access, and assistance by way of services rendered within or outside the area of conflict. It can extend from simple "transactional involvement" to full-scale military intervention. Political-diplomatic support includes verbal public statements; diplomatic pressure on one's opponent and its allies and supporters; voting in international organizations; official contacts with the opponent through mediation efforts; expressions of humanitarian concern; and formal recognition of statehood.

Rothchild and Lake classify external support in three categories, each of which include both tangible and political-diplomatic forms of support. These are noncoercive intervention, coercive intervention, and third-party mediation.[21] Noncoercive intervention, such as sanctions to punish noncompliant regimes, involves the assertion of international norms aimed at raising the costs of unacceptable behavior. Refusals of diplomatic and economic support and the denial (or threatened denial) of recognition similarly aim to change group behavior.[22] Without intervening directly in a conflict, third parties use noncoercive measures to influence the range of options available to an ethnic group contemplating violent means.

Coercive intervention encompasses more direct action. It includes the direct engagement by military forces in support of one group or a state-owning group. It also encompasses peacekeeping missions to enforce ceasefires and other negotiated settlements.[23] Coercive intervention is not limited to third-party military forces. It also includes the provision of humanitarian services in a conflict zone and activities undertaken to build a new regime (monitoring of elections, rebuilding of infrastructure, temporary administration). Although coercive intervention is undertaken to force parties to moderate their demands or their behavior, it creates opportunities that ethnic groups can exploit. A weaker party can use a ceasefire to rearm or secure alternate sources of support to strengthen its position relative to ethnic strangers. A stronger party (often the state-owning ethnic group) can use the reduction in tension to rapidly escalate violence and defeat an unsuspecting opponent before third parties can react.

Third-party mediation describes action undertaken by states and organizations to encourage peaceful settlement of conflict.[24] In the bargaining that ensues, contending groups may exploit linkages with sponsoring states to attempt to secure a more favorable settlement. Even the hint of preference from a sponsoring organization or state may prompt the weaker party to resume violence or reject a ceasefire for more favorable auspices. Although mediation aims at resolving conflict, it can also trigger the outbreak or resumption of ethnic violence.

This wide range of external support is undertaken by an equally wide range of third-party actors. They include ethnic kindred in neighboring states, diasporas, non-state armed groups, regional powers, superpowers, and international organizations. Third parties intervene for a myriad of reasons, including hegemonic ambitions, concerns about regional stability, ethnic sympathy for oppressed groups, a sense of international responsibility, and humanitarian concerns.[25] External support, however, "seems longest-lived when it comes, not from strong, established states with clear-cut interests, but from irregular forces across porous, remote borders."[26] And when it comes from ethnic kin, support will include the most intense forms of assistance.[27]

Although external support sustains the effort against ethnic strangers, it rarely enables ethnic groups to be successful.[28] Herein lies the paradox of third-party intervention: intervention is necessary to sustain a group's effort against ethnic strangers and is essential for conducting a strategy of ethnic war, but in securing that support, groups risk losing control of their strategy to actors whose long-term interests may diverge from those of the ethnic group.

External support involves significant costs and risks. A group's image may be tarnished by ties to an external "disreputable" source.[29] Groups may become overly dependent on outside support only to find themselves abandoned with few qualms by their former patrons. Unless the group finds alternative source(s) of support, its efforts likely will fail. In addition, once secured, foreign support is undependable. This risk adheres even if the supporting state is controlled by ethnic kin, for "no government ever acts exclusively from affective ethnofraternal considerations."[30] The willingness of a state to intervene in support of ethnic kin is a direct function of its relative interests in the issue.[31] Third parties are generally motivated to intervene for reasons that rarely coincide with the grievances of the rebelling group, and although third parties may assure groups of their support for ethnic group aims, often those aims are supported only as long as third parties derive more benefit than cost from their involvement.[32] Once the cost-benefit ratio exceeds a certain level (often a much lower level of acceptability for outsiders than for the groups themselves), the ethnic group will find itself abandoned.

Third parties may also switch their support from the rebelling ethnic group to the state in order to suppress further escalation when there is danger that the conflict will negatively affect the intervening state's own interests in the region.[33] Not only will the ethnic group find itself abandoned, but it will also be subjected to suppression by its former patron.[34] The ultimate hazard is the group's betrayal in the interest of its patron's *raison d'état*.[35]

Because external support brings significant material and nonmaterial benefits to ethnic groups in conflict with ethnic strangers, securing that support remains a paramount goal despite the inherent risks. Ethnic leaderships use the promise of external support to undermine or co-opt moderate or extremist factions, consolidate support for their strategy within the group, and recruit support and aid from ethnic kin in neighboring states and from ethnic diasporas. Groups also rely on third-party support to neutralize or limit the extent of third-party support for the central government or for ethnic strangers. External support brings legitimacy for the group and its claims. External support can also raise awareness of the group's plight and bring international condemnation and pressure against the opposing, state-owning group. Finally, third parties are critical to mediation efforts for ceasefires, autonomy agreements, or settlements, particularly when a group is in conflict with a group that owns the state.

When an ethnic group secures either tangible or political-diplomatic support, or both, from external states, international organizations, and non-state actors, the group's ability to adopt violent means is enhanced. Despite the significant risk of undue dependence on external parties, groups will adopt strategies of ethnic violence against ethnic strangers if external support is deemed sufficient for groups to secure their goals—either through the positive realization of those aims or by denying an opponent the ability to secure its goals. The impact of external support on a group's choice of violent means is reflected in the following proposition:

> If an ethnic group secures external support for its conflict with ethnic strangers, then the ethnic group will be more likely to adopt violent means (Proposition 7).

How external support prompts groups to adopt violent means can be explained by four interrelated scenarios: escalation, division, mediation, and recognition. Each establishes a causal link between external support and the choice of violent means.

Escalation

The first scenario whereby external intervention prompts ethnic groups to adopt violent means is *escalation*. A conflict is said to escalate when it extends in space from the local to the wider regional or international; in number from two to three or more conflicting parties; or in intensity from limited engagements to full-scale war.

In the escalation scenario, one group secures external support, forcing rival groups to seek to offset the advantage by securing the necessary support from other external sources. When ethnic competitors own the state and thus its resources, the group will seek to offset the considerable advantage of the state-owning group.[36] As each group vies to secure reliable support, a cycle of escalatory, third-party support is created that may involve the direct engagement of foreign forces and, in the extreme, result in a proxy war. At each step, the likelihood of short-term success for the beneficiary group increases while the likelihood of long-term realization of group goals diminishes. As third-party support increases, the conflict escalates, as does the likelihood of violence. This suggests the following subproposition:

> If ethnic competitors secure third-party support, then the ethnic group will seek to offset the advantage, triggering escalation of the conflict and increasing the likelihood of violence (Proposition 7.1).

In the escalation scenario, it is not only the support or intervention of a single third party that triggers further escalation of violence, but also the escalatory cycles that are likely as groups seek to offset the advantage when third parties lend support to ethnic rivals.

Division

A second scenario occurs when third-party support triggers *division* within and among contending ethnic groups. By extending noncoercive, coercive, or mediation support to one group or faction, a third party can (1) deepen existing cleavages, (2) spark mobilization of previously quiescent ethnicities, or (3) trigger factionalism and within-group conflict. In each case, the likelihood that conflict will escalate to ethnic violence increases.

Ethnic cleavage refers to the degree of divided political loyalties between and among ethnic groups within the state.[37] Cleavages are akin to boundaries, although they need not be physical. When groups mobilize against ethnic strangers, the degree of political closure and the intensity of conflict between a group and the other deepen existing cleavages. At the group level, cleavages can deepen when ethnic group leaderships, particularly ethnic entrepreneurs, evoke images of past injustice at the hands of ethnic strangers to widen the gap between the group and the other. Chauvinist policies define these divisions in even starker terms of superiority and inferiority. At the state level, repression and exclusion are likely to trigger political closure when the threat comes from a state controlled by ethnic strangers. At the international level, external support for ethnic strangers prompts the consolidation of group identity in a "rally-round-the-flag" scenario.[38] Much as an external threat will trigger populations to unify, so too will ethnic identities converge when ethnic strangers secure external support that is perceived as either materially improving the opposing group's likelihood of success or potentially undermining the group's own chances for securing support or achieving success.

Second, when a third party intervenes by extending noncoercive, coercive, or mediation support for one group in a multiethnic state, or when its actions are viewed as biased in favor of one group over others, previously quiescent ethnicities are likely to mobilize in defense of their interests. As a result, the conflict expands to include additional groups with ethnic claims against the state and each other. Ethnic alliances may form between two weaker groups against a dominant or state-owning group, and newly mobilized groups will look to secure external support to counter the threat. The end result is that the likelihood of violence increases, as does the likelihood of a widened war between multiple groups. If the state is weak, or if ethnic kindred in neighboring states intervene in support of one group, the conflict is also likely to internationalize, sparking an interethnic war with regional and even international implications.

Finally, when a third party intervenes in favor of one ethnic faction within a group engaged in conflict against ethnic strangers, internecine warfare may trigger an escalation of the conflict not only between within-group factions, but also between each contending faction and ethnic strangers. In this scenario, each faction will seek to secure external support in an attempt to co-opt, sideline, or defeat rival factions, greatly increasing the likelihood that the conflict will both escalate and widen. Predatory states and regional powers with an interest in undermining a regional competitor will be tempted to intervene to further their own interests. Additionally, regional powers may choose to alternate support for one rival faction and then the other in an effort to weaken the ethnic group, particularly if the state fears the mobilization of ethnic kin within its own borders.

When third-party support deepens divisions within and among groups, the likelihood that groups will adopt violent means increases. Cleavages deepen, previously quiescent groups may mobilize, and within-group conflict will likely expand the levels of violence between competing factions and between the ethnic group and the ethnic other. This scenario suggests the following proposition:

> If third-party support deepens existing cleavages, awakens latent identities, or triggers factionalism and within-group conflict, then the likelihood of interethnic violence will increase (Proposition 7.2).

The division scenario increases the intensity of conflict or the number of ethnic groups or factions engaged in conflict, both of which increase the likelihood of interethnic violence. The division scenario also increases the likelihood that all issues and claims will be framed in exclusively ethnic terms.

Mediation

Because ethnic conflicts have a high likelihood of being internationalized, particularly in the event of state collapse, third parties are likely to intervene in an effort to resolve the conflict short of violence or to prevent its escalation to international war. Here we find a third scenario whereby external support through *mediation* triggers ethnic war. How third parties intervene to prevent or resolve conflict has a high likelihood of triggering ethnic violence or the resumption of ethnic war. The manner in which third parties undertake mediation efforts, through (1) perceived bias, (2) exclusion, or (3) by defining the issues and actors in exclusively ethnic terms, significantly increases the likelihood that groups will adopt or resume violent means.

If mediation is viewed as biased in support of one of the contending parties, the threatened group may resume violence to secure friendly third-party support and force a change of auspices. The resumption of violence undermines the legitimacy of third-party mediation efforts. It also demonstrates, to both third-party mediators and the international community, that the group remains a serious threat and that its claims must be addressed if there is to be peace.

Mediation has a high likelihood of triggering groups to adopt or resume ethnic violence when that mediation is viewed as exclusionary. Because of what is at stake in ethnic conflict, an excluded group is likely to adopt violence because it has little interest in the continuation of negotiations in which it is not included. Because the group stands to lose by acquiescing to an exclusionary settlement and a great deal to gain by forcing mediators to broaden the negotiations to include the group in the final settlement, excluded groups have a strong incentive to adopt or resume violence even when the likelihood of success is low. This scenario is particularly significant when conflict centers on a contested homeland. As we suggested in Chapter 2, homeland wars tend to be protracted because homeland ownership is viewed as zero-sum. When the ethnonationalist group is denied homeland ownership by the exclusionary actions of third-party mediators, the group is likely to adopt or resume violence because of what homeland ownership means for the group's identity and its survival.

Finally, mediation is likely to trigger violence when third parties define the nature of the conflict in exclusively ethnic terms. How third-party mediators define both issues and actors in conflicts involving ethnic groups can prompt groups to adopt violent means. A separatist conflict will be transformed into an ethnic conflict when mediators make autonomy or cultural rights, rather than statehood, the basis for settlement. A conflict over territory can be transformed into an ethnic conflict when mediators define the territorial unit in terms of its titular nationality rather than its status as a federal unit or subunit of a state. Similarly, a conflict over federal power and institutions becomes an ethnic conflict when mediation ignores nonethnic interests. In each of these cases, mediation serves as a trigger of political closure as excluded parties— either dispersed ethnic groups or nonethnic federal units—vie to challenge the mediators' assumptions about the issues and parties at stake. In no case is this scenario more evident than the former Yugoslavia. Third parties deliberately ignored the federal center in favor of the titular nationalities and thus defined the conflict over Yugoslavia's future exclusively in ethnic terms. When mediation defines the issues and actors in conflict in exclusively ethnic terms, third-party mediators effectively deny the claims of the disadvantaged group(s). This effort creates an incentive for a disadvantaged group to adopt or resume violent means to secure alternate third-party mediation efforts or to force mediators to redefine the actors and the issues at stake.

The link between third-party mediation and an ethnic group's choice of violent means is captured in the following subproposition:

> When third-party mediation is either biased or exclusionary, or when it selectively denies group aims, then the disadvantaged group will be more likely to adopt or resume violent means (Proposition 7.3).

Although third-party mediation aims at the reduction or resolution of ethnic violence, how that mediation unfolds can create new incentives for groups to adopt violent means.

Recognition

A final scenario whereby external support triggers ethnic violence is selective *recognition.* In this scenario, third parties—namely regional states or superpowers— recognize the independence of one ethnic group, usually a group that is regionally concentrated, while denying that same right to competing groups, who are usually regionally dispersed. This scenario is likely following state collapse, as the case of Yugoslavia shows, and was extremely rare prior to the end of the Cold War. Although selective recognition may be founded on the realities of group settlement patterns, groups denied the right to a state of their own are likely to view this recognition as either punitive or unjust.

The result is to create a dynamic of permanent exclusion in which the excluding party is an external state and the group is literally denied state ownership. In much the same way that the domestic exclusion of an unranked group is likely to trigger ethnic war, so too will the denial of a group's right to statehood trigger what is by definition an international war over the right to own the rump state or to secede. Under these conditions, mobilization and the choice of violent means are likely to be rapid given what is at stake. This is expressed in the following subproposition:

> If third parties recognize the secessionist bid of one or more groups while denying it to ethnic competitors, then the ethnic group will adopt a strategy of ethnic violence to claim the rump state or to secede (Proposition 7.4).

This scenario is also likely to trigger more extreme forms of ethnic violence when the contested territory is home to two or more groups who are regionally dispersed or when that territory is a contested homeland. If groups perceive that recognition will be extended only to groups that are regionally concentrated or to territories that are ethnically homogenous, then third parties effectively create an incentive for ethnic cleansing. The selective recognition of republics in Yugoslavia with little regard for ethnic realities on the group prompted widespread ethnic cleansing to buttress claims to self-determination. In an effort to resolve or prevent violence, third parties thus unwittingly create a scenario whereby groups are likely to adopt violent means aimed at ethnic homogenization. This scenario suggests the following subproposition:

> If third parties recognize the independence of one or more regionally concentrated groups while denying it to regionally dispersed groups, then the excluded groups will be more likely to adopt strategies of ethnic cleansing (Proposition 7.5).

When third parties become involved in either material or nonmaterial ways in an ethnic conflict between groups or between groups and the state, ethnic groups are more likely to adopt violent means. Four scenarios describe the impact of systemic actors on ethnic conflict. Each of these scenarios—escalation, division, mediation, and recognition—describe distinct ways in which third parties impact a group's choice of violent means.

THE RESOURCE MODEL

Without the necessary arms and resources to sustain violent conflict against ethnic competitors or the state, ethnic conflict is unlikely to escalate to ethnic war. Arms are a necessary precondition both for sustained ethnic violence and for the achievement of group aims. Regardless of the strength of group claims, the severity of the threat to group survival or a group homeland, or the effectiveness of an ethnic leadership, sustained ethnic violence is effectively impossible without access to arms. These arms need not be sophisticated, as the machetes, spears, and knives that produced large-scale human carnage in Rwanda demonstrate.[39] Yet advanced armaments "facilitate faster killing."[40] They are also necessary when groups challenge the professional or paraprofessional soldiers wielded by the state.

The Resource Model suggests that crossing the threshold from protest to violence requires arms, ammunition, spare parts, financial resources, and the expertise necessary to sustain violence against ethnic strangers or the state controlled by ethnic strangers. Although unsophisticated weapons may be sufficient to initiate sporadic violence, sustaining a strategy of interethnic warfare requires a reliable supply of arms. Whereas states tend to purchase heavy weapons, substate actors tend to focus their efforts on acquiring light or small arms that are easier to move and conceal. As Aaron Karp suggests, "the availability of these weapons directly affects the pace and direction of ethnic conflict."[41]

Arms and related support can be purchased or seized from a myriad of sources, including domestic armories, arms suppliers, and states. Groups may acquire some weapons from domestic sources (government armories, battlefield capture, or domestic manufacture). But evidence shows that most arms are procured from external suppliers, particularly nearby states.[42] Sislin and Pearson show that states remain the most secure form of resupply and the main guarantor of sophisticated arms and spare parts.[43]

The preference for state suppliers is shaped by the significant constraints under which groups operate when attempting to procure or seize the necessary arms and supplies for interethnic war. Without safe havens, groups are also constrained in their ability to stockpile weapons, particularly heavy weapons that are harder to conceal. The state supplier is thus more likely to be near the zone of conflict, preferably bordering the conflict or in the same region. Ethnic groups are also more likely to have multiple suppliers than are states.[44] Whereas states acquire arsenals over many years, ethnic groups are frequently forced to acquire arms under significant time constraints. This suggests that, once acquired, there is a premium on use. In the case of Rwanda, studies have shown that there was a direct linkage between the importation of small arms and the outbreak of violence—a time span of only a few months.[45] Proving a direct causal linkage between the importation of light arms and violence is difficult given the paucity of data on the movement of small arms. In a detailed study in 2001, Sislin and Pearson found that heavy arms flows to an ethnic group were associated with subsequent escalation, a conclusion supported by a subsequent study of arms flow to the LTTE (Liberation Tigers of Tamil Eelam) in Sri Lanka by Pearson in 2006.[46]

One exception is the case of state collapse. Under these conditions, groups are likely to acquire heavy weapons from former government stockpiles. Because former military members are likely to accompany these more sophisticated weapons, their expertise and training will allow the ethnic group to employ them against ethnic rivals and remnants of the state. Numerous examples of such heavy weapons transfers from defecting military can be found in the Nagorno-Karabakh War, as well as in other conflicts in the former Soviet Union. The Kurds have similarly proved adept at seizing heavy weapons from Iraqi and Iranian forces at various times in their decades-long conflict.

Although the global arms market is said to be awash in small-arms supply, acquiring these weapons in sufficient numbers and in a consistent manner is no easy task. Absent direct military sales by foreign governments, ethnic groups must rely on a myriad of external sponsors whose supplies vary over time and who offer no contractual assurances of resupply, parts and technical advice, warranties, or ammunition.[47] Groups thus face real challenges in establishing a reliable supply chain, which, combined with constraints on stockpiling arms, adds to the challenge of procuring sufficient arms to escalate from a conflict to a full-scale ethnic war.

Because ethnic groups face significant constraints in securing a reliable supply of weapons over time, they are likely to rely on commercial arms dealers, ethnic kindred, and criminal organizations to augment state supply. Black-market purchases frequently involve elaborate transit schemes, employing other non-state actors such as criminal organizations who have networks in place to move drugs and other contraband. There are numerous examples of the links between ethnic groups and organized crime. In the former Yugoslavia, ethnic groups cultivated links with organized crime groups for profit to fund the purchases of arms and supplies, particularly following the imposition of an arms embargo.

Once sources are identified, groups face the related challenge of payment. Groups in Africa have relied on the diamond trade to fund their operations.[48] Other sources of funds include drug trafficking as well as extortion of local business in conflict zones and reliance on transnational kindred, particularly wealthy diasporas, for vital donations. Groups will also seek to cultivate relationships with friendly foreign states that may choose to subsidize shipments in pursuit of their own regional interests.

These significant limitations, in terms of the reliability and accessibility of supply and the funds necessary to procure arms not available for local seizure or "purchase," impose important constraints on an ethnic group with grievances against the state or ethnic strangers. Groups engage in complex strategic calculations, weighing the quality and quantity of arms, the likelihood of delivery and resupply, and the ability to fund necessary resources to sustain ethnic war. When these constraints are weighed alongside calculations of the likelihood of success, which include assessments of the nature and reliability of external support, groups will determine whether to adopt violent means. This suggests the following proposition:

> If an ethnic group with grievances against ethnic strangers secures sufficient arms and resources to sustain a strategy of ethnic violence, then the group will be more likely to adopt violent means (Proposition 8).

Without the necessary arms and resources to sustain violent conflict against ethnic competitors or the state, ethnic conflict is unlikely to escalate to ethnic war. Arms are a necessary precondition both for sustained ethnic violence and for the achievement of group aims. When groups secure the necessary resources to sustain violent conflict against ethnic strangers, the likelihood that a group will adopt violent means increases, as does the likelihood that violence will intensify.

CONCLUSION

At the third image, we find considerable overlap between the External Support and Resource Models. Many of the states targeted for external support are also the suppliers of arms and resources necessary to sustain ethnic war. In each of the four scenarios detailing the impact of third parties on a group's choice of violent means, the availability of arms significantly increases the likelihood that groups will adopt violent means. Third parties use both support and arms to escalate conflict and trigger within-group conflict in pursuit of their own broader, regional interests. When the escalation and division scenarios operate in tandem with the Resource Model, escalatory cycles of third-party support are likely to be more intensely violent and divisions between and among groups are likely to deepen, triggering the further escalation and intensification of ethnic violence.

The mediation and recognition scenarios are similarly impacted by the Resource Model. A disadvantaged or excluded group will be more likely to adopt or resume violent means when it has the necessary resources to challenge ethnic strangers or the state. When selective recognition denies the aspirations of an ethnic group for a state of its own, access to the resources necessary to sustain war is critical to the decision to adopt or resume violent means to claim the rump state or to cleanse a contested territory of ethnic strangers.

The two third image models complete our multilevel framework for understanding why groups adopt violent means. At each image we developed distinct explanations for the choice of violent means and briefly considered the interaction among them. In the next chapters, we apply this framework to three cases of violent ethnic war. In Chapter 8 we return to each of the models at each of the three images to study the interrelationships among them.

5

Chapter

Three Images
in Yugoslavia

INTRODUCTION

This chapter examines three interrelated conflicts, first in Croatia between Serbs and Croats; subsequently in Bosnia among Serbs, Croats, and Bosnian Muslims; and finally in Kosovo between Serbs and Kosovar Albanians. Because of the multiple parties to the conflict, the overlapping arenas of conflict, and the significant involvement of third parties, this case presents a unique opportunity to test the entire framework.

The myriad causes of violence in Yugoslavia support the contention that ethnic violence is rarely a single-level phenomenon. Yugoslavia's ethnic groups adopted violent means for reasons that had to with group identity; with the eroding authority, capacity, and legitimacy of the Yugoslav state and the unranked structure of its ethnic populations; and with the significant involvement of third parties. We will apply each of the models across the three images of ethnic war to explain why Yugoslavia's ethnic groups adopted violent means and to demonstrate the value of a multilevel approach to understanding ethnic violence.

THE HOMELAND MODEL

The question of Kosovo was central to the wars fought in Croatia and Bosnia long before violence erupted between Serbs and Kosovar Albanians over the contested region. Serbs throughout Yugoslavia mobilized in defense of Kosovo, which triggered a broader airing of Serb grievances and justified a strategy of violence against the Serbs' historical enemies in Croatia, Bosnia, and finally Kosovo itself.

The Homeland Model suggests that ethnonationalists will adopt violence to defend or reclaim a homeland because possession of that homeland is *vital to the identity and continued survival of the ethnic group* (Proposition 1). Both Serbs and Albanians are ethnonationalists, regionally concentrated ethnic groups with a

Figure 5.1 Map of the Former Yugoslavia.

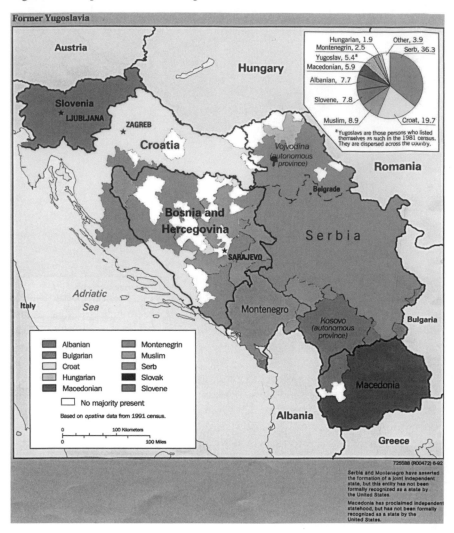

Source: U. S. Central Intelligence Agency, *The Former Yugoslavia: A Map Folio* (1992). Available at http://www.lib.utexas.edu/maps/europe/yugoslav.jpg

history of autonomy or self-rule both in the contested region of Kosovo and in their respective nation-states of Serbia and Albania. Both the Serb and Albanian nations claim the contested region as part of Greater Serbia or Greater Albania. These claims are based on a blending of myth and historical fact. Kosovo, or Kosovo and Metohija as it is known to Serbs, is central to Serbian nationalist mythology. Kosovo symbolizes a centuries-old struggle against historic enemies, as well as the victimization and martyrdom of Serbs under Ottoman occupation.[1] The tragic defeat of the Serbian Army of King Lazar at the battle at Kosovo Polje in 1389 by the Ottoman Army of Murad I is still celebrated on June 28, St. Vitus' Day. Kosovo is also the seat of the Serbian Patriarchate at Pec and the cradle of the medieval Serbian kingdom.[2] During foreign occupation, the Serbian church became the focus of Serb identity.

Serbs buttress their rightful ownership of Kosovo on claims of blood and tenure. The Serb kingdom of the Nemanjić monarchs ruled over portions of modern-day Kosovo during the early Middle Ages; the churches built under their auspices in Pec and Gracanica, and the monastery of Visoki Decani, provide proof of Serbian rule in Kosovo before the Ottoman invasions. According to the Serbian Association of Writers, "There is so much Serbian blood and so many sacred relics that Kosovo will remain Serbian land, even if not a single Serb remains there."[3]

Albanians reject the Serbian argument that Kosovo's population was overwhelmingly Serb until recently. Their argument is founded on a claim of first possession: the ancient Illyrians and Dardanians, early ancestors of Kosovar Albanians, lived there long before the Slav invasions of the six and seventh centuries.[4] Albanian historians further dispute claims that the medieval population of Kosovo was predominately Serb, arguing that Albanians were the majority population and that forced assimilation explains the predominance of Slavic names in the church registries of the period.[5] During the centuries of Ottoman rule until 1912, significant demographic shifts through conversion, migration, and refugee flows of ethnic Albanians into the region and Serbs out of the region altered the population balance in favor of ethnic Albanians.

In modern history, Serbs buttress their claims to Kosovo on Serbia's liberation of the province from Ottoman rule in 1912. Widely celebrated among Serbs, the capture of Kosovo was a disaster for its majority Albanian inhabitants, destroying their hopes that Kosovo would be included in the newly created state of Albania. In 1918, Kosovo became part of the Kingdom of Serbs, Croats and Slovenes—renamed Yugoslavia in 1929. In 1941, German forces invaded Yugoslavia, and Serbia was divided. Portions came under Hungarian and German rule, and the rest was annexed to the Independent State of Croatia (NDH). Kosovo was divided into three sectors: Bulgarian, German, and Albanian zones. The Albanian-controlled territory was briefly attached to Albania, which had been conquered by the Italians. In 1943, no Kosovar Albanians were present when the foundations for a new Yugoslavia were negotiated at the Second Anti-Fascist Council for the National Liberation of Yugoslavia (AVNOJ) on the basis of the right to self-determination for all peoples. In 1954, Kosovo was formally annexed to Serbia and subsequently declared an autonomous region of Serbia within the new Federal People's Republic of Yugoslavia.

Until February 2008, when Kosovo declared independence, the province remained an integral part of Serbia. Although the number of Serbs in Kosovo had declined in both absolute and relative terms (see Group Survival Model below), Serbs still "owned" Kosovo. After Milosevic revoked its autonomous status, the province came fully under Serbian control. The Homeland Model thus fails to provide an explanation for a Serb strategy of violence aimed at *reclaiming* the homeland because Serbia "owned" Kosovo.

The Homeland Model does provide a persuasive explanation for a Serbian strategy of violence to *defend* Kosovo against the threat from the majority Albanian population. Demographic changes combined with the loss of the Serbian Republic's authority over its autonomous region made the issue of Kosovo ripe for exploitation.

In the spring of 1981, a protest movement by university students sparked demonstrations throughout the province with slogans such as "Kosovo-Republic!" and "We Want a Unified Albania!"[6] The riots had a tremendous impact on Yugoslavia. They sparked a nationalist revival among Serbs that destroyed the Titoist policy of national coexistence. The relative freedom of post-Tito Yugoslavia meant that the status of Serbs in Kosovo could be openly discussed. Many Serbs left the province after the riots, and throughout the 1980s petitions were circulated by Serbs in Kosovo demanding an end to Kosovar Albanian aggression in the province. This argument became a centerpiece of the famous *Memorandum of the Serbian Academy of Sciences and Arts*, portions of which first appeared in the press in 1986. The Memorandum claimed that Serbs were subjected to genocide and that 200,000 Serbs had been forced to leave Kosovo in the previous two decades.[7] Efforts on the part of Kosovo Albanians to create an ethnically pure Albanian state threatened the loss, once again, of their "Jerusalem" to Muslim "aliens."[8] Not only were Serbs being forced to leave their historic homeland, nationalists claimed, but Albanian desires to claim Kosovo for Greater Albania were also threatening the Serbian homeland in Kosovo and all that it symbolized for Serbs—not just in Kosovo, but throughout Yugoslavia.

Milosevic skillfully exploited the issue of Kosovo to mobilize Serbs in support of a strategy of interethnic violence aimed at redrawing the boundaries of Serbia to include Serbs living in Croatia and Bosnia. The symbolism of Kosovo—of a valiant and heroic struggle and of victimization and martyrdom—proved crucial in mobilizing Serbs throughout Yugoslavia in defense of the province. Although violence erupted in Croatia and Bosnia, not Kosovo, the symbology of Kosovo remained central to the nationalist movement and the aim of securing a Greater Serbia out of Yugoslavia's collapse. The centrality of Kosovo to the Serb adoption of a strategy of violence *outside of Kosovo* illustrates the rallying power of a widely perceived threat to an ethnic homeland. The case of Yugoslavia suggests that the Homeland Model can explain the choice of violent means to defend a homeland, even when the violence does not occur in that homeland. Defense of an ethnic homeland is a powerful source of ethnic group mobilization.

After the 1995 Dayton conference, Kosovar Albanians became increasingly dis-illusioned with their leadership's policy of peaceful resistance and began to support a more confrontational strategy. A new, armed resistance group, the Kosovo Liberation Army (KLA), began mounting attacks that sparked Serbian reprisals. In October 1988 the Holbrooke-Milosevic agreement set the stage for the withdrawal of Serbian police and armed forces from Kosovo. The KLA exploited the vacuum created by a reduced Serbian presence to escalate its attacks on Serbs.[9] As the threat to Serbs in Kosovo escalated, Serbia launched a large-scale operation in February–March 1999, dubbed "Operation Horseshoe," a strategic plan aimed at solving the Kosovar Albanian homeland claim by cleansing a broad, horseshoe-shaped swath of territory of its Kosovar Albanian inhabitants.[10] Thousands of Kosovar Albanian refugees began to flee the province as NATO's bombing campaign began on March 24, and a week later 300,000 refugees had crossed into Albania and Macedonia. Within a few weeks the number of refugees had increased to 850,000, some forcibly deported on trains, and others fleeing voluntarily.[11] The intent of this strategy of ethnic homogenization was to defend Serbia's ownership of Kosovo by expelling ethnic strangers, the Kosovar Albanians (Proposition 1.2).

The Homeland Model also explains the Kosovar Albanian decision to adopt violent means following the 1995 Dayton Accords. Until the 1995 conference, Kosovar Albanians supported Ibrahim Rugova's policy of peaceful resistance, in part due to a fear that the violence in Croatia and Bosnia might engulf Kosovo, as well as a belief that Yugoslavia's collapse would eventually allow Kosovo's Albanian population to claim ownership of its homeland. Within Kosovo there was a widely shared hope that, through international auspices, Kosovo's population would eventually be reunited with Albania. The Dayton accords shattered this hope and propelled Kosovar Albanians who had questioned the wisdom of Rugova's policy to mobilize and recruit support from among Kosovar Albanians and the wider Albanian diaspora for a strategy of violence. The choice of violent means aimed not only at drawing attention to the Kosovar Albanians' plight but also sought to deny Serbia's right to rule over the province's non-Serb population. Violence was aimed not at securing autonomy or cultural rights for the province's Albanian population. Instead, homeland ownership prompted the adoption of violent means to secure Kosovo's independence (Proposition 1.1).

The case of Kosovo demonstrates that ethnonationalists are rarely willing to settle for autonomy, because homeland ownership is central to group identity and survival. At the peace talks at Rambouillet in 1999 that set the stage for NATO's bombing campaign, the Kosovar Albanians warned, "The armed struggle will not stop until the independence of Kosovo."[12] A successful conclusion to the negotia-tions hinged on the future status of Kosovo. The Albanian negotiators were adamant that no agreement would be accepted unless it provided for a referen-dum and eventual independence, and the Serbs were equally adamant that they would "not give Kosovo-Metohjia away even at the cost of bombardment."[13] The case of Kosovo illustrates how claims of homeland ownership and homeland defense will propel groups to adopt violent means even when the likelihood of success is low, the strategy is likely to incur significant costs, or the violence is likely to be protracted.

THE ETHNOCHAUVINISM MODEL

The Ethnochauvinism Model suggests that a widely held belief in the superiority of the group, and thus its right to dominate the ethnic other, will spur a reexamination of history (particularly of violence perpetrated by historic enemies), awaken feelings of national danger, and promote desires for revenge. Frequently driven by fear—of group extinction, of eroding identity, of loss of dominance—ethnochauvinism assuages group angst by lauding the great achievements of the group and justifying its right to primacy over the inferior other. The Yugoslav case, and particularly the example of Serb ethnochauvinism, clearly demonstrates how fear and opportunity combined to prompt Serbs throughout Yugoslavia to support chauvinist polices aimed at creating a Greater Serbia and the violent means necessary to achieve it.

The roots of Serbian ethnochauvinism can be traced to the Serbian nationalist revival sparked by the 1981 riots in Kosovo. Confined first to the intelligentsia, the reexamination of the Serb nation's history in Kosovo—and more broadly, in Yugoslavia—soon received wide coverage in the press. The nationalist reawakening centered on two seemingly contradictory themes: the collective heroism of the Serb nation symbolized by the mythology of Kosovo, and the history of Serb martyrdom and victimization most recently cemented by the 1974 Yugoslav constitution. Both were used to justify the Serbs' right to dominate and exclude the ethnic other in Croatia, Bosnia, and Kosovo.

Cloaked in the language of injustice, a Serb narrative of superiority emphasized the collective heroism of the Serb nation. The myth of Kosovo was central to this narrative. Before a crowd of millions of Serbs who had flocked to Gazimestan to celebrate the six hundredth anniversary of the battle of Kosovo Polje on June 28, 1989, Milosevic stated, "the Kosovo heroism does not allow us to forget that *at one time we were brave and dignified and one of the few who went into battle undefeated* . . . Today, six centuries later, we are again fighting a battle and facing battles. They are not armed battles, although such things cannot yet be excluded."[14] As the narrative of past injustice melded with the present, Serb ethnochauvinism justified the adoption of violent means in a battle against the Serbs' historic enemies in modern guise.

The situation of Serbs in Kosovo was at the center of the Serb nation's battle against its enemies. According to the Memorandum, Serbs in Kosovo were subjected to "physical, political, juridical and cultural genocide."[15] The plight of the Serbs in Kosovo was in part a consequence of Serbia's "unequal" position within the Yugoslav federation.[16] According to Mihailo Markovich, "the borders of the Serbian republic [after Word War II] were so drawn that millions of Serbs remained minorities in other republics . . . Serbia found itself in the absurd political position with a third of its population in other republics, divided into three parts in its own republic, [and] deprived of any legal or political status in its central part."[17] The Memorandum's sharpest attacks were aimed at the 1974 constitution: "a worse historical defeat in peacetime cannot be imagined."[18] It denied the Serb nation a position and influence equal to Yugoslavia's other nations. Even worse, the constitution had practically effaced Serbia's sovereignty over its two autonomous provinces, Kosovo and Vojvodina.[19]

In the summer of 1990, the emotional evocation of the massacre of Serbs by the Ustase forces during World War II fed the chauvinist impulse to avenge past wrongs and dominate historic enemies. It awoke feelings of national danger, solidarity, and hatred against the Croatian fascists who perpetrated the atrocities, as well as the Albanians and Bosnian Muslims for their "genocidal acts" against the Serbian people.[20] Nationalist Serbian intellectuals dwelled at length on the massacres and mutilations of Serbs, "none too subtly implying that Croats as a people were 'genocidal.'"[21] The preoccupation with the massacres of World War II and Serbia's wartime sufferings had a significant impact on the general populace, not just in Serbia but also throughout Yugoslavia, heightening tensions in those regions where large Serb populations resided.

In the Krajina, Serbs claimed that they confronted "an open state of terror."[22] Although there was no evidence of genocide, nationalist leaders and propagandists in Belgrade successfully mobilized Serbian opposition to Zagreb by convincing a majority of local Serbs that they were indeed threatened by genocide.[23] Following the election of Tudjman's Croatian Democratic Union (HDZ) in April 1990, this fear had turned to panic. As it became clear that Croatia would secede from Yugoslavia, Milosevic stated,

It has not occurred to us to dispute the right of the Croatian nation to secede from Yugoslavia, if that nation decides of its own free will in a referendum . . . but I want to make it completely clear that it should not occur to anyone that a part of the Serbian nation will be allowed to go with them. Because the history of the Serbian nation in the Independent State of Croatia is too tragic to risk such a fate again.[24]

The media portrayal of a new fascist Croatian government intent on exterminating all Serbs was given added ammunition when the newly elected Croatian government passed constitutional provisions adopting traditional Croatian ethnic symbols that Croatia's Serbs associated with the hated Ustase regime. The reemergence of this symbolism was, for Krajina's Serb leaders, certain evidence of the reemergence of Croatian fascism.

Fear of renewed injustice at the hands of the Serbs' historic enemies fueled a desire to avenge past wrongs and to secure Serbia's rightful place in Yugoslavia. As this belief gained greater support among Serbs throughout Yugoslavia, Serb ethnochauvinism justified violent means against the Serbs' modern enemies. Slovenia and Croatia's declarations of independence in the summer of 1991 triggered the first deliberate use of violent means to avenge past injustice and secure Serbia's rightful place in Yugoslavia. The Serb-dominated Yugoslav People's Army (JNA) deployed to Slovenia and fought a ten-day war to seize control of the republic and prevent Yugoslavia's disintegration. In Croatia the Serbs adopted violent means to secure the Krajina's inclusion in Greater Serbia, which the Serb leadership believed it had a right to dominate, and to protect the Serbs in Croatia from renewed injustice (Proposition 2).

The chauvinistic nationalism emanating from Serbia also had a significant impact on Serbs living in Bosnia-Herzegovina. Serb nationalists questioned the true intentions of Bosnia's Muslims, alleging that their aim was to create an Islamic fundamentalist state.[25] Serb nationalists cited Bosnian President Alija Izetbegovic's "Islamic Declaration," which advocated the creation of an Islamic community from Morocco to Indonesia and the "destr[uction of] the existing non-Islamic power," as proof.[26] Serbia's enemy in Bosnia had become the allegedly fundamentalist Muslim population that was seeking to impose an Islamic state and perpetrate genocide against the Bosnian Serbs.[27] As Serb refugees from Croatia fled to Bosnia, their stories increased this fear and made the chauvinistic Serb rhetoric all the more appealing.

In Bosnia, ethnochauvinism prompted Serbs to adopt violent means to secure historic Serb territories that belonged to Greater Serbia. Because Serbs were intermingled with Croat and Bosnian Muslim populations in those territories, violent means were employed to deport, expel, or exterminate ethnic strangers (Proposition 2.1). Ethnochauvinism also justified more extreme forms of violence against enemies who stood in the way of a plan to create a Greater Serbia that Serbs would dominate (Proposition 2.2).

In Kosovo, ethnochauvinism prompted strategies aimed at avenging Kosovar Albanian violence against the Serb population of the province while ensuring Serb dominance. The end of the war in Bosnia did not alter Serbian policies in Kosovo. Rather, it focused Serb nationalist efforts on securing Kosovo through increasingly repressive measures that culminated in Milosevic's 1999 campaign aimed at the ethnic homogenization of Kosovo by expelling its ethnic Albanian population.[28] Serbian ethnochauvinism justified Serb domination of Kosovo and its majority Albanian population (Proposition 2.1) and prompted a strategy aimed at ethnic homogenization (Proposition 2.2), both of which were justified by the Serbs' right to dominate, if not destroy, the ethnic other.

Ethnic chauvinism created a zero-sum environment that precluded negotiation with the "viciously anti-Serbian" other. Ultimately, it prompted Serbs to adopt an offensive strategy of violence that aimed to cleanse parts of Croatia and Bosnia and, in attaching them to the Serbian republic, realize the historic dream of a Greater Serbia. In Kosovo, it precluded any negotiations over the status of the province that Serbs claimed solely for the Serb nation. Militant chauvinistic rhetoric promoted patterns of exclusivism, intolerance, and hatred and created the belief among Serbs in Yugoslavia that the adoption of a strategy of violence to "protect" the Serbian nation by expanding it and to redress past injustices by expelling non-Serbs was both morally justified and historically validated.

GROUP SURVIVAL MODEL

The Group Survival model does not provide an explanation for ethnic violence in Yugoslavia despite claims of ethnic and cultural genocide and demonstrable patterns of demographic change. This model suggests that groups will adopt violence in self-defense when group members perceive *a real threat to their survival as a distinct ethnic group* (Proposition 3).

One factor that leads groups to perceive a threat to their survival is the *decrease in group size*. The high birthrate of 32 per 1,000 of the Albanian population in Kosovo, combined with the continued and growing exodus of Serbs and Montenegrins from the province, resulted in a marked decline in the Serbian and Montenegrin populations while the Albanian population continued to increase, both in absolute and relative terms. In 1948 Albanians numbered 498,000. By 1981 they numbered 1,227,000. As a percentage of the total population, Albanians increased from 68.5 percent of the population in 1948 to 77.5 percent of the population in 1981.[29] During this same period the Serbian population increased only in absolute terms from 199,961 in 1948 to 236,526 in 1981. In the decades after the riots, however, the Serb and Montenegrin population declined in both absolute (Proposition 3.1) and relative terms (Proposition 3.2). Table 5.1 details the shift in population numbers in both relative and absolute terms.

By 1987 Serbs and Montenegrins together comprised only 10 percent of the population in Kosovo.[30] Clearly, the Serbian and Montenegrin population had decreased both in absolute and relative terms. Serb nationalists did indeed conclude that the survival of Serbs and Montenegrins *in Kosovo* was threatened. When violence broke out in the Krajina and later in Bosnia, however, its aim was not the survival of the Serbs in Kosovo. Although the Serb and Montenegrin populations in Kosovo did have legitimate grievances, there is no evidence of genocide. The importance of Kosovo for Serbian mythology, however, and its potential "loss" to ethnic Albanians, did present a dangerous threat to Serbs, both inside Kosovo and in the rest of Yugoslavia. Yet the survival of Serbs as a distinct

Table 5.1 Population of Kosovo[1]

Population in Kosovo	1948	1948 (% of Population)	1981	1981 (% of Population)	1991	1991 (% of Population)
Albanians	498,242	68.5	1,226,736	77.4	1,607,690	82.2
Serbs and Montenegrins	199,961	27.5	236,526	14.9	213,346	10.9
Other	29,617	4.0	121,179	7.7	153,711	6.9
Total	727,820		1,584,441		1,974,747	

[1] Steve Reiquam, "Emigration and Demography in Kosovo," *Radio Free Europe Research*, Yugoslav Background Report 186 (August 4, 1983): [2] See also Tim Judah, *Kosovo: War and Revenge*, 2nd ed. (New Haven: Yale University Press, 2002), Appendix One.

ethnic group was not at risk; rather, Serbian possession of its homeland was threatened by the decline of the Serb population in the region. These significant population shifts thus triggered violence in defense of the Serb homeland. When violence erupted in Kosovo in 1998 and 1999, that violence aimed at securing the contested province for Serbia.

A second factor that may lead a group to conclude that its survival is threatened is the loss or lack of cultural autonomy (Proposition 3.3). Whereas in Kosovo the threat was one of "ethnic genocide," in Croatia, Serb nationalists claimed that Serbs were facing "cultural genocide."[31] The new government of Franjo Tudjman elected in April 1990 adopted a number of policies that radically changed the status of the Serbian population in Croatia. Whereas Serbs had enjoyed full rights as one of the titular nations of Yugoslavia, once Croatia declared independence, Serbs in Croatia became a national minority.

Tudjman did make an effort to include the Serbian leadership in the new government, which it refused to accept. However, Tudjman ignored its pleas to wait on adopting the constitutional changes, thus weakening the faction in the Serbian leadership that would have been willing to negotiate with the new Croatian government. Tudjman's hasty adoption of these measures to realize the "thousand-year-old dream" of Croatian statehood alienated moderate Serbs and strengthened more militant leaders, who were eventually able to sideline the moderate leadership and embark on a strategy of violence. This more militant faction of the Serbian leadership began preparing for war with Croatia well before the elections that brought Tudjman to power had taken place and well before the measures used as evidence of impending cultural genocide had been adopted.[32]

The Croatian government under Tudjman acted too hastily in its adoption of a new constitution and in its dismissal of Serbs throughout the republic. Furthermore, its adoption of the symbols of the Croatian nation, with little regard for the historical meaning its Serbian population attached to these symbols, was an ill-planned strategy that gave little thought to the potentially dangerous implications. Although Serbs in Croatia were not physically threatened, and although there was no evidence of "genocide,"[33] the actions on the part of the Croatian government made it a simple task for Serbian nationalists to persuade the Serbian population otherwise. As in the case of Kosovo, despite claims to the contrary, Serbs were not subjected to genocide and the continued survival of the Serbs as *a distinct ethnic group* was similarly not at risk. Both instances suggest that the choice of violent means can be better explained by other models at the group level as well as by the models at the state and international levels.

THE ETHNIC LEADERSHIP MODEL

Arguably the most important cause of ethnic violence in Yugoslavia was the decision by the Serbian leadership in Croatia, Bosnia, and Serbia that violent means were necessary to secure first a Serb-dominated Yugoslavia, and, subsequently, a Greater Serbia that would include all Serb-populated and historic

Serb lands (Proposition 4). This leadership secured the resources necessary to embark upon violence, employing the resources of the Yugoslav Army (JNA), creating and supplying ethnic militias, and pre-positioning forces in advance of each phase of the conflict's escalation from Croatia, to Bosnia, and finally to Kosovo. Yet the leadership ultimately failed to secure the necessary external support for its strategy, misread the interests of international actors, and undermined its own goals through the escalation of violence, particularly in Kosovo. These fundamental miscalculations ultimately cost Serbia the loss of the Krajina and of Kosovo, and it left Serbs in Bosnia with a much smaller territory than they controlled at the height of the war in 1992.

Although the leaderships of the other Yugoslav republics all bear responsibility to some degree for the events that led to the gradual collapse of Yugoslavia following Tito's death, it was the Serbian leadership, especially Slobodan Milosevic, whose strategies provoked interethnic violence. The Serbian leadership used the opportunity provided by Tito's death, and the lack of consensus among the other republican leaderships about Yugoslavia's future, to launch a war aimed at realizing the dream of a Greater Serbia. The early success of this strategy was ultimately the result of the rise to power of the single most important post-Tito Yugoslav leader and avowed Serbian nationalist: Slobodan Milosevic.

Milosevic's central role in the outbreak of violence in Yugoslavia demonstrates both the *charismatic leader scenario* (Proposition 4.1) and the *militant leader scenario* (Proposition 4.2). Milosevic drew support from among Serbs throughout Yugoslavia by effectively using the Serbs' plight in their historic homeland, the desire for a national unification of all Serbs within a Serb-dominated state, and the need for national defense against the Serbs' historic enemies in Croatia, Bosnia, and Kosovo. He was also effective at building support among the nationalist intelligentsia, particularly among the more extremist Serb elite, to sideline or otherwise silence moderate Serbs who opposed the destruction of Yugoslavia.

The Kosovo crisis propelled Milosevic, a hitherto little-known bureaucrat with ties of friendship to the head of the Serbian Communist Party, into the limelight. Deeply impressed by the claims in the Memorandum, Milosevic saw it as an opportunity to expand his own power. On April 24–25, 1987, Milosevic attended a meeting in Kosovo Polje of 300 party delegates, most of whom were Kosovar Albanians, that was to address the deteriorating situation in the province. Some 15,000 Serbs and Montenegrins attempted to gain access to the meeting, but were rebuffed by the Kosovar Albanian police wielding clubs. Milosevic raised his hands and signaled to the police to let the Serbs into the meeting, telling them, "Nobody, either now or in the future, has the right to beat you."[34] With these words, Milosevic was "assured a place in Serbian mythology."[35] Milosevic sided with the demonstrators and told them,

> The first thing I wish to tell you comrades, is that you must remain here.
> This is your land, your houses are here, your fields and gardens, your

memories . . . It was never characteristic of the spirit of the Serb and Montenegrin people to knuckle under to difficulties, to demobilize itself when it must fight, to become demoralized when the going is tough. You must remain here on account of your ancestors and descendants. Otherwise, we would be shaming the ancestors and disillusioning the descendants.[36]

Milosevic emerged from that meeting profoundly changed. He suddenly realized that he had power over people.[37] Milosevic urged them to resist and, in so doing, "hijacked the nationalist movement."[38] He used the plight of Kosovo to launch his own career and to promote a strategy that would seek to redress the injustices outlined in the Memorandum, which became, in effect, Milosevic and the Serbian Nationalists' manifesto. Under Milosevic, the Serbian party organization was turned into *the* party of Serbian nationalism.

Once Milosevic replaced Stambolic as president of Serbia, he implemented a four-part strategy to ensure Serb dominance in post-Tito Yugoslavia and to secure Kosovo for the Serbs. Milosevic's first step was to assume full control of Serbia itself, which required a pliant press.[39] A pliant press proved critical to "uncovering" atrocities against Serbs in Albania. Milosevic was so successful in his consolidation of power that "it became impossible for Serbs to criticize Milosevic publicly and retain jobs of any importance."[40]

Milosevic's next task was to remove the danger of being outvoted by reformists in the other republics and of facing a federal level alliance of reformists.[41] Milosevic undertook a series of measures to secure his control over Serbia's two autonomous provinces and over neighboring Montenegro. The successful implementation of this strategy would give Serbia control of four of the eight federal votes, ensuring that the federal presidency could not take a single decision without Milosevic's approval.[42] Milosevic exploited the issue of Kosovo, using the Committee for the Protection of Kosovo Serbs and Montenegrins, established in 1988, to bring the provinces and Montenegro under Serbian control. Through orchestrated demonstrations, first in Vojvodina and then in Kosovo and Montenegro in 1988 and 1989, Milosevic forced the resignations of the local leaderships and their replacement with loyal followers.

Milosevic's third step involved changing the Serbian constitution and reversing the 1974 constitutional provisions that had removed Serbia's control over its two provinces. In February 1989 Milosevic successfully pushed though constitutional changes that eliminated the provinces' autonomy.[43] The new constitution also gave the president of Serbia an unusual new prerogative: it granted the president the power to declare war and conclude peace.[44]

By mid-1989, Milosevic controlled half the votes on the Yugoslav Federal Presidency. To dominate the presidency, however, Milosevic would need at least five of the eight votes.[45] Milosevic thus implemented the fourth part of his strategy: the removal of the republican leaderships in the remaining Yugoslav republics and their replacement by loyal conservative leaderships willing to acknowledge

Serbian supremacy in a recentralized Yugoslavia. Milosevic again relied on mass rallies under the guise of explaining "the truth" about Serb persecution and genocide in Kosovo.

Milosevic's strategy of subverting the other republican leaderships backfired. It emboldened the reformists and radicalized the other republican parties, while weakening conservatives who were accused of being allied with Milosevic and his aggressive rhetoric. Milosevic's efforts to recentralize the federal party at the Fourteenth Party Congress in January 1990 failed. Multiparty elections were scheduled in Croatia and Slovenia for spring 1990, and openly antisocialist parties were campaigning to loosen, rather than tighten, political ties.

The original goal of Serbian conservatives had been to recentralize Yugoslavia. By 1990, however, the reformist backlash in the other republics meant that Serbian conservatives now faced a critical choice: either they had to accept defeat and Yugoslavia's transformation into a confederalist system, or they could fight to create a new, Serb-dominated state. They chose the latter, adopting a strategy known as "Project RAM" that sought to "use military force to expand Serbia's borders westward and create a new Serbian Yugoslavia."[46] At this critical juncture the Serb leadership chose to adopt violent means to secure its goals, and in so doing, undermined moderates in the other Yugoslav republics and sealed the fate of Yugoslavia.

Nationalists and private militias began provoking confrontations and violent incidents in the Krajina and in Bosnia. The Serb leadership in Belgrade took over the Serbian Democratic Party (SDS) in Croatia, replacing moderate leaders with hardliners such as Milan Babic. The more militant Serbian leadership in Croatia, with Belgrade's prompting, rejected all compromises with Zagreb, organized mass rallies and demonstrations, and threatened Serbs in Croatia—most of whom supported a moderate reformist course—to accept the new confrontational strategy. Local forces in the Krajina provoked armed incidents with the Croatian police, stormed villages adjacent to regions already under Serb control and annexed them to their territory, and proclaimed the establishment of the "Republic of Serb Krajina." Moderate Serbs were threatened and silenced by paramilitary groups, many from Serbia itself, who played an important role in cleansing mixed villages of ethnic Croats. Their efforts made it increasingly difficult for more moderate Serbs to pursue negotiations with the Croatian government or Croatian opposition parties.

Belgrade's strategy in the Krajina was closely tied to events within Serbia itself. As the fighting in Croatia spread from the Krajina, where Serbs were in the majority, to other areas in Croatia—such as Slavonia, where Serbs were often in the minority—the Serbian leadership faced massive demonstrations by the political opposition in Belgrade in early March 1991. At the end of March, to forestall Croatia from taking advantage of his weakened position, Milosevic met secretly with Tudjman and agreed to the division of Bosnia-Herzegovina.[47] At the same time, the media charged opposition leader Vuk Draskovic with plotting to destabilize Serbia in secret alliance with Tudjman's "Ustase regime."[48]

To insulate itself further from any opposition, the ruling Socialist Party of Serbia (SPS) entered into an open alliance with the militant Serbian Radical Party of Vojislav Seselj, whose "Chetnik" guerrilla groups were at the forefront of cleansing Serb regions in the Krajina and Slavonia of Croats. In an interview with *Der Speigel*, when asked what he would do if he were Serbia's president, Seselj responded, "I would immediately mobilize all Serbs, amputate Croatia in a blitzkrieg, and then inform the international community of the new Serbian borders."[49] When asked where those borders would be, Seselj answered, "the current Serbia, including the provinces of Vojvodina and Kosovo . . . [and] the republics of Bosnia-Herzegovina, Macedonia, and Montenegro, and the Serbian areas of Croatia."[50] In comparison with the extremist Seselj, the SPS and Milosevic appeared a more moderate option.

By the end of 1991 the opposition, which seemed poised to defeat Milosevic in April, was in shambles. Milosevic had successfully marginalized and weakened the democratic opposition. However, the costs of the war were beginning to mount, Croatian forces were beginning to regain ground, and the European Community was preparing to recognize Croatia. In addition, Serbia's reputation abroad had begun to suffer, particularly following the destruction of Vukovar and Dubrovnik.[51] Milosevic thus shifted his strategy, finally conceding that a ceasefire was necessary. In December 1991 Milosevic reversed his opposition to the deployment of UN peacekeepers and pressured the Krajina leadership to accept the deployment of UNPROFOR in Serb-occupied areas of Croatia. Milosevic was forced to exert a great deal of pressure on local Croatian Serbs to obtain their agreement, for which he was subsequently praised by the international community.

Serbian tactics in Bosnia-Herzegovina were identical to those employed in Croatia, although the scale was much greater. Serbian strategy involved the proclamation of "autonomous" Serbian regions that declared their independence from the government in Sarajevo, held their own referendum, proclaimed the creation of the Serbian Republic of Bosnia-Herzegovina, and eventually declared their independence and desire to join Serbia. When violence erupted in Bosnia-Herzegovina in April 1992, again the overriding goals were to secure Serbian-populated areas and cleanse them, and to create a land corridor linking territories in Croatia with Serbia proper.

In 1992 Serbs controlled large territories in the Krajina and Croatia, as well as all of "inner Serbia." However, when Croatia launched a campaign to retake the Krajina in 1993, Serb forces began to retreat. The loss of the Krajina, combined with international pressure, created fissures in the Serb leadership and shattered Serb morale throughout the former Yugoslavia. Milosevic ultimately abandoned the Krajina after it became clear that only a full-scale Serbian war would save it. Milosevic concluded that the best alternative was to put Serbian gains "on hold" by agreeing to diplomatic initiatives that would safeguard Serb territories and buy time. The fissures among the Serbian leadership doomed this strategy to failure. Hard-liners in the Krajina rejected a negotiated settlement, having become closely tied to the more hard-line Bosnian Serb leadership, which rejected the Vance-Owen plan in May 1993 despite Milosevic's efforts to force the Bosnian Serb parliament to ratify it. Had they done so, the Serbs would have secured a more favorable settlement than the Dayton plan that Milosevic ultimately signed, ending the war in 1995.

Yet another fundamental miscalculation would end in the loss of Kosovo. The Dayton plan affirmed that Kosovo, as a province and not a republic, was to remain part of the rump Yugoslavia. The EU recognized the Federal Republic of Yugoslavia (FRY) with Kosovo as an integral part of Serbia, prompting a shift in strategy by the KLA. By the time of the Rambouillet negotiations, it was clear that nothing short of a referendum, and thus independence, would be accepted by the Kosovar Albanians. Milosevic and the hard-line Serb leadership chose to suppress the rebellion. They launched an ethnic cleansing campaign aimed at physically removing large numbers of Albanians from the province. Milosevic drew the wrong lessons from Bosnia, and fundamentally underestimated NATO's will to continue bombing. Ultimately, these fundamental missteps led to the loss of Kosovo and Milosevic's ouster.

The war in Bosnia-Herzegovina and the war in Croatia were waged to create a Greater Serbia on the ruins of Tito's Yugoslavia. The Serbian leadership mobilized the Serbian nation around the alleged genocide of Serbs first in Kosovo and then in Croatia, adopted a strategy of deliberately destroying interethnic peace to justify violent means, and embarked upon a strategy of interethnic violence to realize the dream of a Greater Serbia.

THE WEAK STATE MODEL

In Yugoslavia, we find competing and overlapping arenas of ethnic conflict. The first is the Yugoslav state itself, which faced a fundamental crisis of legitimacy following Tito's death that undermined both its authority and capacity to accommodate the divergent demands of Yugoslavia's powerful republics. Once Yugoslavia collapsed, the successor states—notably Croatia, Bosnia, and Serbia—emerged as new arenas of conflict, each with their own authority, capacity, and legitimacy deficits that constrained these new states' abilities to respond to ethnic demands.

The Weak State Model suggests that authority, capacity, and legitimacy deficits constrain a state's ability to accommodate ethnic-based challenges and increase the likelihood that conflict will escalate to violence. Three factors contributed to Yugoslavia's emergence as a weak state and its descent into ethnic warfare. First, Yugoslavia's federal system was fundamentally weakened by a devolution of power that transformed the federal center into little more than a committee whose decision-making authority was entirely consensus-based. Second, the devolution of power increased the number and power of Yugoslavia's federal actors from six to nine: it elevated Serbia's two provinces, Vojvodina and Kosovo, to federal actors equal to the republics, and it increased the prominence of the Yugoslav People's Army (JNA). Finally, the unintended consequence of Yugoslavia's constitutional reform was the destruction of Yugoslavia's legitimacy, which had been derived from an inclusive idea of the state that rested on the Titoist concept of multiethnic coexistence. As a result, the federal Yugoslav government did not have the resources or capabilities to reach accommodation with the far more powerful republics. It also lacked the means to repress the emergence first of Serbian ethnic chauvinism and then of other Yugoslav nationalisms. The powerful republics, led by Serbia and Slovenia, set out to destroy the Yugoslav system. The federal center and the Yugoslav republics that remained committed to a federal Yugoslavia were too weak to respond. Yugoslavia's failure either to repress the destructive policies of its republics or to offer concessions and broker compromise resulted in its collapse and the outbreak of ethnic violence (Proposition 5).

The decentralization of Yugoslavia's federal system was initially prompted by a decade of economic decline in the late 1950s and 1960s. Aimed at integrating Yugoslavia's republics and lessening regional disparities among them, decentralization was ultimately derailed by a conservative backlash that reversed the economic reforms but left the devolution of power in place. Yugoslavia became a confederation[52] of eight largely autonomous federal actors.[53] Yugoslavia's republics were granted vast political, cultural, and administrative autonomy, as well as an effective veto in many areas of federal legislation. These fundamental changes were enshrined in the 1971 constitutional amendments and subsequently in the 1974 constitution.

The devolution of power eroded Yugoslavia's authority, capacity, and legitimacy. The federal center became, in effect, a committee of eight republican representatives who decided matters of federal jurisdiction by consensual agreement.[54] As long as Tito was alive, he could force the republics to accept changes that were harmful to their interests. However, his death in 1981 revealed the weakness of a system that depended on Tito's authority to function. The weakened federal center was ill-equipped to manage the divergent interests of the republics.

A second cause of Yugoslavia's interrelated authority, capacity, and legitimacy deficits was the increase in the number of federal actors that resulted from the 1960s reforms. Until the 1960s there were six actors in the federal system, the six socialist republics of Yugoslavia (Serbia, Croatia, Slovenia, Macedonia, Montenegro, and Bosnia-Herzegovina). Kosovo and Vojvodina, Serbia's two provinces, had no independent representation in federal bodies. In the late 1960s, however, Serbia's two provinces began pressing for more equal treatment, and riots in 1968 in Kosovo finally prompted Tito to meet some of their demands. A series of constitutional amendments granted the two provinces extensive legislative and judicial powers. Because of these measures, the provinces enjoyed the same degree of administrative autonomy as the republics and were treated by the other federal actors as republics in everything but name. In terms of the power they wielded, the provinces were equivalent to the republics. The consequence for the federal center, however, was to increase to eight the number of actors required for consensus in order to act.

In 1987 Milosevic reasserted Serbia's control of its two provinces, which the consensus-based system was unable to prevent. Because of the increase in the number of actors at the federal level, Milosevic, by controlling the votes of Serbia's two provinces, was subsequently able to control three of the eight actors at the federal level. In effect, Milosevic would use the changes that had weakened Serbia in the 1970s to strengthen Serbia's position in the 1980s in a way that Tito's devolution never intended. The weakened federal center was unable to counter Milosevic's efforts to increase Serbia's weight at the federal level. Milosevic's actions threatened the power of the other Yugoslav republics and destroyed support for Yugoslavia's confederalists who sought to renegotiate a new Yugoslav federation in the early 1990s.

The weakened consensus-based federal system was further compounded by the addition of a ninth actor. As a result of the conservative backlash of the early 1970s that led to the ouster of liberals in all the republics and ultimately derailed Yugoslavia's economic reforms, Tito elevated the JNA such that its party organization became, in effect, "the ninth republic" at the federal level.[55] Following the purges, Tito declared that the JNA "must participate" in political affairs within Yugoslavia. Within a few years, army officers comprised 12 percent of the central committee membership, a significant increase from only 2 percent in 1969.[56] Even more ominous, Tito charged the army with ensuring domestic political order against external *and* internal enemies.[57] While Tito was alive, the army remained a neutral actor, loyal to the idea of a multiethnic Yugoslavia. After his death, however, the preponderance of Serbs and Montenegrins within the officer corps would prove critical to the functioning of the Yugoslav center. Entrusted with protecting the Yugoslav system, the JNA resisted changes proposed by the liberal Slovenian and Croatian party leaderships and increasingly supported the position of conservatives such as Milosevic. Eventually Slovenia and Croatia would stop sending recruits to the JNA and cease funding its budget, strengthening the link between the JNA and the two republics of Serbia and Montenegro.

As the federal government began to collapse, the JNA found it increasingly difficult to remain neutral. By 1991 the federal government had lost control of the Yugoslav Army. The "ninth" republic allied itself with the Serbian block. Gradually it became involved in the conflict, deploying to Slovenia to prevent its secession and to the Krajina and Bosnia-Herzegovina to fight for the interests of the rump Yugoslavia. With the state it was entrusted to protect gradually disappearing, the JNA became the army of the Serbs and Montenegrins in Yugoslavia.

Two unintended consequences from the expanded authority of Yugoslavia's republics and provinces were the destruction of the Titoist concept of multiethnic coexistence, and thus of Yugoslavia's legitimacy, and the rise of nationalism to fill this void. Devolution "elevated the republics and provinces to the status of being the only legitimate bearers of openly competing interests within the system."[58] Except for the populations of Bosnia-Herzegovina and Vojvodina, which were highly heterogeneous, the titular nationalities of the other republics and Kosovo accounted for at least two-thirds of their populations. In four of the republics, this percentage was as high as three-quarters of the republics' populations.[59] Republican leaders could thus claim to represent the ethnic interests of their titular nationality and portray themselves not only as republican leaders but also as defenders of "the nation."

The emergence of increasingly exclusive national identities ultimately eroded support for Yugoslavia's multiethnic identity. The elevation of national over broader, nonethnic interests blocked the formation of cross-republican alliances that were so critical to building the necessary consensus for the continued functioning of the federal center. It also destroyed any remaining hope of salvaging the existing system either through full confederalization or through recentralization. At the Fourteenth Party Congress in January 1990, three days of deliberation over the fate of the party ended in deadlock. The Serbs sought to recentralize Yugoslavia, which Serbia would effectively control, while the confederalists, led by Slovenia and Croatia, demanded the further devolution of power to the republics. The Slovene and Croat delegations ultimately walked out and subsequently severed links with the League of Communists of Yugoslavia (LCY), which effectively collapsed, taking with it the last vestige of Titoist Yugoslavia.[60]

During the first six months of 1991, the leaders of Yugoslavia's republics convened a series of conferences to overcome the impasse on the future structure of Yugoslavia. Both Slovenia and Croatia's referenda for independence demonstrated broad support for their secession. Macedonia and Bosnia-Herzegovina eventually supported the confederalist option, but Montenegro and Serbia's continued insistence on recentralization led to deadlock. The federal authorities were too weak to accommodate demands from Yugoslavia's ethnic groups and prevent further escalation (Proposition 5.1). On June 25, 1991, both Croatia and Slovenia declared their secession from Yugoslavia. The JNA deployed to Slovenia, prompting a ten-day war that ultimately failed to repress Slovenia's secession (Proposition 5.2). Within two months the JNA deployed to Croatia in an attempt first to repress both Croat and Serb violence by forcibly separating the two parties and subsequently to fight alongside the Krajina Serbs in an attempt to prevent the Krajina's secession as part of Croatia from the rump Yugoslavia (Proposition 5.2). Both attempts by one of the remaining federal actors to repress the secession of two of Yugoslavia's nations failed.

As Yugoslavia collapsed, new arenas of conflict emerged in Croatia, Bosnia-Herzegovina, and Serbia. Serbs in Croatia rejected the new Croatian state's right to rule, demanding autonomy for the Serbs in the Krajina. The newly independent Croatian government was effectively a weak state. It had yet to consolidate its rule and could ill afford to accommodate the Serbs, many of whom supported a more moderate solution to the conflict (Proposition 5). With no effective military forces to maintain a monopoly on the use of force, Croatian police units attempted to repress the Krajina Serbs and failed, prompting the Serbs in the Krajina to adopt violent means (Proposition 5.2).

In Bosnia-Herzegovina, a fundamental vertical and horizontal legitimacy deficit ensured that the weak republic could not accommodate the demands of its multiethnic population nor suppress ethnic mobilization when Bosnia's Serbs boycotted the 1992 referendum for independence (Proposition 5). Despite attempted negotiations over Bosnia's future under international auspices, more than a third of its population rejected the idea of a Bosnian state and adopted violent means to secure secession. With no effective Bosnian state to resist, the Bosnia Croat and Muslim groups attempted to suppress the Serb effort to dismember Bosnia, prompting the Serbs to escalate their strategy of violence (Proposition 5.2).

In Kosovo, Serb repression prompted Kosovo's Albanian population to refrain from adopting a strategy of violence (Proposition 5.3), yet repression ultimately destroyed support among Kosovar Albanians for a solution short of secession. In 1999 the Kosovar Albanian policy of peaceful resistance was rejected in favor of ethnic violence aimed at securing international recognition for independence.

In each of the arenas of conflict in Yugoslavia, state weakness limited the ability of the state—both the federal government and the individual Yugoslav successor states—to accommodate exclusivist demands. Devolution fundamentally weakened the federal government and created a legitimacy void that nationalism filled with disastrous results. The impact of the weak state arenas at each stage of the conflict presents a significant state-level explanation for both the outbreak and the escalation of violence.

THE EXCLUSION MODEL

Ethnic groups in Yugoslavia reflected a parallel or unranked structure such that each group constituted an "incipient whole society." This unranked structure was given a degree of permanence by Yugoslavia's federal system, which granted the major nationality groups in Yugoslavia their own republic. In multiethnic Bosnia-Herzegovina, the three major ethnic groups were similarly unranked, as were the Kosovar Albanians and Serbs in Kosovo. The Exclusion Model suggests that unranked ethnic groups faced with exclusion or the threat thereof will adopt violent means to protect their status or to claim ownership of the state for themselves, effectively transforming the system into a ranked one (Proposition 6).

The Serbs in both Croatia and Bosnia-Herzegovina adopted a strategy of violence to prevent their relegation to the status of a minority and their exclusion from participation in the polities in which they found themselves upon Yugoslavia's collapse (Proposition 6.1). Because Yugoslavia was also a deeply divided society, this exclusion, by virtue of the Serb percentage of the population in both Croatia and Bosnia, seemed permanent. Rather than be ruled by Croats, or by Croats and Muslims in a seemingly permanent alliance, the Serbs in Croatia and Bosnia adopted violent means to create a state of their own (Proposition 6.3). In Kosovo, exclusion prompted the Kosovar Albanians to adopt violence after the Dayton Accords effectively denied their demands for self-determination and determined Kosovo's post-Yugoslav future as a province *within* Serbia (Proposition 6.3).

As Yugoslavia proceeded to disintegrate in the late 1980s and early 1990s, Serbia sought first to transform Yugoslavia into a ranked system through a strategy of recentralization that would have ensured Serb dominance of a new

Yugoslav state. When this strategy proved unworkable, Serbia sought to create an enlarged Serb state, a Greater Serbia that would include Serb areas of Croatia and Bosnia-Herzegovina with Serb populations. Serbia's efforts first to decentralize and then to destroy multiethnic Yugoslavia directly threatened the power and status of the other republics, particularly Slovenia and Croatia, who had no interest in remaining in a state dominated by Serbia. Consequently, Slovenia and Croatia declared independence and seceded from Yugoslavia.

Slovenia's secession was not seriously contested, because it was a homogeneous state: no ethnic groups were "orphaned" when Slovenia seceded. However, Croatia's secession directly threatened the status of its significant Serb minority. The secession of Croatia and Slovenia left Bosnia-Herzegovina with the choice of remaining in a Serb-dominated rump Yugoslavia, which its Muslim and Croat population opposed, or opting for independence, which its Serbian population opposed. Either option meant exclusion of one or more of Bosnia's ethnic groups. As Yugoslavia's republics declared independence, Kosovo's Albanian population faced permanent exclusion in a rump Yugoslavia dominated by Serbs.

Serb Exclusion in Croatia

The new Croatian government elected in April 1990 adopted polices that radically changed the status of Croatia's Serb population, which constituted 12.2 percent of the population of Croatia concentrated in the Krajina, in Slavonia, and in Zagreb itself.[61] In May 1990, on the day that the Zagreb parliament appointed Tudjman president, it adopted a new constitution that revoked "some of the finest Titoist legislation protecting the rights of minorities."[62] It elevated Croats to the rank of "sole nation of the state" and accorded Croatia's Serbs the status of an official minority, a radical change from their position under the constitution of the old socialist Yugoslav state. Under the terms of the 1974 constitution, Serbs were not a minority, but one of the six constituent nations of Yugoslavia.[63]

Serbs had had considerable influence in Croatia's Communist Party before Tudjman was elected, constituting roughly 25 percent of the membership of the Croatian Communist Party despite their much smaller percentage of Croatia's population.[64] In addition, some professions, such as the police, were completely dominated by ethnic Serbs.[65] Tudjman sought to end the privileges accorded to the Serb community. Across the republic, thousands of Serbs were sidelined or fired. When the war began in earnest a year later, thousands of Serb police officers, who might otherwise have been persuaded to live in an independent Croatia, enthusiastically joined the rebels.[66]

Serbs feared that Tudjman planned to sever Croatia from Yugoslavia, either by creating a loose confederation or by outright secession.[67] Either option would leave the Serbs at the mercy of a Croatian majority and a nationalist government that had, in its first few months of rule, succeeded in alienating its Serb population. These measures persuaded many moderate Serbs that confrontation, rather than negotiation, was the better strategy for pursuing their interests within Croatia.

In early May 1991 more than 90 percent of Croatia's population voted in favor of independence. The Serbs boycotted the Croatian referendum and then held their own referendum on secession from Croatia, declaring the Krajina to be a "federal unit" of Yugoslavia.[68] Territorial or political autonomy within Croatia was no longer a viable option. Faced with separation from Yugoslavia and exclusion in a new Croat-dominated state, the Serbian minority in Croatia embarked upon a strategy of violence to secede from Croatia and create a state of their own (Proposition 6.3).

Serb Exclusion in Bosnia-Herzegovina

In Croatia, the contest over group worth was fought between two ethnic groups, the Croats and the Serbs. The situation in Bosnia-Herzegovina, however, was far more complicated. The population in Bosnia-Herzegovina was divided among three ethnic groups with diametrically opposed goals and strategies. In the last census of 1991, Bosnia's population was 43.6 percent Muslim, 31.3 percent Serb, and 17.3 percent Croat.[69] In addition, Bosnia was composed of 109 municipalities, each with different ethnic majorities. Of these municipalities, 37 had an absolute Muslim majority, 32 had an absolute Serbian majority, and 13 had an absolute Croat majority. In addition, 15 municipalities had a simple Muslim majority, five a simple Serb majority, and seven a simple Croat majority.[70] To complicate matters further, only the Croat municipalities were regionally concentrated, in western Herzegovina, with the important exception of Mostar.[71] The Muslim populations were concentrated in urban centers, and the Serb population was mostly concentrated in rural areas such that the Serb areas constituted, before the war, well over 50 percent of Bosnian territory.[72]

In the first multiparty elections held in November 1990, political leaders mobilized support along ethnic lines, using ethnic stereotypes to simplify voters' choices and avoid debate on difficult issues.[73] As a result, nonethnic or multiethnic alternatives were sidelined.[74] In addition, because of links between Zagreb and the Bosnian branch of the HDZ in Croatia and similar links between Belgrade and the Serbian Democratic Party (SDS) in Bosnia, the propaganda and ethnic demonization that characterized the election campaign were not confined to Bosnia alone.[75] Forty-one parties contested the election, and, predictably, three national parties gained votes and seats almost directly proportional to the selection of ethnic identity in the 1981 census.[76] The three parties agreed to govern in a trilateral power-sharing arrangement much like that of the federal government.

This tenuous power-sharing arrangement managed to survive through most of 1991 despite the proclamation of six Serb autonomous provinces in Bosnia-Herzegovina that proclaimed allegiance to the Yugoslav federation. In October 1991, the Hague Peace Conference on Yugoslavia made its conditional offer of recognition to any Yugoslav republic that wished it. Although the Croats preferred to be ruled by Zagreb, remaining in a rump Yugoslavia dominated by Serbia was unacceptable. Croats thus joined the Bosnian Muslims in support of independence. In October 1991, after the definitive withdrawal of Croatia and Slovenia from the Yugoslav Federation, Izetbegovic proposed a declaration of sovereignty as a way of avoiding war. However, the Serb members denounced it as a veiled attempt at secession and a violation of the power-sharing arrangement. The Serbs withdrew from the power-sharing arrangement and, in January 1992, declared an independent Serbian Republic in the 66 percent of Bosnian territory controlled by the SDS.[77] Ninety-nine percent of the voters (in a turnout of 85 percent) supported the creation of a Serbian republic if Bosnia were to secede from Yugoslavia.[78]

Despite the continued opposition of Serb members, the Muslim and Croat deputies in the Bosnian parliament authorized a referendum in accordance with the criteria established in January 1992 by the Badinter Arbitration Commission attached to the EC peace conference. The commission had recommended that a "referendum of all citizens of [Bosnia-Herzegovina] without distinction" take place before any further consideration could be given to extending recognition to Bosnia-Herzegovina.[79]

The referendum was held on February 28 and March 1, 1991, without the participation of Bosnia's Serbian population. Indeed, "all citizens" did not participate in the decision on Bosnia's future as the commission had instructed. With the Serb abstention, 63 percent of Bosnia's population participated in the referendum. The Muslims and Croats, forming an automatic majority, voted 99 percent in favor of Bosnian independence. On April 5, two days before the United States and the European Community recognized Bosnia-Herzegovina, full-scale hostilities broke out in Sarajevo.

Bosnia's Serbs were firmly opposed to Bosnian independence. As the decision over the referendum on independence had clearly shown, a Muslim-Croat alliance would ensure that the Serbs remained permanently excluded from the governance of the state and subject to Muslim-Croat rule.[80] Invoking their right to self-determination, Bosnia's Serbs adopted violent means to secede from a state in which they perceived their exclusion would be permanent (Proposition 6.3).

Kosovar Albanian Exclusion in Kosovo

Unlike the Serbs in Croatia and Bosnia, the Kosovar Albanians had long been excluded from the administration of the province. The ethnic Albanians constituted a clear majority of the population, and the size of the Albanian population had continued to increase relative to the Serb population. In the 1960s, riots in Kosovo prompted Tito to grant Kosovo a significant degree of autonomy, which was further extended after the 1981 riots such that Kosovar Albanians ruled the province. During the 1970s and 1980s, Kosovo's administration was "Albanianized"[81] and Serbs lost their privileged position, which prompted many Serbs to leave for Serbia proper. Combined with higher birthrates among Albanians, significant demographic shifts occurred during the decades of Albanian autonomy in Kosovo that Serb nationalists later termed "genocide." Until Milosevic reversed Kosovo's autonomy in 1988, the Serbian minority was effectively excluded in Kosovo. Kosovar Albanians "owned" the province and enjoyed the rights and privileges of a Yugoslav republic at the federal level.

Once Milosevic assumed power in Serbia, however, Kosovo's autonomy and the Albanianization of the province were rapidly reversed, such that the majority Kosovar Albanian population was again excluded in Kosovo. Despite the passage of several hundred new laws and decrees solidifying Serb rule over Kosovo, exclusion did not prompt violence.

A number of factors explain the lack of widespread violence in the early 1990s. First, the Kosovar leadership, under Ibrahim Rugova, adopted a policy of peaceful resistance aimed at creating a Kosovar Albanian government-in-waiting in Serb-controlled Kosovo. In December 1989 the newly founded Democratic League of Kosovo (LDK) began to take a series of steps to separate Kosovo from Serbia—but not yet from Yugoslavia—through peaceful means. As interethnic war erupted in the Krajina, Kosovo's deputies to the disbanded Kosovar Parliament voted for the "Resolution on Independence and Sovereignty of Kosovo." A subsequent referendum registered 99.87 percent in favor of independence, with Serbs in Kosovo abstaining.[82] The violent wars in Croatia and then Bosnia proved the wisdom of Rugova's policy. A violent policy of resistance without sufficient arms to sustain it or to defend the population from Serb reprisals would likely lead to a similar fate for the Kosovar Albanians. With Serbia's attention focused on these two violent conflicts, Kosovo's Albanians thus worked to construct their government-in-waiting.

The Exclusion Model suggests that the perception of *permanent exclusion* from a polity will lead a regionally concentrated, excluded group to adopt violent means to secede (Proposition 6.3). Serb exclusion of its Kosovar Albanian population in Kosovo was not permanent. The final status of the rump Yugoslavia's republics and provinces had not yet been established, and Kosovar Albanians widely believed that negotiations, under international auspices, would eventually secure Kosovo autonomy within Yugoslavia, if not independence. The risk inherent in a more violent resistance to Serb exclusion, the as-yet undetermined final status of the rump Yugoslavia, and a widespread belief that the international community would eventually grant Kosovo autonomy, if not independence, created broad support for a policy of patience and peaceful resistance.

The Dayton Conference on Bosnia in November 1995 shattered Kosovar Albanian faith in the international community's commitment to Kosovar autonomy and the wisdom of the LDK's strategy of peaceful coexistence. Aimed at ending the war in Bosnia, the Dayton negotiations were never intended as a general settlement of outstanding issues in Yugoslavia. All the major parties to the negotiations supported the Serb claim that Kosovo was an integral part of Serbia. Unwilling to risk the collapse of the negotiations, the issue of Kosovo was never addressed. Once the agreement was formally signed in Paris in early 1996, the EU recognized the rump Yugoslavia as the Federal Republic of Yugoslavia (FRY), and, with it, Kosovo as an integral part of Serbia. Kosovar Albanian exclusion in the Serb-dominated FRY now seemed permanent.

The effective transition of rule from the rump Yugoslavia to an integral part of a Serb-dominated state prompted the Kosovar Albanians to adopt violent means (Proposition 6). The Kosovo Liberation Army (KLA) began to mount violent attacks against Serb police officers and to challenge the policy of the ruling LDK. By the end of 1997, a more active policy of resistance was receiving wide-spread support among the population of Kosovar Albanians. Addressing a crowd of some 20,000 people assembled at the funeral of a Kosovar activist, masked KLA fighters addressed the crowd: "Serbia is massacring Albanians. The KLA is the only force which is fighting for the liberation and national unity of Kosovo! We shall continue to fight!"[83] This open defiance of Serb rule, and of the LDK's passive pol-icy, received widespread coverage. Violence rapidly escalated as the KLA seized areas in central Kosovo and along the Albanian border, leaving the major roads to the control of Serb forces. Finally, two attacks on important coal mines in Belacevac and Trepca triggered a Serb counterattack by the police and the army on KLA-held areas. By August 1998 an estimated 100,000 Kosovars had been displaced by the fighting, galvanizing international efforts to stop the violence.[84]

The KLA-led shift to violent resistance forced the international community to pay attention to the plight of Kosovo in ways that the LDK's policy had failed to do. The UN Security Council passed Resolution 1199, demanding an end to the fighting.[85] As the international community became increasingly involved in nego-tiating an end to the conflict, it became apparent that Kosovar Albanian willing-ness to contemplate a settlement short of autonomy had disappeared. Faced with permanent exclusion in any arrangement in which Kosovo would remain within FRY, the Kosovar Albanians adopted a strategy of violence to secede from the rump Yugoslavia and claim their independence (Proposition 6.3).

THE EXTERNAL SUPPORT MODEL

Tangible and political diplomatic support by third parties to influence the course of violence, to prevent it, or, alternatively, to end it directly influenced the choice of violent means first in Slovenia, then in Croatia and Bosnia, and finally in Kosovo (Proposition 7). The External Support Model describes four scenarios whereby groups adopt strategies of ethnic violence, all of which operated, often simultaneously, in the case of Yugoslavia.

Escalation

The escalation scenario describes a situation in which external involvement extends the conflict in space, number, intensity, or all three. As one group secures external support, competing groups will seek to offset the perceived advantage by securing the necessary support from other external sources, triggering a cycle of escalatory third-party support that increases the likelihood that groups will adopt violent means (Proposition 7.1).

Serbs in Croatia mobilized rapidly once Croatia's intent to secede gained international support. On June 25, 1991, Slovenia, followed by Croatia, declared its secession from Yugoslavia. Slovenia's secession was critical in that it established a precedent that Croatia would follow.[86] Both the European Community and the United States sent signals encouraging Yugoslav unity and discouraging the planned secession of Slovenia and Croatia in June 1991. U.S. Secretary of State James Baker's opposition to secession, expressed in meetings in Belgrade on June 21, 1991, was interpreted by the JNA and the Serbian leadership as support for military intervention on the part of the federal government if Slovenia and Croatia were to proceed with their planned secession from Yugoslavia.[87] Four days after Baker's visit, Slovenia and Croatia declared independence. The federal parliament and cabinet ordered JNA units in Slovenia to assert Yugoslav sovereignty over its borders and in Croatia, initially, to separate the warring factions.[88] The perception of U.S. support for Yugoslavia's territorial integrity prompted the Serb-dominated JNA to use force to prevent Yugoslavia's dismemberment, thereby triggering further escalation of violence, particularly in Croatia, and widening the war (Proposition 7.1).

International support for Croatia's independence also triggered an escalating conflict between Croats and Serbs in the Krajina. In 1991, as violence escalated in Croatia, the European Community took steps to negotiate a ceasefire while Germany's open support for Croatian independence created an incentive to escalate it. A cessation of hostilities was not in the least desirable from the Croatian point of view; the more violent the conflict, the more likely that Croatia's supporters, notably Germany, would recognize Croatia's independence. As a result, Croatia's strategy was as much aimed at physical control of territory as it was at securing foreign support and influencing international public opinion. External support for Croatia's recognition triggered the escalation of violence among Croats and Serbs in Croatia. It also prompted the Serbs to declare the Krajina to be a federal unit of Yugoslavia in a bid both to secure international support and to counter the significant external support for Croatian independence (Proposition 7.1).

Despite an UN-brokered ceasefire that eventually halted the war in Croatia, the conflict among Yugoslavia's ethnic groups continued to escalate. Only the venue changed. The agreement called for the withdrawal of JNA forces, but made no provision for where they were to withdraw. The JNA thus took up strategically important positions in Bosnia, and command was transferred to local Bosnian Serbs. Milosevic subsequently withdrew the JNA from Bosnia-Herzegovina in May 1992, but it left behind the bulk of its weaponry and 80,000 troops who were Bosnian citizens, including General Ratko Mladic, who became the commander in chief of the Bosnian Serb Army.[89] Paramilitary groups and private militias also entered the war in Bosnia, looting and expelling Muslim and Croat populations by threat, intimidation, and massacre.[90] Gradually Serb forces secured control of some 70 percent of Bosnia-Herzegovina and forcibly expelled most of its non-Serb population.[91]

The escalation of war to Bosnia was a direct consequence of external support for Bosnian independence. In Bosnia-Herzegovina, the offer of recognition after the Hague Peace Conference on Yugoslavia led to the unraveling of the power-sharing agreement and, in January 1992, to the escalation of violence among its complexly intermingled ethnic populations. To secure the agreement of the other EC states for Croatia and Slovenia's recognition, Germany had agreed to maintain unity among its members by extending the offer of recognition to all six Yugoslav republics. Republics were given a week to apply. On December 20 the Bosnian government, despite misgivings and without the involvement of the Bosnian Serbs, requested recognition. The next day the conflict escalated dramatically when the Bosnian Serbs declared their intent to create a Serbian republic in Bosnia. By linking Croatian and Slovenian recognition to the recognition of all of Yugoslavia's republics, the European Community triggered rapid escalation of the conflict (Proposition 7.1). On April 5, days before the United States and the European Community recognized Bosnia-Herzegovina, full-scale hostilities broke out in Sarajevo.

Division

External support strengthened the already severe divisions in Yugoslavia and fostered new ones, triggering ethnic violence by way of the division scenario (Proposition 7.2). The constitutional changes that strengthened the national republics at the expense of the federal center institutionalized Yugoslavia's ethnic divisions and elevated the leaders of Yugoslavia's titular nationalities to positions of power on par with the federal center. Thus the leaders of Yugoslavia's national republics, notably Croatia, Slovenia, and Serbia, were able to pursue national policies and, in the case of Croatia and Serbia, effectively speak for ethnic kin not only in their own republics but also throughout Yugoslavia. Whereas Serbs and Croats had national republics to represent their interests, Yugoslavia's Muslim population had no such advocate. The multiethnic population of Bosnia-Herzegovina (particularly its Muslim population), and the population of Yugoslavia's autonomous provinces (notably Kosovo), depended at the federal level on "Titoists"—those who continued to support a Yugoslav identity and a multiethnic federal state founded on the concept of peaceful coexistence—to promote and protect their interests against the increasingly chauvinistic policies of the national republics.

When international actors intervened in the conflict in the early 1990s, they did so almost exclusively in support of Yugoslavia's national leaders and its federal republics, effectively sidelining the federal center. The West's involvement was so biased in favor of the republics that the federal government was treated, at best, as perfunctory. By November 1991 it was no longer even included in negotiations over Yugoslavia.[92] According to Susan Woodward, while supporters of a federal Yugoslavia were sidelined, nationalist leaders were "promoted by EC, CSCE, and UN negotiators to the status of statesmen, leaders of nations struggling for independence."[93] International actors, perhaps unwittingly, enabled the strategies of

Yugoslavia's national leaders who sought to shift the debate from reform to independence. By ignoring those who supported Yugoslavia's survival as a federal state, international actors became the effective allies of Yugoslavia's national leaders and of their policies to destroy Yugoslavia. In choosing to undermine the proponents of a multiethnic Yugoslavia, international actors further exacerbated Yugoslavia's divisions.

Through their mediation and noncoercive support, international actors also ignored Yugoslavia's ethnic groups that were without republican representation. As recognition was gradually extended to the national republics, the divisions between Yugoslavia's titular nationalities and its "orphaned" ethnic groups in the secessionist republics and in multiethnic Bosnia-Herzegovina further intensified. The result was to deepen significantly ethnic cleavages and to frame the conflict over Yugoslavia's future exclusively in ethnic terms. As divisions among Yugoslavia's ethnic groups intensified, the likelihood of interethnic war increased (Proposition 7.2). By excluding supporters of a federal Yugoslavia, and by elevating Yugoslavia's titular ethnic groups, external support so deepened divisions that Yugoslavia's collapse became inevitable.

Mediation

The West's preference for the individual republics at the expense of the federal government not only exacerbated ethnic cleavages; it also determined who would be included in the negotiations over Yugoslavia's future and who would be excluded. External support through mediation describes a third scenario, whereby the involvement of third parties to resolve conflict before it escalates, or to prevent its spread, triggers the outbreak or resumption of ethnic violence. When that mediation is perceived as biased in favor of one of the contending parties, when it excludes one or more parties to the conflict, or when it defines the issues in exclusively ethnic terms, the disadvantaged group is likely to adopt violent means (Proposition 7.3). Violence serves an important purpose. It can elevate the threat, forcing third parties to contend with the excluded group. It can also buy time to secure alternate third-party mediators, and it can destroy a settlement that threatens group goals. Although third-party mediation aims to reduce or prevent violence, how that mediation is conducted can create new incentives for groups to adopt violent means.

The policy of the 12 members of the European Community, and of the Western nations more generally, was fundamentally inconsistent. Almost from the outset, EC involvement was viewed as biased.[94] Germany's partisan view of the Yugoslav conflict forced a break in the European Community over the question of recognition, with France, the United Kingdom, and Spain firmly opposed, making any EC involvement automatically suspect by some parties to the conflict, notably the Serbs. Support for Slovenia and Croatia on the part of Austria, Hungary, Germany, Denmark, the Vatican, and Italy led both republics to expect political and economic support for independence and encouraged them to believe that they could "join"

Europe quickly,[95] giving added impetus to their efforts to secure recognition. It also "proved" Serb suspicions that they faced both a revived World War II Axis alliance and German revanchism, and thus inadvertently strengthened Milosevic's appeal.[96] Such fundamental inconsistencies, in addition to undermining the effectiveness of EC efforts aimed at ending the conflict, furthered the perception among Serbs that the European Community was heavily biased against it.[97]

Successive attempts on the part of the European Community to negotiate a ceasefire in Croatia failed due to Serbian resistance to the involvement of what Serbs believed to be a hostile body. By mid-1991, Serbia's reputation abroad had suffered blow after blow; EC recognition of Croatia, as a result of German pressure, appeared imminent;[98] and Serbian forces were beginning to sustain losses.[99] The Serbian leadership thus began to favor a solution to the crisis that would neutralize the anti-Serbian European Community. Serbia turned to the United Nations and particularly to the United States, which it believed would be supportive of Serbian interests and could act as a counterforce to Germany. It was thus no coincidence that the 15th ceasefire, brokered by UN envoy Cyrus Vance, held firm when previous EC efforts had all failed.[100]

Efforts to resolve the conflict in Croatia, on the part of both the European Community and the United Nations, "proceeded with little regard for the consequences in the rest of Yugoslavia."[101] Outside mediators treated the conflict in Croatia as a discrete problem and failed to address the broader implications of the Serb-Croat conflict in Croatia for the rest of Yugoslavia. The ceasefire agreement made no provisions for the withdrawal of JNA forces in Croatia beyond simply ensuring that they would be withdrawn. It also left the final status of the Serbian enclaves in Croatia vague, failing to achieve a definitive solution to the Serb-Croat conflict.[102]

The tendency to define each ethnic conflict as a discrete problem directly contributed to the escalation of violence elsewhere in Yugoslavia. The failure at Dayton to acknowledge that the war in Bosnia-Herzegovina was not only ethnic and not only confined to Bosnia, but also tied to the larger issue of state collapse, prompted the Kosovar Albanians to reject their policy of peaceful resistance for one of violence. Dayton confirmed that Western mediation was aimed only at resolving the status of Yugoslavia's republics and not its provinces. It also confirmed that the international actors would not protect the "orphaned" populations in Yugoslavia's former republics. Thus, international mediation directly contributed to the Kosovar Albanian rejection of Rugova's policy of peaceful resistance in favor of violent confrontation (Proposition 7.3). Led by the KLA, Kosovar Albanians adopted violent means to draw attention to the plight of Kosovo's Albanian population, as well as to demonstrate to the international community that the conflict over Kosovo could not be ignored.

Recognition

A third scenario whereby external support may trigger ethnic violence is selective *recognition* (Proposition 7.4). This scenario is likely following state collapse when external powers recognize the secessionist bid(s) of one or more parties to the conflict and deny this same right to competing groups. In the case of Yugoslavia, both the piecemeal process whereby recognition was granted to Yugoslavia's republics and the fact that recognition was granted to its republics but not its provinces triggered the outbreak of ethnic war, first in Croatia, then in Bosnia, and finally in Kosovo.

As Yugoslavia began to collapse, the right to self-determination was inconsistently applied. It was denied to Serbs outside Serbia and to Kosovo's Albanian population in Serbia, while it was recognized as legitimate for the Slovenes, Croats, and for the Muslims in Bosnia.[103] Inconsistent application of the right to self-determination forced those for whom this right was denied, namely the Serbs and the Kosovar Albanians, to fight for territory, cleanse it of ethnic strangers, and achieve by force the right to determine in what state they would live and under what conditions. The denial of the right to self-determination prompted both the Serbs and the Kosovar Albanians to adopt violent means aimed at forcing the international community to recognize their right to self-determination (Proposition 7.4).

The short-lived Slovene war began the process of selective recognition that contributed to the escalation and intensification of violence aimed at claiming ownership of the rump state or secession. While Germany pushed for immediate recognition of Slovenia, the United States resisted, arguing that the breakup of Yugoslavia would be highly destabilizing and could not occur without war.[104] On July 7, 1991, EC-sponsored negotiations produced the Brioni Accords, which in effect recognized the Slovenian military victory. The agreement also made Slovenia and Croatia the subject, de facto, of international law, preparing the way for their eventual recognition.[105] Of even greater import, the Brioni agreement accomplished an important goal of the Serbian nationalists: it established a precedent for redrawing internal Yugoslav borders.[106] Western involvement had thus opened the door to war in Croatia, Bosnia Herzegovina, and Serbia's province of Kosovo.

In December 1991 Germany persuaded the other members of the European Community to recognize Slovenia and Croatia. As Woodward notes, this step was taken "despite warnings that without a comprehensive political settlement for the whole of Yugoslavia, the tens of thousands of dead, hundreds of thousands of refugees and displaced persons, and massive destruction of many villages and towns in Croatia would seem a picnic beside a war in Bosnia-Herzegovina."[107] German support for recognition was based on the argument that imminent recognition of Croatia had deterred further Serbian aggression, which Germany argued was the cause of the war in Yugoslavia. On December 23, 1991, Germany recognized Slovenia and Croatia, forcing the EC member states to follow suit, despite pleas from Bosnian President Izetbegovic to delay recognition for fear of its impact on Bosnia.[108]

In order to secure the agreement of the other EC states for Croatia and Slovenia's recognition, Germany agreed to maintain unity among them by extending the offer of recognition to all six Yugoslav republics. This offer was accompanied by a number of conditions: first, that each of the republics request formal recognition by December 23, 1991; and second, that each meet the criteria established by the Badinter Commission.[109] With only a week to apply, the coalition government in Bosnia was forced to make a rapid decision. On December 20 the Bosnian government, without the involvement of the Bosnian Serbs, requested recognition. The next day, the Bosnian Serbs declared their intent to create a Serbian republic in Bosnia.

The Badinter Commission imposed an additional condition for recognition of Bosnia-Herzegovina: it required that the republic hold a referendum on independence to prove that its request for recognition had popular support. On February 29 and March 1, 1992, the ill-fated referendum on Bosnian independence took place without the involvement of over a third of Bosnia's population and in direct violation of the power-sharing agreement. The power-sharing arrangement collapsed, and the Croats and Serbs prepared for war while Izetbegovic hoped that his compliance with each of the requirements for recognition would secure Western support for Bosnia should the Serbs attempt to secede. As tensions in Bosnia escalated, pressure for the recognition of Bosnia-Herzegovina, led by the United States, began to build. Because Croatian recognition appeared to have halted the war in Croatia, international policy makers hoped that, by recognizing Bosnia-Herzegovina, they might prevent the violent incidents already taking place in Bosnia from escalating to full-scale war. The ill-fated decision to offer recognition to a republic in which a well-armed third of the population was violently opposed to secession was directly responsible for the outbreak of violence in Bosnia. It also created an incentive for ethnic cleansing.

The Badinter Commission established a requirement that recognition be sanctioned by a referendum, thus creating a policy that unwittingly would reward ethnic cleansing. As a result, the Serb blitzkrieg campaign at the outset of the conflict, which secured the bulk of Serb territorial holdings in Bosnia-Herzegovina, was accompanied by a systematic campaign of ethnic cleansing aimed at permanently altering the population balance in each of these territories. Ethnic cleansing would ensure that those territories under Serb control would subsequently vote correctly in any future referendum on Bosnian Serb independence and would justify administration of that territory by Serb leaders (Proposition 7.5).

Ethnic cleansing was not restricted to Serb forces alone. In fact, the Bosnian war involved ethnic cleansing by all parties in order to secure not just military occupation, but permanent control over territory. Where ceasefires were brokered, ethnic cleansing did not cease. The methods simply changed. Population exchanges between individual towns occurred both in Croatia and in Bosnia after ceasefires were negotiated. Although less violent, these methods were hardly more voluntary.[110] Cleansing ensured that, once ethnic strangers vacated a particular territory, their ethnic leadership lost political control over that territory.[111] The cleansing group was thus rewarded with an ethnically homogenous territory to buttress its claims to self-determination.

Recognition triggered ethnic violence because it was selectively applied to Yugoslavia's ethnic groups with little regard for the multiethnic character of Yugoslavia's republics. Ethnic groups denied the right to self determination thus faced permanent exclusion and mobilized rapidly to demand the right to secede. In ethnically mixed territories, selective recognition triggered ethnic cleansing. Control over territory was not enough; populations had to be sufficiently homogeneous to buttress claims to ownership.

THE RESOURCE MODEL

Crossing the threshold from protest to violence requires access to the arms and resources necessary to conduct and sustain a strategy of ethnic violence. Arms are not only a precondition for ethnic war. They are also vital for the achievement of group goals. In Yugoslavia, that threshold was rapidly crossed. The massive amount of weaponry available locally, combined with the availability of arms from external sources despite the imposition of an arms embargo, ensured that the various ethnic groups had the arms and funding necessary to sustain interethnic war. Whereas Serb forces were armed mostly by the JNA, the Croats and Bosnian Muslims were forced to rely on outside sources to secure the necessary weaponry and the financial resources to purchase them, circumventing the arms embargo in the process. The imposition of an arms embargo in September 1991 made the acquisition of the necessary resources more complicated, but it did not prevent the various ethnic groups in Yugoslavia from acquiring the necessary weaponry. In fact, it encouraged an arms race as the various actors sought to secure the necessary resources from various outside sources and from the JNA itself.

The Serbs in the Krajina began acquiring arms from the JNA as early as 1990, following Croatia's elections. Arms were acquired both from individuals in the Interior Ministry in Belgrade and from the local 9th Corps in Knin. In October 1990 cargo trains bearing arms without their usual armed escort were unexpectedly routed through Knin, where local Serbs relieved the trains of their cargo.[112] In other instances, arms were smuggled on trucks from Montenegro to Knin, via Bosansko Grahovo in Bosnia.[113] Radmilo Bogdanovic, a close associate of Milosevic and, until March 1991, Serbian Interior Minister, later admitted that the Krajina Serbs had been armed by Serbia's Interior Ministry throughout 1990 and 1991.[114] Most of the weaponry, however, came from local sources in the Krajina, from JNA garrisons in Croatia, and from military officers stationed in the Krajina, most of whom were ethnic Serbs and Montenegrins.[115] By early autumn 1990, there were numerous instances of arms "theft" from army stores in Croatia. Officially, the Knin militias stole their weapons, although there were no comparable thefts elsewhere in Croatia. The extent of this covert arming operation became evident when violence first erupted following the Krajina Serb referendum in August 1990. Initially the Serbs fought with hunting rifles. By the end of the summer, they were armed with large numbers of sophisticated weaponry that could only have come from JNA stores.[116] When Croatia subsequently held a referendum on independence, the Serbs were prepared to resist Croatia's secession from Yugoslavia by force. They had the necessary means to embark upon a strategy of violence as well as sufficient resources to sustain it (Proposition 8).

Beginning in 1991 the Serbs in Bosnia benefited from the same policy of covert arms shipments by the JNA and the Serbian Interior Ministry.[117] The JNA had made careful preparations prior to the outbreak of war in Bosnia. With the imposition of the arms embargo in September 1991, JNA troops were moved out of Bosnian cities; JNA control over Bosnia's defense industries was strengthened; and, in some instances, whole factories were moved to Serbia.[118] In addition, the JNA disarmed the Territorial Defense Forces (TDF), an all-people's civilian militia under the control of the individual republics. As a result, some 200,000 small arms in the custody of the TDF were returned, with the exception of the weaponry of the TDF staffs in western Herzegovina, which ignored the general staff's order.[119]

The bulk of Bosnian Serb arms, however, were directly transferred from the JNA to the army of the Bosnian Serbs in early May 1992, when the JNA officially withdrew from Bosnia-Herzegovina and became the army of the new Serb-Montenegrin federation. Only 20 percent of its personnel, those who were citizens of Serbia or Montenegro, withdrew. The JNA left behind 80,000 troops and the bulk of its weaponry, including two-thirds of its ammunition and most of its heavy artillery and equipment.[120] Thus, when the Bosnian Serb Army inherited the lion's share of the JNA, it acquired a well-equipped army that had made careful preparations for eventual war (Proposition 8). These weapons and forces enabled the rapid expansion of war in the spring of 1992.

The JNA also proved to be an important source of arms for the Croatian government. Croatia embarked upon a massive rearmament effort after the outbreak of war in the Krajina and in Slavonia. On September 14, 1991, the Croatian National Guard laid siege to 33 JNA garrisons across the republic.[121] One by one, the garrisons surrendered, allowing Croats to confiscate JNA weaponry. The TDF in Croatia had been disarmed by the JNA, such that Tudjman's incoming government had no armed forces capable of acting independently of the JNA except for the police, which he organized into a national guard.[122] The weaponry confiscated from the JNA was thus critical to the initial Croatian war effort.

Although Serb forces were armed mostly by the JNA, the Croats and the Bosnian Muslims were forced to rely on outside sources to secure the necessary weaponry and the financial resources to purchase them, circumventing the arms embargo in the process. Neither group was severely limited in its search for reliable and sustainable arms and resources. Croatia relied on its émigré network abroad to purchase and traffic arms and organize gun-running operations that included drugs-for-arms arrangements. Private individuals in Croatia reportedly purchased arms from South Africa, and Croatian émigrés in Chile arranged arms shipments through black-market dealers.[123] Croatia used funds provided by its network of émigrés to purchase 36,000–50,000 Kalashnikov rifles and antitank rockets from Hungary, SAR-80 automatic rifles from Singapore, Spanish pistols from Austria, and other weaponry from private companies in Austria, Germany, Belgium, Switzerland, Italy, Great Britain, the United States, and Spain.[124] In addition, Argentina, Panama, and Israel sold arms on the Yugoslav market.[125] Many of these weapons were imported under the cover of import-export companies in Zagreb.[126] During 1992, Croatia had reportedly spent some $250 million buying weapons on the black market.[127] In 1993, Croatia had sufficiently armed to challenge Serb control over Croatia territory. In January, Croat forces seized key strategic points in the Krajina, and by May 1995, Croatia had succeeded in crushing Serb forces in western Slavonia.[128] Two months later, Croatian forces secured control of the Krajina (Proposition 8).

Because of the arms embargo, the weaker Bosnian Muslim forces were almost entirely dependent on outside sources of support. Beginning in 1992, Iran began purchasing arms for the Bosnian Muslims and persuaded the Croatian government to transport these arms across its territory in exchange for a share of each shipment, usually a third.[129] Based on what was seized, Iranian arms shipments included a 32-truck convoy of surface-to-air missiles and Stingers, accompanied by Afghan Mujaheddin, an Iranian aircraft carrying 4,000 automatic weapons destined for Sarajevo but seized in Zagreb, and another Iranian shipment of over 60 tons of explosives and weapons-manufacturing equipment.[130] Sent under the guise of "humanitarian aid," many of these shipments were confiscated by the United Nations and the Bosnian Serbs.[131] Although the transit of weapons to Bosnia was not always reliable, Iranian shipments remained the most important source of arms for the Bosnian Muslims. Continued shipments of these weapons and of ammunition were crucial to the Muslims' ability to fight the better-equipped Serbs. Bosnian Muslim forces also benefited from the arrival of foreign fighters, notably Mujaheddin from Pakistan, Afghanistan, Morocco, Sudan, Lebanon, Algeria, Turkey, Saudi Arabia, and Iran; members of Hezbollah also became involved in the Bosnian war, fighting alongside Bosnian government forces and establishing training camps for Bosnian Muslim soldiers.[132]

The Kosovar Albanians were perhaps the most constrained in their ability to secure arms, which led in part to the LDK decision to adopt a strategy of peaceful resistance for most of the 1990s. Dayton demonstrated the failure of this policy, and the loose network of KLA forces began to search for suppliers and resources to acquire the necessary arms. Unrest in neighboring Albania in 1997 opened a significant corridor for weapons shipment as well as reliable and cheap arms. By 1998, KLA operatives in western Europe were able to secure some $10,000–15,000 per month from the Albanian diaspora, which was used to buy the necessary arms and ammunition to sustain a campaign of ethnic violence against Serb forces.[133] By the late 1990s, the KLA had sufficient resources to launch a violent campaign that sparked Serb reprisals and focused international attention on the plight of the Kosovar Albanians (Proposition 8).

The relative weakness of the Bosnian Muslims and the Kosovar Albanians meant that their strategy for fighting the stronger Serbian forces had to have, as its central aim, the continued active involvement of the West. Arms were necessary not only to secure territory and defend populations, but also to continue violent resistance on a scale large enough to hold international attention and garner sympathy for their causes. The arms embargo thus prompted a strategy that aimed as much at international public opinion as it did at securing success on the ground.

CONCLUSION

Each of the models, with the exception of the Group Survival Model, identifies why Yugoslavia's ethnic groups adopted violent means. Although interethnic tensions were heightened by competing Serb and Kosovar Albanian claims to a homeland in Kosovo, violence did not erupt in Kosovo until much later. However, the symbol of a threatened homeland proved critical to the mobilization of Serbs throughout Yugoslavia. Ethnochauvinism describes why the Serbian ethnic leadership was able to mobilize such a broad base of support for violent means and for the extensive cleansing of ethnic strangers in Serb-occupied territories throughout Yugoslavia. In addition, Serbia's ethnic leadership was critical to the development and implementation of a strategy of violence to secure a Greater Serbia upon Yugoslavia's collapse. These are the group-level causes of violence.

At the state level, we find additional reasons why Yugoslavia's ethnic groups adopted violent means. Yugoslavia's fundamental authority, capacity, and legitimacy deficits undermined the ability of the federal leadership to accommodate competing ethnic demands. The void created by the devolution of power decades before the outbreak of violence demonstrates that the state arena critically shapes group interaction and conflict. Additionally, Yugoslavia's unranked ethnic structure explains why Yugoslavia's ethnic groups adopted violent means once they were excluded from the states in which they found themselves upon Yugoslavia's collapse. These significant state-level causes of violence enhance our understanding of how the state arena shapes both the choice of violent means and the intensity of ethnic violence.

The final elements of our framework are the two third image models, which in the case of Yugoslavia are essential to understanding why groups adopted violent means and why they resumed fighting despite numerous attempts at mediation by international actors. Indeed, third-party support and intervention created incentives for some of the most extreme violence in Yugoslavia. Finally, the vast resources of the JNA, and the ease with which Yugoslavia's groups were able to circumvent the arms embargo, provide additional explanations for the explosion of ethnic violence in Yugoslavia. At each level, we find clear reasons why groups adopted violent means. The application of the models to the Yugoslav case suggests that there is also a considerable degree of interaction among them. In Chapter 8, we return to the question of interaction, drawing on the conclusions from each of the three case studies to define how the models interrelate across the three images of ethnic war.

6
Chapter

Three Images in
Nagorno-Karabakh

INTRODUCTION

The Nagorno-Karabakh war erupted in 1988 over the long-standing Armenian demand to transfer the Nagorno-Karabakh Autonomous Oblast (NKAO) from the Azerbaijan Soviet Socialist Republic (SSR) to the Armenian SSR. The war was fought in overlapping and competing arenas of conflict. It began as a "war of petitions," sparked by a mass-led movement of Armenians in the NKAO to win approval from the Soviet authorities in Moscow to change the region's territorial status. Armenians in the Armenian SSR mobilized in support and the war of petitions expanded, sparking a later mass movement in Azerbaijan as the threat to Azerbaijan's territorial integrity became apparent. As ethnic violence escalated, Moscow intervened in all three of its federal units in an effort to accommodate the competing demands and then, finally, to repress the violence and buttress the local Communist authorities. When the Soviet Union collapsed, the arena of conflict was transformed. What had begun as an internal ethnic conflict over the status of a Soviet autonomous region became an international war that was simultaneously irredentist and secessionist between two newly independent, post-Soviet republics. Following the ceasefire agreement negotiated under Russian Federation auspices in 1994, the conflict was essentially frozen—large-scale, interethnic violence came to a halt, but the underlying causes of violence remain unresolved.

THE HOMELAND MODEL

At its root, the Nagorno-Karabakh war is a conflict over territory—not just any territory, but an ethnic homeland. Nagorno-Karabakh is an enclave in the mountains of Azerbaijan with a majority Armenian population. Both Armenians and Azerbaijanis are ethnonationalists, regionally concentrated ethnic groups with a history of autonomy or self-rule in the contested region of Nagorno-Karabakh

Figure 6.1 Map of Nagorno-Karabakh.

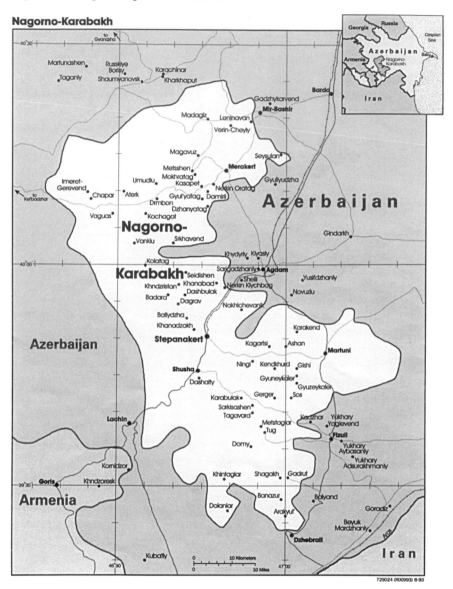

Source: U.S. Central Intelligence Agency, *Nagorno-Karabakh (Political) 2003.* Available at http://www.lib.utexas.edu/maps/commonwealth/nagorno-karabakh.gif

and in their respective nation states of Azerbaijan and Armenia. Both nations—the Armenian and the Azerbaijani—claim the contested region as a homeland. The Homeland Model suggests that ethnonationalists will adopt violence to defend or reclaim a homeland because *possession of that homeland is vital to the identity and continued survival of the ethnic group* (Proposition 1).

The Armenian claim to Nagorno-Karabakh, or "Mountainous Karabakh," is based on three arguments. The first is founded on tenure and first possession: because Armenians have maintained a continuous presence in Karabakh for millennia, they are the true indigenous people in Karabakh and, by virtue of their indigenousness, have the exclusive right both to possess and rule the region—a right that transcends any claims by ethnic strangers. The second is based on a history of Armenian victimization at the hands of their historic enemies. The Karabakh issue, for Armenians, is the latest in a series of historic wrongs perpetrated by the Turks and their proxies in the region, the Azerbaijanis. The third argument is a legal one: Karabakh's initial inclusion in Azerbaijan was illegal.

Azerbaijanis counter that tenure notwithstanding, the modern history of Karabakh is an Azerbaijani one: overwhelmingly Muslim until the mid-nineteenth century, the region has been an integral part of the Azerbaijani state for nearly a century. It is also an integral part of the Azerbaijani homeland. They refute the Armenian claim to a Karabakh homeland, arguing that it cloaks simple territorial aggrandizement at Azerbaijan's expense.

The Armenian claims to tenure and first possession of Karabakh, or Artsakh in Armenian, date back to the ninth century B.C.E. Armenian scholars trace a nearly continuous Armenian presence in the contested region to the modern era.[1] In the mid-fourth century B.C.E., an Armenian dynasty under the Ervandunis united much of Armenian-inhabited territory, including all or part of Artsakh, into a single state. In the first century B.C.E., under Tigran the Great, the Armenian Kingdom expanded to include all of Nagorno-Karabakh and regions north of it.[2] Armenians contend that Artsakh and lower Karabakh, or Utik, remained part of the Armenian Kingdom until its fall in 428 C.E.,[3] although others date this split to 387 C.E. when Armenia was divided between the Byzantines and the Persian Sassanids.[4] Artsakh and Utik were thus separated from Armenia and incorporated in Caucasian Albania, where they remained relatively autonomous until the Arab invasions of the seventh century. Quoting Arab sources, Armenians contend that the Arranshahik princes continued to rule Artsakh and Utik and, in the ninth and tenth centuries, established two Armenian-Albanian kingdoms on their lands in Artsakh.[5]

In the eleventh century, a Turkic people, the Seljuks, invaded and occupied nearly all of Armenia and eastern Transcaucasia. All that remained of the Kingdom of Greater Armenia were a number of small enclaves hidden in the mountains.[6] Karabakh is thus seen as a refuge that sheltered Armenian princes, heirs to the Arranshahiks, through successive invasions by the Mongols, the Ottomans, and the Safavid Persians. "This region was the only part of Armenia to preserve indigenous, hereditary Armenian power and a degree of national sovereignty without interruption until the late middle ages."[7]

At the end of the Persian-Ottoman wars of the sixteenth century, the territory came under the control of the Persian Safavid Empire. The Persians established a series of hereditary Khanates: the Khanate of Karabakh (excluding upper or Mountainous Karabakh), the Khanate of Ganja, the Khanate of Erevan, and the Khanate of Nakhichevan. Armenians contend that in the Armenian highlands of Karabakh, local Armenian nobles (meliks) continued to rule the region alongside the Khanates. According to one Armenian author, "the importance of these powers, even though diminished, should be stressed in the case of Armenia, which had lost its sovereignty long before and found itself divided between the Ottoman empire and Safavid Persia, its population stripped of protection. Under these conditions, the meliks constituted the only authority capable of . . . maintaining national traditions."[8]

Karabakh's independence over the centuries ensured that the Armenian nation survived intact and that the Armenian link with its historic territories was continuous. Karabakh is a vital Armenian homeland: a refuge for threatened Armenians, a bastion of Armenian culture, and the cradle of Armenian civilization. A leading Armenian historian notes that "for the Armenians, this region has a particular importance, in that while the rest of Armenia was submerged under foreign control, a flicker of freedom was maintained in Karabakh, albeit under Iranian suzerainty."[9]

The Azerbaijanis use similar claims of tenure to prove that the contested region is part of their historic patrimony, the cradle of their national culture.[10] Azerbaijanis contend that Karabakh was controlled not by Armenian princes, but by Azerbaijanis under nominal Persian suzerainty: the Karabakh Khanate, centered in Shusha, was one of the major Azerbaijani states prior to Russia expansion.[11] As Russia expanded into the region, the Khanates were dismantled, and in 1867 Transcaucasia was divided into four Russian *gubernii*.[12] All of the territory of the former Khanate of Karabakh was included in the Elizavetopol Gubernia.[13] The Azerbaijan Democratic Republic, an Azerbaijani state that was briefly independent from 1918 to 1920, included both the Elizavetopol and the Baku gubernii. In April 1920, when Azerbaijan was reconquered by Moscow, Karabakh was included in the new Azerbaijan SSR.

Azerbaijanis buttress their claim of tenure by arguing that the population of the contested region was overwhelmingly Muslim prior to the mass migration of Armenians from Persian and Ottoman lands, which was encouraged and organized by Russia after the 1828 Treaty of Turkomanchai.[14] Citing official Tsarist population records, Azerbaijanis maintain that Armenians were not a majority in Karabakh until the 1840s. Azerbaijanis view the region as part of their historic patrimony. Many Azerbaijani artists, composers, poets, and other literary figures hailed from the region, particularly Shusha, and played a key role in the emergence of an Azerbaijani national identity in the early 1900s.[15]

Armenians cite their tragic history of victimization and loss during the last century to justify ownership of Karabakh on moral grounds. The massacres of 1894 to 1896 and the genocide of 1915 to 1917, which resulted in the loss of more than half of the Armenian population,[16] "virtually eliminated Armenians from nine-tenths of Greater Armenia stretching into eastern Anatolia, leaving them only the small, mangled territory in the Russian Caucasus."[17] Promised an independent state in the Treaty of Sèvres at the end of World War I, Armenians were again denied national independence. The territories that were to have formed an independent Armenian state were instead incorporated in the Turkish Republic. According to Richard Hovannisian, "it was bitterly ironic for the Armenians that, of the several defeated central powers, Turkey alone expanded its prewar boundaries and this, only on the Armenian front."[18]

In 1921, as Soviet power was reestablished in the Transcaucasus, the Armenians again faced the loss of historic Armenian territory to the Azerbaijani "Turks" as a result of Stalin's "arbitrary reversal" of the decision to include Nagorno-Karabakh in the newly created Armenian SSR.[19] Denied the right to self-determination, the Armenian majority in Nagorno-Karabakh was separated from the Armenian SSR, and ties between the oblast and the Armenian republic were restricted. In a letter to Brezhnev in 1977, Armenians in Nagorno-Karabakh argued that "the Armenian population of Mountainous Karabakh has never accepted willingly its destiny of today which has meant its separation from the motherland . . . Such a 'destiny' is, in itself, an injustice."[20]

Armenians viewed the loss of Karabakh to the Azerbaijani "Turks" as a continuation of Turkish attempts to destroy the Armenian nation, a belief that was strengthened by the massacre of Armenians by Azerbaijanis in Sumgait in February 1988.[21] Virtually every Armenian family retains living memories of close relatives who died during the Azerbaijani massacres of 1905 and 1918–1919 and the Turkish genocide. In Karabakh alone, approximately 20 percent of the population died in internecine clashes from 1918 to 1919 when Turkish forces, at the invitation of the Azerbaijani Mustavat party, massacred residents of captured Armenian villages.[22] According to one Armenian living in Karabakh, "Our only misfortune was to live among the Turks. And no Christian people can live successfully in a sea of Muslims."[23]

Exclusive Armenian ownership of Karabakh is further justified by the illegality of the contested region's transfer to Azerbaijan. After Armenia was reconquered by Moscow in late 1920, the new Soviet authorities promised that Karabakh would be transferred to Armenia. On July 3, 1921, the Caucasian Bureau of the Russian Communist Party (Kavbiuro) declared Nagorno-Karabakh "an integral part of the Socialist Republic of Armenia."[24] Two days later, however, "expediency overruled ethnic self-determination"[25] and the decision was reversed. "Mountainous Karabagh was taken away from Armenia by Stalin's criminal hands."[26] According to Armenians, the transfer was part of a conspiracy between the Turks and the Azerbaijani Communists to claim the disputed region for Azerbaijan.[27] Armenians contend that "Karabagh has never, legally or otherwise, belonged to a sovereign, independent Azerbaijan."[28]

Homeland possession is a defining feature of an ethnonationalist group's identity. The Armenians view Karabakh as a symbol of national resistance and survival.

Nagorno-Karabakh represents, in the words of an Armenian poet, the "soul of this great Armenian body, dismembered and scattered throughout the world."[29] Nagorno-Karabakh is also the cradle of their national culture.[30] It is one of the last historic Armenian territories not lost to Armenia's enemies, the Turks—and, by extension, the Azerbaijanis, whom Armenians view as the Turks' proxies in the region. According to one Armenian interviewed after the February 1988 demonstrations, "Karabakh . . . strikes at the core of our collective essence."[31]

Ethnonationalists are rarely willing to settle for autonomy in their homeland. Even when a group enjoys genuine autonomy, ownership of the homeland remains with the state, as does the power to shape state-level policies that could undermine group ownership. The shifting demographic balance in favor of Azerbaijanis, combined with deliberate neglect of the region and restricted cultural rights, detailed in the Group Survival Model below, buttress the Armenian claim that only transfer of the region to Armenia would protect the homeland. After repeated petitions to the central Communist authorities failed to win their support for transfer, Armenians in Nagorno-Karabakh adopted violent means to reclaim ownership of their homeland (Proposition 1). Because the Nagorno-Karabakh homeland was part of the Azerbaijan SSR, reclaiming ownership prompted secession (Proposition 1.1).

Homeland claims are rarely unopposed. As conflict between Armenians—both in Armenia and the NKAO—and Azerbaijanis intensified, both groups began to cleanse their territories of the ethnic other. The first population shifts occurred as early as 1987, when the petition drive began in Armenia. In northern Azerbaijan, violent clashes erupted between Armenian and Azerbaijani villagers in Chardakhlu in October 1987.[32] A month later, Azerbaijanis in Southern Armenia were forcibly expelled from the region and transferred by train to Azerbaijan.[33] Many of these displaced persons participated in the Sumgait pogrom in February 1988, prompting some 14,000 Armenians to flee.[34] In 1989, the reciprocal expulsion of the ethnic other continued, and all remaining Azerbaijanis in Armenia were expelled. In January 1990 the last Armenians in Azerbaijan, particularly in Baku, were forced to leave. In some instances ethnic cleansing was sparked by violence, yet in other cases it proceeded from deliberate homogenization policies. Population exchanges were arranged between the two Soviet republics such that refugees were given homes in deserted villages that had once housed the ethnic other.[35] A similar pattern of ethnic cleansing was apparent in the oblast, although the population exchanges there occurred between ethnic Armenian and Azerbaijani towns within the oblast.

As violence escalated following the imposition of direct Soviet rule, increasingly violent measures were used to cleanse the ethnic other. The Azerbaijani authorities implemented a plan termed "Operation Ring" in early 1991. The plan called for the encirclement of Armenian villages to check Soviet internal passports and to expel any Armenians who were not registered to the village. The operation was conducted by units of the Soviet 4th Army, Azerbaijani paramilitary units, and Azerbaijani villagers, and it had the effect of cleansing the villages of all their inhabitants and subsequently resettling them with Azerbaijani refugees from Armenia.[36] By the end of the year, Armenian paramilitary forces had regrouped. In early 1992, as the war shifted from a guerrilla to a full-scale conventional war, Karabakh Armenian forces seized all of the oblast and the remaining Azerbaijanis were expelled. The Armenians sought to secure ownership of their homeland and the Azerbaijanis sought to defend it. Both these aims prompted a strategy of expulsion and population exchanges to cleanse the contested region of the ethnic other (Proposition 1.2). Ethnic homogenization extended to the populations in both the Armenian and Azerbaijani republics as competing claims to the contested homeland cemented the violent political closure of both nations.

THE ETHNOCHAUVINISM MODEL

The Ethnochauvinism Model does not provide an explanation for ethnic violence in the Armenian-Azerbaijani war over Nagorno-Karabakh, despite a process of boundary demarcation and political closure that created enemies out of neighbors within a year of the first protests in Stepanakeart. Although cleavages between the two ethnic groups deepened, neither group's "myths of ethnic chosenness" were founded on claims of ethnic superiority. Neither the Armenians nor the Azerbaijanis adopted chauvinist policies based on their alleged superiority, and neither group claimed the right to dominate the other (Proposition 2).

Both the Armenians and the Azerbaijanis claimed to be the victims of the ethnic "other," those deemed responsible for the group's loss. The Armenians claimed to be the victims of Stalin, the Azerbaijanis, and, by extension, the Turks, whereas the Azerbaijanis claimed to be victims of the Armenians, Gorbachev, and even the international community. Claiming to be the victim of the ethnic other, the Armenians fought to safeguard their homeland and ensure their continued survival, and the Azerbaijanis fought to prevent the dismemberment of their national homeland. Although interethnic hatred and ethnic cleansing were certainly part of the Nagorno-Karabakh war, the adoption of violent strategies was not driven by ethnic chauvinism.

THE GROUP SURVIVAL MODEL

A second important source of ethnic violence at the group level in the Nagorno-Karabakh war is the belief shared by Armenians, both in Armenia and Nagorno-Karabakh, that *their survival as a distinct ethnic group was threatened by the policies and actions of ethnic strangers*, the Azerbaijanis who controlled the autonomous oblast (Proposition 3).

One factor that leads ethnic groups to conclude that their survival as a distinct ethnic group is threatened is the *decrease in group size* through out-migration, assimilation, and forced resettlement (Proposition 3.1). Armenians claim that an Azerbaijani policy of "Turkification" deliberately caused the decline of the Armenian population of the NKAO.[37] In a letter to Krushchev requesting transfer of the NKAO to Armenia, Armenians in Nagorno-Karabakh argued that Azerbaijan's "underhanded measures . . . intended to bring about the deterioration in the economy of the Armenian population and eventually to force the latter's exodus from the region."[38] They also claimed that Azerbaijan was repopulating Armenian villages with Azerbaijanis.[39] Finally, the letter concluded that "in the last twenty-five years there is a total lack of increase in the growth rate of the Armenian population of Mountainous Karabagh . . . [This] decline has made it possible to populate Karabagh with Azerbaijanis."[40] According to the population figures for the NKAO shown in Table 6.1, the Armenian population did in fact decrease from 117,000 in 1926 to 110,000 in 1959.[41] In subsequent years, however, the Armenian population increased in absolute terms.

Between 1921 and 1979, the Armenian population of the NKAO decreased from 124,000 to 123,100. However, in 1987, when Armenian efforts to transfer the region to Armenia intensified, the Armenian population had increased in absolute terms to 133,200. Figures for the entire period of Soviet rule also show an increase in absolute numbers.[42] Although the rate of increase declined during the period of Soviet rule, the claim to a decrease in the absolute size of the Armenian population in Nagorno-Karabakh is not supported by the census figures.

A second factor that leads groups to determine that their survival as a distinct ethnic group is threatened is the fear of domination created by a *decline in a group's size relative to ethnic strangers* (Proposition 3.2). The Armenian percentage of the population of the autonomous oblast steadily declined, while the absolute and relative size of the Azerbaijani population increased dramatically. Between 1921 and 1987 the Armenian percentage of the population declined from 94.4 percent to 74.0 percent, while the Azerbaijani percentage of the population increased from a mere 5.6 percent to nearly a quarter of the total population of Nagorno-Karabakh. A number of factors are responsible for this demographic shift. Azerbaijanis have a higher rate of population growth, one of the highest among the Soviet Muslims,[43] as well as a slower rate of migration to the cities.[44] As Armenians left Nagorno-Karabakh in search of economic opportunities, Azerbaijanis moved into those areas.[45] Armenians contend that "this exodus was not fortuitous and is clearly related to the persistent policies of Baku which has sought the 'Nakhichevanization' of the territory: first cultural de-Armenianization, followed by physical exodus."[46]

Table 6.1 Relative Population of Nagorno-Karabakh, 1921–1987[1]

Year	1921	1926	1939	1959	1970	1979	1987
% Armenian	94.4%	89.1%	88.1%	84.4%	80.6%	75.9%	74.0%
% Azerbaijani	5.6%	10.9%	11.9%	15.6%	19.4%	24.1%	24.4%

1. Claude Mutafian, "Karabagh in the Twentieth Century," in *The Caucasian Knot*, Levon Chorbajian, Patrick Donabedian, and Claude Mutafian, eds, 109–170 (London: Zed Books, 1994), 142; A. N. Yamskov, "Ethnic Conflict in the Transcaucasus: The Case of Nagorno-Karabakh," *Theory and Society* 20 (1991): 645. The 1987 figures include 1.6% of the population listed as "other."

The significant demographic shift in the NKAO represented a direct threat to the survival of the Armenian nation in its homeland. By the 1980s the rate of increase on the part of the Azerbaijani population was such that, if trends were to have continued for another fifteen to twenty years, the Armenians in Nagorno-Karabakh would have lost their majority status.[47] Armenians feared their demographic decline would replicate the fate of Nakhichevan, another historically Armenian region where the Armenian population declined from 15 percent in 1926 to 1.4 percent by 1979.[48] The significant decline relative to the Azerbaijani population of Nagorno-Karabakh, combined with the belief that the continuation of such rapid growth on the part of the Azerbaijani population would ultimately result in the "Nakhichevanization of Nagorno-Karabakh," prompted Armenians in Nagorno-Karabakh to conclude that their survival was indeed threatened (Proposition 3.2).

A third factor that leads groups to conclude that their survival as a distinct ethnic group is threatened is the *lack of cultural autonomy* (Proposition 3.3). As an autonomous oblast within the Azerbaijan SSR, Armenians in the NKAO were guaranteed the right to develop and use their own language and culture and the right to an education in their native language. In practice, however, these rights were circumscribed.[49]

Whereas most Soviet Republics outside the Caucasus were subject to demographic and linguistic Russification, the three Transcaucasian republics (Armenia, Azerbaijan, and Georgia) enjoyed an unusual degree of cultural and political autonomy.[50] A policy of "nativization" (korenizatsiia) first instituted in the 1920s ensured that native cadres were promoted within each republic and that education was conducted in the language of each republic with provisions made for ethnic minorities. This political and cultural autonomy meant that local elites had a limited degree of freedom to implement policies of exclusion toward their ethnic minorities. Over time, local elites in Azerbaijan and Armenia developed a system of patronage that favored the titular nationality, whereas ethnic minorities such as the Armenians in Nagorno-Karabakh experienced "a progressive marginalization and discrimination."[51] Over the years, these policies led to the "steady erosion of cultural rights in the oblast,"[52] prompting Armenians in Nagorno-Karabakh to conclude that, "there is in fact no Autonomous region."[53]

Although Armenians in the NKAO were granted the right to primary education in the Armenian language, course content and instructor training were limited by the Azerbaijani authorities. Armenian teachers were not allowed to study in Yerevan, books from Armenia were not permitted in the schools in the NKAO, and NKAO schools were not permitted to teach Armenian history.[54] "The low level of work in the field of education" meant that Armenian students in Karabakh performed poorly in tests "to gain entrance to higher education institutions in the Armenian SSR."[55]

The Armenian language and its unique alphabet are central to the Armenian identity. "Language remains an emotive issue for Armenians, who consider the Armenian language . . . to be one of the factors responsible for their long survival as a distinct ethnic entity."[56] According to Vazken I, the head of the Armenian Church,

> Our language is one of the most important treasures of our culture. It is a genuine creation of the Armenian people. The image of the Armenian nation's spirit is in our mother tongue. *Without the Armenian language it is difficult to remain and survive as Armenians*, not to say impossible . . . The Armenian language is our existence, it is our dignity, it is our identity and it is the mold of realization of all our expectations. *We cannot live without our mother tongue.*[57]

Thus, cultural and educational restrictions in the NKAO threatened more than Armenian opportunities for educational and economic advancement; they translated into a direct threat to the Armenian nation, to its "existence . . . dignity . . . [and] identity."[58] This profoundly significant threat to the Armenian identity *in Nagorno-Karabakh* prompted the Armenians to conclude that their survival as a distinct ethnic group was threatened (Proposition 3.3). Although Armenian identity was protected in the Armenian SSR, Azerbaijan's ability to restrict interaction between the oblast and the republic meant that a threat to Armenian cultural rights in Nagorno-Karabakh was viewed as a threat to group survival.

A fourth factor that leads groups to conclude that their survival as a distinct ethnic group is threatened is *pressure on group lands and resources* (Proposition 3.4). When a group's lands and resources are encroached upon by ethnic strangers or by a state controlled by ethnic strangers, then the group may conclude that its survival is threatened. The tendency to perceive a threat to group survival is heightened when the land and resources under threat are part of an ethnic homeland.

Armenians claimed that Azerbaijan deliberately kept the region backward to encourage Armenians to emigrate in an attempt to duplicate the dramatic population shift in Nakhichevan. In a petition to Krushchev in 1964, Armenians in Nagorno-Karabakh argued that, since its creation,

> the rights of the autonomous region were gradually curtailed and presently are almost entirely arrogated. The Armenian population of the Azerbaijani SSR has been subjected to chauvinistic policies creating extremely unfavorable conditions of life. At the inception of the autonomy, certain positive steps were undertaken for the development of industry and agriculture in the region. Subsequently, however, every enterprise has been thwarted, and established institutions have either been inhibited from functioning or have been transferred to regions inhabited by Azerbaijanis . . . These underhanded measures . . . were intended to bring about a deterioration in the economy of the Armenian population and eventually to force the latter's exodus from the region.[59]

The petition cited industries that were transferred out of the region or placed under the jurisdiction of Azerbaijanis and Armenians who were "flatly dismissed" and "replaced by Azerbaijanis."[60] Furthermore, "in forty years, not one kilometer of new road has been constructed between villages and the regional center; nor have existing roads been repaired."[61] The petition further argued that "no possibilities have been explored for developing new agriculture in the region," reservoirs erected in the region benefit "only Azerbaijani villages," and Armenians have not been given the right "to utilize the waters of their own rivers."[62] The petition concluded that "these unilaterally harmful measures have deprived the Armenian population of the region of its livelihood and well-being and forced it to abandon its own ancestral homeland."[63]

Many of these same concerns were recognized by Arkady Volsky, the USSR Supreme Soviet's representative in Nagorno-Karabakh, more than a decade later. According to Volsky, the economy of the region was in "an extremely neglected state, especially in the social area, with respect to the satisfaction of the people's priority needs for housing, water and power supply, medicine and food."[64] A year later, he noted that "during my travels throughout the country, I have never been confronted with such a state of abandonment, such scorn for the destiny of people as in Mountainous Karabakh."[65] This persistent and deliberate neglect represented a clear threat to group lands and resources. The encroachment of ethnic strangers, whose intent was to force the Armenian population to abandon its homeland, constituted a clear threat to the lives and livelihoods of Armenians in their homeland (Proposition 3.4).

The nature and extent of the threat led Armenians to conclude that their very survival was at stake. Armenians in Nagorno-Karabakh thus sought to transfer the oblast to Armenia to protect the group from the policies of the Azerbaijani government. When this strategy proved unsuccessful, Armenians, believing that their very survival in the region was at stake, adopted a strategy of violence to defend the group against the policies and actions of the Azerbaijanis (Proposition 3).

THE ETHNIC LEADERSHIP MODEL

The conflict over Nagorno-Karabakh was triggered by a mass-led movement that propelled the formation of ethnic leaderships, first in Armenia and Nagorno-Karabakh in 1988, and a year and a half later in Azerbaijan. Both ethnic leaderships emerged in response to mass protests, seizing on the settlement of the long-standing grievance over the status of Nagorno-Karabakh to adopt violent means to challenge the ruling Communist authorities in both republics and Moscow (Proposition 4).

The status of Nagorno-Karabakh was central to the "national awakening" of both Armenians and Azerbaijanis. An Armenian ethnic leadership was the first to emerge in response to the grassroots movement to transfer Karabakh to Armenia. When the petition for transfer was denied by the Soviet authorities, the Armenian leadership openly defied Moscow's decision, declaring the oblast's secession from Azerbaijan, its subsequent transfer to Armenia, and Armenia's independence. The Armenian ethnic leadership seized the opportunity created by a mass-led movement to develop a unified leadership structure of Armenian intellectuals, political activists, and Communist Party officials. They then secured a broad base of support for a well-coordinated and executed strategy of ethnic violence to unify the oblast with Armenia.

Azerbaijan's national awakening was similarly driven by mass protests over the issue of Karabakh, yet the Azerbaijan Popular Front (APF) was deeply divided from the outset. Whereas the Armenian national movement comprised various organizations with a common goal, the Azerbaijani movement was a loose association of individuals with vastly different goals and strategies. Small groups of intellectuals had begun to organize following the Sumgait trials, but mass support for a national agenda did not emerge until the demonstrations in November 1988.[66] As in the case of Armenia, the galvanizing issue was Karabakh—particularly the Azerbaijan Communist Party's failure to assert its sovereignty over the NKAO. In a clear example of the *militant leader scenario*, the threat from an increasingly powerful opposition movement forced the Communist Party to adopt a hard-line position to outflank and undermine the opposition. By 1991 the growing power of the APF and the radicalization of the Karabakh issue prompted the Azerbaijani Communist leadership to adopt a strategy of ethnic violence that propelled Azerbaijan into a war for which it was ill prepared (Proposition 4.2).

Gorbachev's policy of glasnost, first announced at the 27th Congress of the Communist Party of the Soviet Union (CPSU) in February 1986, created an opportunity for Armenians to pursue their long-suppressed desire for the oblast's transfer to Armenia. Karabakh Armenians mobilized quickly, submitting the first of a series of petitions requesting transfer in late 1986.[67] A subsequent petition in January 1988 garnered some 80,000 Armenian signatures, 31,000 from the oblast and the rest from Armenia proper.[68] The initial petitions were organized by a network of individuals, mostly members of the Armenian intelligentsia and non-government political leaders. In February 1988, as momentum in support of transfer continued to build, this assortment of Armenian leaders formed the Krunk Society (Crane Society), "named after the Armenian symbol of longing for one's homeland."[69] As its petition-writing effort progressed, Krunk secured support from local Communist Party leaders.

That same month Moscow rejected the petition for transfer, triggering an upsurge of public protest in Nagorno-Karabakh. Popular pressure in the form of strikes, student boycotts, and protest rallies in the oblast capital of Stepanakert forced the local governing councils (soviets) to respond. Four out of five soviets in Nagorno-Karabakh passed a resolution calling for the transfer of the region to Armenia, and on February 20, the Supreme Soviet of the NKAO endorsed the request, overriding its Azerbaijani members.[70] Krunk effectively organized the upsurge of mass sentiment into a massive petition movement that ultimately gained the support of the local Communist Party leadership. This strategy was to gain strength with the expansion of the movement to the Armenian SSR.

In Armenia, the Karabakh issue prompted a massive letter-writing campaign and a formal petition from the Armenian Academy of Arts and Sciences in the fall of 1987. It gained the support of a number of leading Armenian scholars and Soviet advisors who were ethnic Armenians, and, with that support, it raised expectations that the Armenian petition would be favorably received. On February 21, when the Politburo rejected the NKAO Supreme Soviet's request, demonstrations erupted in Yerevan. Initially some 50,000 people participated in the protests; as each day passed, the numbers grew larger, and by month's end some million protesters assembled in Yerevan demanding the region's transfer.[71]

These mass demonstrations prompted the formation of an organizational structure to manage and direct the upsurge of public sentiment. In March 1988 a number of Armenian nationalist organizations formed the Karabakh Committee. When the Armenian Supreme Soviet met in June, the Karabakh Committee organized a demonstration of some 700,000 Armenians in Yerevan to pressure the legislators to endorse their demands over Karabakh. The strategy proved successful; the Armenian legislators endorsed the NKAO request. The Karabakh committee organized additional strikes and protests in July against the Communist First Party Secretary, Suren Harutiunyan, and occupied Yerevan's airport. Interior ministry troops were dispatched to deal with the protestors.

Rather than quell the movement, the death of one protestor further radicalized popular support. The Spitak earthquake in Armenia brought a temporary halt to the movement; it provided the Communist authorities with the opportunity to jail hundreds of Karabakh Committee activists and most of their leadership on charges that they were obstructing earthquake relief from Azerbaijan.[72] The movement's repression only served to significantly expand its popularity among Armenians. Upon their release in May 1989, the Karabakh Committee merged with other, smaller political groups to form the Armenian National Movement (ANM). In elections in May 1990, the ANM became the largest block in the parliament, and Levon Ter-Petrosyan became the chairman of the parliament.

The imposition of direct rule in Nagorno-Karabakh by Moscow under the authority of the Volsky Commission further unified the Armenian ethnic leadership in the republic and the contested region. Armenians interpreted direct rule by Moscow as an important step in the eventual unification of the region with Armenia. Direct rule, along with the imposition of an embargo by the APF, prompted closer coordination among the leaderships in Armenia and Nagorno-Karabakh. As violent incidents continued to escalate in Nagorno-Karabakh, members of the suspended Karabakh soviet created the Nagorno-Karabakh National Council. After Soviet direct rule was abolished and the oblast returned officially to Azerbaijan's control in November 1989, the Armenian Supreme Soviet passed a resolution recognizing "the fact of the self determination of Nagorno-Karabakh."[73] It instructed the Armenian authorities and the Nagorno-Karabakh National Council "to take all necessary measures arising out of this resolution to effect a real merging of the political, economic, and cultural structures of the Armenian Republic and Nagorno-Karabakh into a unified state-political system."[74]

While the Armenian leadership in the republic and the oblast sought to transfer the region using the institutions of governance in both territories, it simultaneously supported the formation of paramilitary organizations that would be able to secure Armenian ownership of the region by force. When the Karabakh National Council proclaimed the independence of Nagorno-Karabakh in September 1991, Armenian paramilitary forces were prepared to secure control over the region. As Azerbaijan revoked the autonomous status of the oblast and the remaining Soviet forces withdrew, the Karabakh National Council organized a referendum in which 99 percent of the votes favored secession.[75]

The results of the Armenian ethnic leadership's strategy of coordination and preparation were readily apparent when the conflict escalated to full-scale war in 1992. Armenian forces were well-armed and well-prepared (Proposition 4). They rapidly seized full control of the oblast and the Lachin land corridor linking the oblast to Armenia. This corridor ensured a continued flow of supplies and people such that a strategy of violence could be sustained.

In contrast to the Armenians, Azerbaijan's national awakening was belatedly sparked by the Armenian effort to secure Moscow's sanction for transfer. As Azerbaijani refugees fled Armenia for Azerbaijan, violence erupted in Sumgait in February 1988 between Armenians and Azerbaijanis, many of whom were refugees from Armenia. In May, tens of thousands of Azerbaijanis protested the trial of officials charged with failing to prevent the Sumgait programs. Although these early incidents widened the scope of participation and demonstrated the eroding authority of the Azerbaijani Communist leadership, there was no organizational direction to the movement.

In November 1988, mass demonstrations erupted in Baku and elsewhere in Azerbaijan over the Communist Party's failure to assert its authority over Nagorno-Karabakh.[76] As in the Armenian case, the mass demonstrations prompted a group of intellectuals and political activists to form an opposition movement, but it was repressed. The Communist authorities imposed "special regulations" along with widespread arrests.[77] Finally, in March 1989, after their release from prison, Azerbaijani activists and intellectuals from the Baku Academy of Sciences organized an "initiative group" for an Azerbaijan Popular Front (APF).[78] Unlike the Karabakh Committee, the APF was a grouping of diverse individuals of varying interests and political orientations. Thus "the APF contained within its own internal organizational structure the possibility of sharp political divisions and eventual fragmentation."[79]

At its founding congress on July 16, 1989, the APF denounced the use of force and declared its commitment to the themes of humanism, democracy, pluralism, internationalism, and human rights.[80] Yet in the months following its formation, the APF "remained largely an isolated group of intellectuals that failed to win either the active participation of the Baku-based Azerbaijani intellectual elite or effective support from Azerbaijani society at large."

Although there was little support for the APF's moderate agenda of democratization, there was intense interest in the Karabakh issue. The APF organized a series of strikes and mass rallies to secure legalization of the organization, using a rising anti-Armenian sentiment and a growing dissatisfaction with the Communist

Party's mishandling of the Karabakh crisis to bring tens of thousands of Azerbaijanis into the streets.[81] The most active element of Azerbaijani society, and also the most anti-Armenian, was the refugee population, many of whom lived in abject conditions with little or no access to social services. Mobilizing the Azerbaijani population thus meant mobilizing this more radical element of society. The APF activists "faced the unhappy prospect that only an anti-Armenian NKAO-oriented platform could bring thousands of Azerbaijani supporters into the streets."[82]

The APF adopted an increasingly extreme position on the Karabakh issue to secure a broad base of support with which to challenge the ruling Communist authorities.[83] It abandoned its broader social and political goals to focus exclusively on Karabakh, and, in so doing, increased its popular support and its threat to the ruling Communist authorities.[84] In this *militant leader scenario*, the APF shift in strategy succeeded in mobilizing popular support, but it did so at the cost of increased internal divisions that ultimately caused the organization to splinter into three main factions. A moderate faction continued to advocate Azerbaijan's democratization within the USSR, while a national democratic faction argued for Azerbaijan's secession from the USSR and eventual unification with an Azeri-inhabited region of Iran known as Southern Azerbaijan. A third faction of radical religious and ultra-leftist groups increasingly came to dominate the organization, marginalizing the more moderate factions.[85] Wary of the radical APF, the mainstream intelligentsia organized an alternative group, the Committee for Aid to Karabakh, and won the official sanction that had thus far eluded the APF.

The APF intensified its efforts and organized a strike by railway workers that managed to nearly isolate Armenia from the remainder of the Soviet Union.[86] The continuing strikes weakened the Communist leadership's hold on power in Azerbaijan, and its failure to terminate the blockade of Armenia and the NKAO elicited threats from Moscow. Both left the Communist leadership with little choice but to grant a series of concessions to the APF. In mid-September a special session of the Azerbaijan Supreme Soviet was held on the issue of the NKAO. In addition, the Supreme Soviet voted to abolish the Volsky Committee and to begin drafting laws on Azerbaijan's political and economic sovereignty. Strikes continued into October until tense negotiations finally resulted in the legalization of the APF. In exchange, the APF agreed to call off the blockade. But the APF was unable to uphold its end of the bargain. Weakened by internal divisions, the APF found that it had little control over the popular movement it had sparked. In December 1989, activists claiming to be a part of the APF attacked Party and Ministry of Internal Affairs offices in Lankaran and Jalilabad in Azerbaijan and along the Soviet-Iranian border in Nakhichevan.

In yet another clear example of the *militant leader scenario*, growing popular support for the opposition movement propelled the Communist leadership to adopt a similarly hard-line position as its hold on power became increasingly desperate. To demonstrate its newfound resolve to protect Azerbaijan's territorial integrity, the Communist government abolished the autonomous status of

Nagorno-Karabakh in November 1991.[87] As Moscow withdrew its forces from Karabakh in December, the Communist leadership dispatched Azerbaijani forces to the region and began bombing Stepanakert, marking the conflict's transformation into a full-scale war.

The increased radicalization of the Communist Party's policy toward Karabakh as a result of the APF's own radicalization demonstrates how conflict between within-group factions can propel groups to adopt increasingly militant policies in an effort to sideline and undermine within-group competitors. In this scenario, violence will escalate even when the choice of violent means undermines group goals. Azerbaijan was ill prepared for a full-scale war with Armenian forces, as it belatedly discovered in 1992. When Armenian forces launched their offensive in May to seize control of the oblast, the Communist leadership kept Azerbaijan's best-trained and best-equipped forces in reserve, guarding Baku against a potential coup by the APF. Massive Azerbaijani losses ultimately led to the resignation of the Communist government and, in June 1992, to the election of a Popular Front candidate. Despite a change in government, Azerbaijan was unable to recover from its early failure to develop a coherent strategy. A year later, Azerbaijani forces suffered another series of strategic losses as Karabakh Armenian forces widened the Lachin corridor, and the APF government was overthrown.

The Azerbaijani leadership failed to articulate a clear policy toward the war in Nagorno-Karabakh, develop a strategy based on an assessment of Azerbaijani interests and capabilities, and mobilize and organize the necessary resources and forces necessary to conduct it. The competition between an increasingly radicalized APF and a weakened Communist leadership ultimately undermined Azerbaijan's ability to protect its territorial integrity. Within-group competition propelled the radicalization of Azerbaijan's policy toward Nagorno-Karabakh and the choice of violent means (Proposition 4.2).

THE WEAK STATE MODEL

The eruption of mass-led movements in Armenia and Azerbaijan following the introduction of glasnost and perestroika presented a grave threat to the authority and legitimacy of the Soviet Union, a multiethnic federation comprised of more than a hundred nationalities,[88] most of whom claimed Soviet territory as their homeland. As an authoritarian state that imposed an inclusive Soviet identity upon its inhabitants, the Soviet Union suffered from a fundamental legitimacy deficit: the right to rule was not freely extended. As an authoritarian state, the Soviet Union was effectively a weak state, but one that appeared strong as long as its capacity to repress challenges to its vertical legitimacy continued to exist. Once its authority began to erode, its coercive capacity was likewise undermined, and the state collapsed.

Like the Yugoslav state, the Soviet Union's federal structure was founded on ethnically defined units with a titular nationality, yet not all nationalities were treated equally. Only 53 nationalities were recognized as titular nations and granted a "national" territorial unit—either a Soviet Socialist Republic (SSR) or, within those 15 "union republics," an Autonomous Soviet Socialist Republic (ASSR), an Autonomous Oblast (region), or an Autonomous Okruga (area).[89] Both Armenians and Azerbaijanis were titular nationalities in their respective republics. Within Azerbaijan, Armenians in Nagorno-Karabakh were granted their own autonomous oblast. Although in theory titular nationalities had extensive national rights within their respective republics, in practice Soviet nationalities policy sought to create a new state identity founded on class solidarity that would supplant atavistic ethnic identities. Ethnonationalism was effectively repressed for nearly 70 years until the introduction of glasnost and perestroika triggered a mass national movement—first in Armenia, and later in Azerbaijan and elsewhere in the Soviet Union.

The Soviet Union's interrelated authority, capacity, and legitimacy deficits limited Moscow's ability to respond to Armenian demands to transfer the NKAO. Moscow's effort to repress the escalating conflict ultimately undermined the authority and legitimacy of the Soviet state. Moscow's conciliatory policies created the impression among Armenians that their efforts would ultimately prove successful, while Moscow's repression of the conflict in Nagorno-Karabakh led Azerbaijanis to believe that Moscow would uphold Soviet territorial boundaries. This traditional policy of divide and rule had long been successful while backed by the extensive power of the Soviet state; once that power began to decline, Moscow's vacillating policy only served to fuel the further escalation of violence.

Moscow's inability to accommodate Armenian demands, ensure the security of its citizens, and uphold Azerbaijan's sovereignty over its autonomous oblast prompted both Armenians and Azerbaijanis to adopt violent means (Proposition 5). Moscow's vacillation between concession and increasingly severe repression prompted the Armenians to adopt violent means to secure the contested region and a broad swath of Azerbaijani territory to protect it (Proposition 5.1). Moscow's vacillation also sparked an Azerbaijani national awakening. Opposition groups mobilized against the Communist government and its failure to defend Azerbaijan. Moscow's increasingly repressive measures undermined the Azerbaijan Communist Party, sparked an opposition movement, and propelled Azerbaijanis into a large-scale conventional war to defend their ownership of the NKAO by force (Proposition 5.2).

Armenians were some of Gorbachev's strongest supporters. In demonstrations in February 1988, they flew the flag of Soviet Armenia and carried portraits of Gorbachev. Gorbachev's initial sympathy for Armenian aspirations for unification, followed by his abrupt rejection of their demands, was met with anger, disappointment, and incomprehension in Armenia and quickly undermined his support. According to Silva Kaputikian, one of the Armenian intellectuals who met with Gorbachev in February 1988, "we went out with slogans of trust in the country of socialism, in the Russian people, in perestroika, with portraits of . . . Gorbachev. But they [the Party and government organs, the Soviet media, and the perpetrators of Sumgait] opened fire at us."[90] For Kaputikian, this betrayal was a "spiritual Sumgait."[91]

Although Armenian hopes may have been unrealistic, they were not entirely unfounded. Gorbachev's personal intervention in the crisis and his assurances on numerous occasions that the dispute would be "justly solved" encouraged Armenians to believe that their long-denied desire for unification would be accommodated. Between November 1987 and early February 1988, three delegations of Armenians from Nagorno-Karabakh went to Moscow to lobby the CPSU Central Committee (CC) and the USSR Supreme Soviet.[92] In meetings with senior party officials, the Armenian delegates were reportedly given assurances that a settlement of the NKAO issue was under active consideration in Moscow and were told that their demands were "neither anti-Soviet nor nationalistic."[93]

As Armenian efforts to transfer the region escalated, it became clear that Gorbachev's ability to accommodate Armenian demands was limited by the Soviet Union's legitimacy deficit. Changing the territorial status of the NKAO would set a dangerous precedent in a state with hundreds of potential ethnic-territorial claims. To concede to Armenian demands meant risking the disintegration of the Soviet state. The CPSU CC thus rejected the demands for incorporation of Nagorno-Karabakh into Armenia and dispatched Soviet troops to Armenia to restore order.[94] Faced with a crisis that was rapidly escalating out of control, Gorbachev appeared on television, appealing for calm and "a reasonable approach".[95] In a meeting with two leading Armenian activists, Silva Kaputikian and Zori Balayan, in Moscow, Gorbachev complained that the Armenians were "stabbing perestroika in the back," but he reportedly promised them that the situation in the NKAO would be thoroughly examined in the following months and that a "just solution" would be found.[96] Based on these assurances, which the two Armenians conveyed to the organizers of ongoing mass protests in Yerevan, the demonstrators agreed to halt the demonstrations for a period of one month to allow the central authorities to examine the issue carefully.[97]

On the same day that Gorbachev met with the Armenians activists, he stated in a televised address that exceptions to existing policy could not be made for Nagorno-Karabakh and that existing territorial administrative borders would not be withdrawn.[98] In that same address, however, allusions can be found to the possibility of shifting the NKAO to the control of Armenia. Gorbachev noted that "not a few shortcomings and difficulties have accumulated in the Nagorno-Karabakh Autonomous Oblast. The new leadership of the oblast must adopt urgent measures to remedy the situation." Finally, he ended with the assurance that

> it is intended to devote a special plenum of our party's Central Committee to the development of national relations. It is planned to discuss a wide range of questions on this most important social sphere and, on the basis of the principled gains of Lenin's nationalities policy, to mark out the paths for the concrete solution of social, economic, cultural and other problems.[99]

Armenians thus continued to believe that Gorbachev supported their claims, despite the rejection of those claims by the CPSU CC. Believing that genuine concessions would be forthcoming, the Armenians refrained from adopting violent tactics (Proposition 5.4).

Three days before the month-long moratorium expired, the CC and the USSR Council of Ministers, in a joint session, issued a final decision. Transfer of the NKAO to Armenian was "inadmissible."[100] Instead, Moscow offered to address some of the Armenian grievances in the NKAO with a comprehensive eight-year aid package designed to improve the cultural, economic, and social conditions in Nagorno-Karabakh.[101] These fell well short of Armenian demands. Moscow wrongly viewed the conflict as being primarily economic. It failed to understand that the conflict was, at its root, about mutually exclusive claims to homeland ownership. In offering concessions to the Karabakh Armenians, Moscow failed to recognize the second order consequences of its offer. Although Moscow's aid package intended to address Armenian grievances, the unintended result was to trigger a violent Azerbaijani response that ultimately undermined Communist rule in Azerbaijan.

As the violence continued to escalate, Moscow opted for repression. Armenian activists were arrested, troops were deployed in Yerevan and the NKAO, and in May 1988, Moscow removed the first secretaries of both the Azerbaijan and the Armenian Communist Parties and replaced them with individuals thought to be more amenable to negotiations and compromise.[102] Yet Moscow's repressive measures only emboldened Armenian resistance. With the support of the newly appointed First Secretary, the Armenian Supreme Soviet voted unanimously in favor of the transfer of Nagorno-Karabakh to the Armenian SSR on June 15, 1988.[103] Moscow's effort to strengthen its authority over the region had only led to further escalation. Neither the final ruling by Moscow on the NKAO's transfer nor the package of spending measures prevented the further escalation of violence.

Recognizing the dangers of continued escalation and the growing challenge to Soviet authority, Moscow expanded its repressive measures. It imposed martial law in Stepanakert and Agdam,[104] dissolved the Armenian-dominated NKAO party and government organizations, and finally assumed direct rule over Nagorno-Karabakh.[105] The immediate result was to quell the violence in the oblast—but at the cost of sparking mass demonstrations of Azerbaijanis against the Communist authorities in Baku and emboldening Azerbaijan's opposition movement. Although repression prompted both groups to refrain from interethnic violence (Proposition 5.3), the respite was only temporary.

A general strike in Karabakh and an Azerbaijani blockade that effectively cut all road traffic between Armenia and Nagorno-Karabakh brought the NKAO economy to a halt, triggering violent interethnic clashes in the oblast. In Azerbaijan, huge rallies against the Volsky Committee that ruled the oblast—and against the Communist authorities for their failure to assert Azerbaijan's sovereignty over Nagorno-Karabakh—threatened the Azerbaijan Communist Party's hold on power.

Moscow thus reversed its decision and "returned the region to a virtual status quo ante."[106] A Republican Organizational Committee (Orgkom), appointed by the Presidium of the Azerbaijani Supreme Soviet and staffed primarily by ethnic Azerbaijani officials, was given authority over the day-to-day management of the NKAO.[107] The Azerbaijani republic was also given authority over all security functions in the NKAO. Moscow was desperate to shore up the Azerbaijani Communist Party, which, unlike its Armenian counterpart, had retained its hold on power. Moscow was thus willing to risk further escalation of interethnic violence to secure a pro-Soviet government in Azerbaijan. Its decision was to spark a rapid escalation of interethnic violence.

Armenia announced its decision to annex the territory, and the Karabakh National Council voted for unification of the two territories under a single Armenian government.[108] Armenia announced a budget for the region in January 1990, which "touched off a revolution in Azerbaijan."[109] Radical groups claiming to represent the APF launched a massive wave of attacks against Armenians in Baku that, combined with APF seizures of government buildings elsewhere in Azerbaijan, gave the APF effective control over the republic. Moscow responded with brutal force, triggering a second bloodbath in Baku as Soviet forces reestablished Communist authority in Azerbaijan.[110] Azerbaijan's First Secretary was ousted and replaced with Ayaz Mutalibov.[111] Simultaneously with the invasion of troops in Baku, a state of emergency was declared in Nagorno-Karabakh and an additional 17,000 troops were dispatched to the region to enforce it. Coordinating their efforts with the Orgkom, Soviet troops in the NKAO conducted widespread searches and disarmed Armenian villages.[112]

As Moscow adopted increasingly repressive measures, its authority and capacity were further undermined. The central Soviet authorities were rapidly losing control over the conflict. Paramilitary groups began raiding arsenals and police stations to secure the necessary arms to conduct a guerrilla war against Azerbaijanis and Soviet troops in the spring of 1990. Armenian attacks on Azerbaijani villages and subsequent counterattacks led to a rapid escalation of the war.

By the time of the August 1991 coup d'état, the Soviet Union had lost its monopoly of force within its borders, and repeated efforts to resolve the growing crisis in Nagorno-Karabakh, from concessions to direct rule, had failed to satisfy either side or to quell the violence. Belated concessions were insufficient to meet Armenian demands, and repressive measures, when they were finally adopted nearly a year and a half after the conflict began, only served to escalate the violence. By the time the Soviet Union collapsed in December 1991, the conflict between Armenians and Azerbaijanis had escalated to full-scale war.

THE EXCLUSION MODEL

Although the Armenians were excluded from the Azerbaijani polity, and although they were to a large extent regionally concentrated (despite the sizable Armenian population in Baku), exclusion does not offer an explanation for the outbreak of ethnic violence. The Armenians in Nagorno-Karabakh and in the Armenian SSR were not bidding for a share of power in the Azerbaijani state when they first launched their effort to transfer the region from Azerbaijan to Armenia (Proposition 6). They did not seek to protect their autonomous status (Proposition 6.1), nor did they seek to overturn the prevailing political order *in Azerbaijan* (Proposition 6.2). From the earliest stage of the conflict, the Armenians were intent upon securing their complete exclusion from the Azerbaijani state.

THE EXTERNAL SUPPORT MODEL

The Soviet collapse in 1991 transformed the arena of conflict from an internal ethnic conflict to an international war between two post-Soviet republics. Although Moscow's role was fundamentally transformed by the Soviet collapse, its influence as an external actor continued to drive the escalation of violence. The transformation of the arena of conflict also expanded the number and influence of third-party actors, triggering a competition for influence among them. External support, particularly Russian intervention, enabled Armenian forces to launch a full-scale war to seize the contested region, and it enabled Azerbaijani forces to launch a full-scale counteroffensive in an attempt to reclaim the region (Proposition 7). Two scenarios explain how external support prompted the choice of violent means.

Escalation

The escalation scenario describes a situation in which external involvement extends the conflict in space, number, intensity, or all three. As one group secures external support, its competitor is forced to offset the perceived advantage by targeting the group through violence or by securing competing sources of external support, thereby triggering escalation (Proposition 7.1).

In the Nagorno-Karabakh war, Russian Federation support escalated violence both in space and in intensity. In the first few months after the Soviet collapse, Karabakh Armenian forces began a large-scale offensive to seize all of Nagorno-Karabakh. In late February 1992, Karabakh forces attacked the village of Khojaly—reportedly with the assistance of Russian troops from the 366th MRD.[113] According to eyewitness reports, Russian troops also spearheaded the ethnic cleansing campaign in which fleeing civilians were cut down and then mutilated in the no-man's-land between the two sides.[114] Whether Russian involvement was the work of rogue elements or whether it was directed by the Russian defense ministry, Russian intervention on the side of the Armenians was driven by Russia's broader interests in the region. Armenia was one of Russia's staunchest supporters in the Caucasus. Whereas Armenia openly aligned itself with Russia, signed an agreement establishing Russia's right to station troops and control bases in Armenia, and agreed to join the Commonwealth of Independent States (CIS), the anti-Russian APF demanded the withdrawal of Russian forces and rejected membership in the CIS. Russian involvement in Khojaly and in subsequent battles thus aimed to undermine the APF and expand its influence in a key region of the Near

Abroad. In so doing, Russian intervention escalated the conflict and widened the war.

The battle over Khojaly was in many ways a watershed. It was the first massacre of civilians by regular military forces in the Nagorno-Karabakh war.[115] It was also a major Armenian military success. Unlike the case of the Kurds, when Armenian forces shifted to a conventional strategy, external support proved critical to its success. By May Armenian forces had seized control of a strategic stretch of territory beyond the borders of the oblast connecting Nagorno-Karabakh to Armenia. Control of the Lachin corridor enabled the Armenians to break the Azerbaijani blockade of Nagorno-Karabakh. Subsequently, food, fuel, arms, and "volunteers" entered Karabakh from Armenia, providing crucial assistance for the war effort. Russian support, including the direct intervention of Russian forces, significantly escalated the conflict; it also enabled the Armenians to break the blockade of Nagorno-Karabakh and seize all of Nagorno-Karabakh.

Yet Russian support came at a cost. Prior to the Armenian offensive, international opinion had largely branded Azerbaijan as the aggressor. Following Khojaly, international opinion shifted in favor of Azerbaijan. The Karabakh Armenians were increasingly isolated internationally. This served to heighten the importance of the Lachin corridor as a lifeline for the Karabakh Armenians, and provided the Russian Federation with an opportunity to exert its influence on the Armenians.

Russia also used the string of Azerbaijani defeats in the spring of 1992 to exert its influence over Azerbaijan. The series of losses prompted Azerbaijan to search for external support to offset the clear Armenian advantage. In a pattern that would repeat itself many times throughout the war, Russia extended support to Azerbaijan, which gave it unparalleled influence over the conflict. Beginning in June, Azerbaijan launched a massive counterattack, spearheaded apparently by Russian armor driven by Russian soldiers.[116] With Russian forces, equipment, and training, Azerbaijan regained significant territory in the fall of 1992.

Russia's ability to control events on the battlefield became apparent with the sudden halt to the offensive in October 1992 after the APF government voted to reject membership in the CIS. "Spare parts were not to be had at any price,"[117] and Russian forces stationed in Armenia reportedly launched attacks against Azerbaijani cities near the Karabakh border. By April 1993, a substantially weakened Azerbaijani army lost Kelbajar to Karabakh Armenian forces.[118]

Although Russia cut off the important pipeline of weaponry and parts for the Azerbaijani national army, Russian forces maintained a close relationship with rogue units, controlled by Surat Huseinov, a wealthy merchant who played a key role in procuring Russian arms. By the time of the coup in June 1993, Huseinov had dozens of armored vehicles in the Russian garrison in Ganja. He assumed control over them when the 104th Airborne Division, the last Russian unit in Azerbaijan, pulled out of Azerbaijan on May 28, 1993, a full year ahead of schedule. "The precipitous removal of Russian protection around Huseinov—as well as the prospect of considerable weapons stocks falling into his hands" served as "bait in a well-planned trap for the Elchibey government."[119] After a failed attempt to disarm Huseinov's forces, Elchibey fled Baku, and Heydar Aliyev came to power, committed to repairing Azerbaijan's relationship with Russia.

Although Russian support enabled the APF to reclaim battlefield losses, it did so at great cost. The Azerbaijani government effectively ceded control of its rearmament and thus of the war itself. Armenian forces also paid the cost as Russian support for Azerbaijan secured gains on the ground for Azerbaijan at the Armenians' expense. Russian support for both sides of the conflict significantly escalated the violence. While Russia's 7th Army in Armenia was reportedly involved in the fighting in Nagorno-Karabakh in order to weaken the Elchibey government through losses on the battlefield, Russia was simultaneously supplying the Azerbaijani army, and then suddenly cutting off that supply, to weaken the Azerbaijani government from within. Russian support triggered an escalatory cycle of third-party intervention as both sides sought to offset the balance. In the Nagorno-Karabakh conflict, that escalatory cycle was largely controlled by one third party.

As Moscow's support for Azerbaijan expanded, the Karabakh Armenians and Armenia began to coordinate their efforts more closely to offset the Azerbaijani advantage. Throughout the conflict, Armenians in Nagorno-Karabakh and Armenia maintained an official policy of distance. Although Armenia strongly supported the Karabakh Armenian desire for unification with Armenia, the proclaimed policy was one of secession and independence for the NKAO. Russian support for Azerbaijan's rearmament prompted the direct intervention of Armenian republic forces.[120]

Moscow's support for both the Armenians and Azerbaijanis in the conflict over Nagorno-Karabakh directly contributed to the escalation of violence and the widening of the war (Proposition 7.1). Initial support for Armenian forces prompted the Azerbaijanis to seek to offset the advantage, triggering an escalatory cycle of violence that Russia, because of its role as the primary third party in the conflict, could effectively exploit to secure its own interests.

Mediation

External support through mediation can trigger the escalation or resumption of war when the intervening parties are viewed as biased or their efforts are perceived to be exclusionary (Proposition 7.3). When that mediation aims to resolve a conflict over a contested homeland, the effort is likely to protract the war.

The power vacuum created by the Soviet collapse created an opening for regional powers to compete with Russia for influence in the Caucasus. It also opened the door to mediation attempts by various states and international actors. Turkey's pro-Azerbaijani stance and Russia's intervention on the Armenian side created an opening for Iranian mediation. Because Armenians viewed Iran as an important counterweight to Turkey in the region, the Armenians were particularly supportive of Iranian efforts. In late February 1992, Iran attempted to broker a ceasefire, but the effort quickly collapsed as Karabakh Armenian forces launched an offensive that brought all of Nagorno-Karabakh under Armenian control. A second Iranian effort in May 1992 similarly failed to produce a ceasefire. Azerbaijanis quickly came to view Iran as a biased party,[121] and Iran's role in the region was subsequently marginalized. With Russia and Iran effectively sidelined by one or both groups' refusal to accept their mediation efforts as neutral, the CSCE Minsk Group emerged as the primary third-party mediator. However, by September 1992, its efforts too had failed over Azerbaijan's refusal to recognize the Karabakh Armenian leadership as a party to the negotiations.[122]

The election of Elchibey in June 1992 created a significant shift in the number and nature of third-party mediation efforts. Elchibey's pro-Turkish policies elevated Turkey's role in the region. Encouraged by the West, particularly the United States, to assert its influence in Central Asia and the Transcaucasus, Turkey became Azerbaijan's closest regional ally. With the CSCE initiative stymied by Azerbaijan's refusal to negotiate directly with the Karabakh Armenians, Turkey assumed the role of mediator and proposed a bilateral Turkish-Russian mediation effort. Russia was firmly opposed to the expansion of Turkish influence in the region, and its intervention on the side of the Armenians enabled the Armenian seizure of Kelbajar in April 1993. It also undermined the mediation effort, which the Armenians viewed as biased in favor of Azerbaijan.

The attack on Kelbajar sparked strong reactions internationally, and the UN Security Council condemned the incursion and called for the withdrawal of "foreign and local Armenian forces, whether regular or irregular" from occupied territory, a halt to hostilities in and around Nagorno-Karabakh, and a resumption of the peace negotiations.[123] Three days later, Resolution 822 became the basis for an ambitious tripartite U.S.-Turkish-Russian peace plan. Having suffered severe losses to the Armenian offensives, Azerbaijan endorsed the plan, as did Armenia.[124] Under international pressure, Armenian President Ter-Petrosyan pressured the Karabakh leadership to accept the plan. It was subsequently modified, and on June 14, 1993, the Karabakh leadership signed the agreement. The June 1993 coup d'état that toppled Elchibey's government, with Russian involvement, effectively undermined the peace plan.

The Russian-engineered coup brought Aliyev, a former First Secretary of the Azerbaijan Communist Party, KGB General, and Politburo member, to power. Aliyev engineered a fundamental shift in Azerbaijan's foreign policy: Russian influence came to the fore, Turkey was sidelined, and Azerbaijan opened direct negotiations with the Karabakh leadership. Recognizing that only Moscow could bring an end to the war, Aliyev sought to repair Azerbaijan's relationship with Russia. In a meeting with Yeltsin and Russian Defense Minister Pavel Grachev, Aliyev requested that Russia use "the full authority of the Russian Army, the Defense Ministry and personal relations with the Armenian leadership to seek a resolution to the conflict."[125] At the same time, Aliyev ended Azerbaijan's close relationship with Turkey. He extended Azerbaijan's visa requirement to Turks, who were previously exempt, and then rounded up and deported all Turkish citizens in Baku who did not posses the necessary documentation.[126] Some 1,600 Turkish military experts and volunteers serving in Azerbaijan were dismissed, and many of the agreements between Elchibey and Ankara were reversed.[127]

In an effort to secure much-needed Russian support to end the conflict on favorable terms, Aliyev began to distance himself from both the CSCE and the U.S.-Turkish-Russian mediation process, claiming that they had achieved nothing.[128] At a CSCE Foreign Minister's Meeting in Rome in November 1993, Azerbaijan's Foreign Minster delivered a bitter attack on the Minsk Group's involvement in the conflict, accusing the CSCE of siding with Armenia and tacitly condoning Armenian ethnic cleansing, while at the same time pressuring Azerbaijan to make "unacceptable decisions."[129]

Under the aegis of the Russian Foreign Ministry, Aliyev agreed to hold direct talks with the Karabakh leadership, which produced a ceasefire agreement for Nagorno-Karabakh. Yet peace was short-lived. In October, Karabakh Armenian forces launched another offensive. By the end of the month, Karabakh forces had seized the Zangelan province, leaving them in control of roughly 20 percent of Azerbaijani territory.[130] There is some evidence that the Armenian offensive was supported by Russia in retaliation for Azerbaijan's refusal to agree to Russian jurisdiction over parts of the Caspian Sea and its rich oil deposits, as well as to stationing Russian troops in Azerbaijan.[131] When both Iran and Turkey called on the UN Security Council to condemn the aggression, which it did in UNSC Resolution 874, "there was a deafening silence from Russia."[132] Russia's manipulation of the mediation efforts thus triggered the further expansion of violence as the turmoil in Azerbaijan created new opportunities for Armenian forces to exploit.

Throughout the winter of 1993 to 1994, the OSCE Minsk group mediation process was essentially eclipsed by Russian envoy Vladimir Kazimirov's shuttle diplomacy between the various capitals.[133] The marginalization of parallel OSCE efforts led to mounting criticism of Russia's efforts to monopolize the mediation process, prompting Kazimirov to complain in November that "we feel very little support from other governments for our efforts . . . There is a jealous attitude: why is Russia doing it and not the Minsk group?"[134] Despite criticism of Russia's monopolization of the peace process by OSCE members, Russian efforts produced a ceasefire in May 1994. The negotiations were conducted at the same time as an OSCE visit to the region, yet no OSCE Minsk group representative attended the meeting. "The agreement mark[ed] the culmination of a single-minded Russian effort to wrest the initiative in the Karabakh mediation process away from the OSCE."[135]

Moscow successfully brought Azerbaijan back within its sphere of influence and marginalized competing mediation efforts through the alternating use of force and negotiation. Azerbaijan was faced with little alternative but to acquiesce to the reestablishment of Russian influence in the region, for to fail to do so would have risked more extensive territorial losses to the Karabakh Armenians. The costs of exclusive Russian mediation were high. Russia deliberately protracted the war to secure its influence in Azerbaijan. "Russia strove for a stalemate, and both Armenia and Azerbaijan were its victims."[136] The existence of competing mediation efforts provided the Karabakh Armenians with the opportunity to seize as much Azerbaijani territory as possible, which gave the Karabakh Armenians leverage in the negotiations, created a buffer zone around Karabakh, and forced Azerbaijan to negotiate directly with the Karabakh Armenians (Proposition 7.4). The result was a significant protraction of the conflict over a five-year period of international mediation that Russia manipulated to secure its regional objectives.[137] A ceasefire only became possible when the main third party to the conflict, Russia, had realized its broader interests in the region.

RESOURCE MODEL

The Soviet Union, and after 1991 the Russian Federation, was the primary supplier of arms and resources to both sides of the conflict. Soviet and later Russian weapons were easy to obtain and, when seized on the battlefield, simple to incorporate and operate. The relative ease with which both sides could procure weapons was a significant factor in the rapid escalation of violent incidents to full-scale war in 1992 (Proposition 8).

Soviet military stocks, and after December 1991, the Russian defense establishment, served as the primary supply of weaponry for both the Azerbaijanis and the Armenians. At first, when violence was limited to isolated incidents in Nagorno-Karabakh, the combatants used hunting rifles, shotguns, knives, and an occasional grenade or Molotov cocktail.[138] By the end of 1991, however, both sides had acquired a large stock of weaponry from the disintegrating Soviet armed forces. Some of the weaponry was purchased from local Soviet commanders, but most of it was seized from Soviet barracks and weapons stockpiles. Heavy artillery, rocket-propelled grenades, rocket launchers, tanks, and armored personnel carriers were either sold or "loaned" to both sides, or alternatively were seized from weapons depots or the battlefield.[139] The bulk of Soviet weaponry, however, was acquired by agreements on the allocation of former Soviet weaponry between Russia and the newly independent republics.

The Azerbaijan Armed Forces were established in October 1991, following a decree by the Azerbaijan Supreme Soviet to "nationalize" all property of the Soviet 4th Army located in Azerbaijan. Some 140,000 Azerbaijani conscripts serving in the USSR were recalled to serve in the new army of Azerbaijan. The Azerbaijani Army was equipped with 300 tanks, 800 armored personnel carriers, 330 artillery pieces and rocket launchers, and some 45 combat aircraft, most of which was seized from Soviet military barracks prior to the breakup of the Soviet Union.[140] Having acquired the necessary weaponry, Azerbaijan was able to launch the first large-scale attack by regular forces in the Nagorno-Karabakh war in December 1991. The Azerbaijanis gradually lost their advantage against the more effective Karabakh Armenian forces, who, despite being smaller in number, evidenced strong morale and were better led and trained.[141] As these forces began to acquire weapons on par with the Azerbaijanis, these qualitative advantages help explain the rapid and decisive Armenian victories.

Armenian paramilitary forces in Nagorno-Karabakh were at a significant disadvantage against the larger, better-equipped Azerbaijani forces at the outset of the conflict. In the spring of 1992, however, the balance in military forces shifted. On May 15, the Russian Federation, Armenia, Azerbaijan, and Georgia signed the Tashkent Agreement on the partition and transfer of former Soviet military equipment of the Transcaucasus Military District among the three Transcaucasian states. This massive infusion of military equipment into an already escalating conflict transformed the conflict to a full-scale war.

In Nagorno-Karabakh, Armenian forces secured weapons from the 366th MRD in Stepanakert when it withdrew. These arms were a crucial threshold to the expansion of the war. In the spring of 1992, the Karabakh Armenian forces launched an offensive that left them in control of all of Karabakh and the strategic Lachin corridor in Azerbaijan, linking the enclave with Armenia. This corridor became a major conduit for Armenian supplies, including weaponry, food, fuel, and "volunteers." Although the Azerbaijani forces were much larger and better-equipped than the Karabakh forces, the Azerbaijani Armed Forces were from the outset poorly led and politically divided, with certain units owing loyalty to individual warlords, such as Surat Huseinov, rather than to the state itself. As a result, Azerbaijan failed to create an effective army. The critical influx of weaponry in 1992 thus gave the Karabakh Armenian forces the necessary supplies to launch their spring offensives and defeat the better-equipped Azerbaijani Army.

After the allocation of Soviet weapons stockpiles through the Tashkent Agreement, Russia remained the principle weapons supplier to both sides. Weapons reached both sides of the conflict in three ways: through seizure from Russian stockpiles, through capture in battle, and by purchases from the Russian defense establishment.

Former Soviet Arms depots provided an important source of ammunition and weaponry for both sides. During 1992, there were mysterious fires and explosions at former Soviet Army ammunition dumps outside Baku and Agdam in Azerbaijan and near Yerevan, Armenia.[142] These seizures may have been authorized by local military commanders for personal gain, and then covered up by "remarkably destructive explosions . . . totally incinerating all inventory."[143] According to Philip Remler, a political officer in the U.S. Embassy in Azerbaijan, these explosions were part of a cover-up to "destroy the evidence of what is not because you have already stolen and sold the lot."[144]

A second important source of weaponry, particularly for the Karabakh forces, was the capture of weapons from the Azerbaijani army. The Karabakh Armenian forces acquired a large number of tanks and armored personnel carriers from the Azerbaijani Army through capture on the battlefield, including Soviet T-72 tanks refitted with Turkish communications equipment.[145] A converted tractor repair plant in Karabakh was opened to repair the large number of captured tanks so that Karabakh Armenian forces could recycle them against the original owners.

The third and most important means by which former Soviet and Russian weaponry reached both sides after 1992 was through direct arms purchases, reportedly on easy credit terms.[146] The advantage of Soviet equipment was that anyone who served in the Soviet Army was familiar with it and ammunition was easy to obtain. In Azerbaijan, while the APF was in power, these sales were accomplished through middlemen such as Huseinov, who procured essential weaponry, spare parts, and ammunition for the Azerbaijani Army and for his own units. In Armenia weapons purchases were negotiated directly, and in peak periods some 40 Russian transport planes landed in Yerevan's airport daily.[147] A study in 1997 based on interviews with Russian Defense Ministry officials estimates the total cost of arms deals with Armenia at one billion dollars.[148] Russia supplied Armenia not only with weapons, but also with spare parts and fuel. The embargo by Azerbaijan and, after Kelbajar, by Turkey, created a desperate situation in Armenia, which could only access fuel and other imports sporadically through Georgia. Russian arms and resources were thus central to the Armenian war effort and to its repeated success on the battlefield against the Azerbaijani forces.

As the primary weapons supplier, Moscow was able to influence the course of the conflict and even control events on the battlefield. Both sides were dependent on Moscow for equipment, and Moscow exploited this dependence for leverage to secure its interests in the region, which precluded victory on either side. By controlling the type of weapons systems available to both sides, Moscow could ensure the advantage or disadvantage to either side, or, alternatively, produce a regional stalemate. Thus, neither Armenia nor Karabakh was able to purchase fixed-wing aircraft, but both were able to acquire antiaircraft systems to shoot down enemy aircraft. Azerbaijan was able to acquire fixed-wing aircraft, including Su-25s and MiG-29s, which were used on bombing raids over Stepanakert, but was unable to purchase antiaircraft systems.[149] By controlling the timing, amounts and types of supplies each side was buying, Moscow could award or punish either side, influence the scale and extent of the battles, and determine to a great extent success or failure on the battlefield.

As the primary weapons supplier, Moscow was also able to limit the influence of other regional suppliers. Azerbaijan was able to purchase weapons from Israel, China, and Turkey,[150] and was also able to secure a Saudi aid package worth $100 million.[151] The primary external supplier for the Karabakh Armenians was Armenia itself, which purchased its supplies primarily from Russia, either on easy credit or with funds supplied by the Armenian diaspora. Moscow could effectively nullify the benefit of these arms by increasing the supply of military equipment to the other side, thus ensuring that Moscow remained the dominant source of arms and resources throughout the conflict. Its ability to control the flow of weapons was a significant factor in the choice of violent means and the rapid escalation of the conflict.

CONCLUSION

In the Nagorno-Karabakh case, the choice of violent means is explained by models at all three images of ethnic war. At the first image, competing claims to Nagorno-Karabakh as an ethnic homeland prompted Armenians to adopt violent means to reclaim their homeland and Azerbaijanis to defend it. Significant demographic shifts, the lack of meaningful cultural autonomy, and the encroachment on group lands and resources by ethnic strangers constituted a clear threat to the survival of Armenians as a distinct ethnic group in the NKAO. Finally, the role of the Armenian ethnic leadership in responding to a grassroots protest movement and creating an effective leadership structure and strategy to secure group aims was critical to the choice of violent means when the petition for transfer failed. Yet these group-level causes tell only part of the story.

The protest movement in Armenia over the NKAO triggered the first, mass, ethnic-based challenge to the legitimacy and authority of Soviet rule in nearly 70 years. As the conflict escalated, the inherent weakness of the Soviet state constrained both the central government and the republic authorities' ability to respond. This single, state-level explanation for violence demonstrates the impact of the state as both arena and actor in the choice of violent means.

As the Soviet state collapsed, external actors vied for a role in the conflict, and the competition among them sparked an escalation of violence. However, Russian support and arms were the primary causes of violence at the third image. Russian support—or the withdrawal of that support—granted Russia a significant degree of influence over the conflict. As the primary third party to the conflict, Russia used this influence deliberately to escalate and widen the war in pursuit of its interests in the region.

Each of the six models applicable to the Nagorno-Karabakh war explains the choice of violent means from a different level of analysis. As was clear in the Yugoslav case, these triggers of violence rarely operate in isolation. In the case of Nagorno-Karabakh, we see significant interaction among them. In Chapter 8, we return to the interrelationship of the models across the three images to add this additional layer of complexity to our multilevel framework.

7
Chapter

Three Images in Iraqi Kurdistan

INTRODUCTION

In this final case study, we examine the Kurds' decades-long struggle against a succession of Arab rulers, which began with the creation of the modern Iraqi state and has lasted until the collapse of Saddam Hussein's regime in 2003. Unlike the case of Yugoslavia or Nagorno-Karabakh, the violent conflict between Kurds and Arabs in Iraq allows us to test the framework against a case of ethnic violence that was sustained over several decades. The models at each of the three images of ethnic war explain not only why the Kurds adopted violent means, but also why the Kurds repeatedly resumed fighting. The case of Iraqi Kurdistan, like the Yugoslav and Nagorno-Karabakh cases, demonstrates that violence is rarely a single-level phenomenon. Understanding the complexity of Kurd-Arab violence is best achieved through a multilevel framework of interrelated models across the three images of ethnic war.

THE HOMELAND MODEL

The question of a Kurdish homeland is complicated by the fact that Kurdistan describes a region that straddles the political boundaries of six states: four with sizeable Kurdish populations (Iraq, Iran, Turkey, and Syria), and two with much smaller populations (the former Soviet republics of Azerbaijan and Armenia). The Homeland Model suggests that ethnonational groups will adopt violent means to defend or reclaim an ethnic homeland because possession of that homeland is vital to the group's ethnic identity. Ethnonational groups are regionally concentrated ethnic groups who have a history of self-rule in their homeland. Autonomy or possession of the homeland need not be recent to trigger ethnic violence, but possession of that homeland must be central to the group's identity if the homeland model is to provide an explanation for violence.

Figure 7.1 Ethnoreligious Map of Iraq.

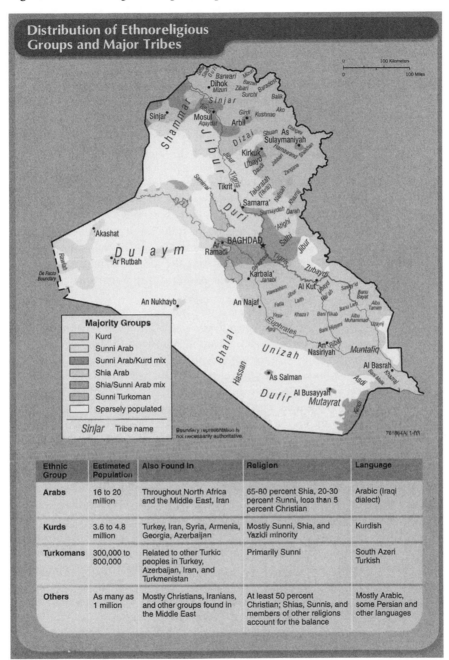

Ethnic Group	Estimated Population	Also Found In	Religion	Language
Arabs	16 to 20 million	Throughout North Africa and the Middle East, Iran	65-80 percent Shia, 20-30 percent Sunni, less than 5 percent Christian	Arabic (Iraqi dialect)
Kurds	3.6 to 4.8 million	Turkey, Iran, Syria, Armenia, Georgia, Azerbaijan	Mostly Sunni, Shia, and Yazidi minority	Kurdish
Turkomans	300,000 to 800,000	Related to other Turkic peoples in Turkey, Azerbaijan, Iran, and Turkmenistan	Primarily Sunni	South Azeri Turkish
Others	As many as 1 million	Mostly Christians, Iranians, and other groups found in the Middle East	At least 50 percent Christian; Shias, Sunnis, and members of other religions account for the balance	Mostly Arabic, some Persian and other languages

Source: U.S. Central Intelligence Agency, *Iraq: Distribution of Ethnoreligious Groups and Major Tribes* (Iraq Country Profile (Map), January 2003). Available at http://www.lib.utexas.edu/maps/middle_east_and_asia/iraq_ethno_2003.jpg

Although the Kurds are regionally concentrated, they have never had a state of their own. The Kurds were promised an independent state in the Treaty of Sèvres, but its provisions were never implemented. In Iran the Democratic Republic of Kurdistan, also known as the Mahabad Republic, survived barely a year even with Soviet backing.[1] In Iraq, however, portions of Kurdish-inhabited territory in the north were designated as an autonomous region for the purpose of controlling the Kurdish population. The Kurds were never granted real self-rule in Iraqi Kurdistan. The Kurds thus have neither a history of autonomy nor of self-rule in any of the regions within Kurdistan. Furthermore, Kurdish ethnic identity, unlike the Serbs or the Armenians, was not centered on the possession of a specific homeland or territory. Rather, the Kurds' ethnic identity has been closely linked to the Kurdish way of life symbolized by "the Mountain." Territory was important only to the extent that the Kurds were allowed to remain in the mountainous regions of Kurdistan.

The decades-long violent ethnic war between the Kurds and their Arab rulers in Baghdad cannot be explained by the Homeland Model. The war was not fought to reclaim or defend a lost homeland, nor was the idea of a specific homeland central to Kurdish identity as it was for the Armenians in Nagorno-Karabakh or the Serbs in Kosovo.

Since 1991, however, the Kurds have enjoyed de facto autonomy in Iraq. If the Kurds come to view this autonomous region as a Kurdish homeland for the Kurds in Iraq or for Kurds throughout the region, then the Homeland Model suggests a possible source of future ethnic violence not only in Iraq, but also more broadly in the region inhabited by Kurds. Fifteen years of self-rule are likely to change the Kurds' perception of their autonomous region, particularly in relation to Kirkuk. It is exactly this scenario that has engendered such fierce resistance to the idea of ethnic rather than territorial autonomy in Iraq by regional powers such as Turkey. Iraqi Kurdistan may become that homeland for the Kurds throughout the Middle East, and Kirkuk may become a symbol of that homeland for the Iraqi Kurds. Both scenarios suggest a high likelihood of future interethnic violence, and they explain why regional powers with Kurdish minorities have been so opposed to autonomy for the Iraqi Kurds. If Kurds come to view Iraqi Kurdistan as a homeland, and perceive continued possession of that homeland as vital to their identity as a distinct ethnic group, then the Kurds in Iraq and in the broader region of Kurdistan may adopt violent means to defend their ownership (Proposition 1), and the Kurds in Iraq may attempt secession (Proposition 1.1). In defending their homeland, the Kurdish majority population may also be prompted to cleanse the homeland of ethnic strangers and claim exclusive ownership, particularly given the number of regional powers with designs on the territory (Proposition 1.2). It is this latter scenario that Turkey has cited as justification for its intervention in support of Kurdistan's Turkomen population.

THE ETHNOCHAUVINISM MODEL

The Ethnochauvinism Model suggests that groups will adopt strategies of ethnic violence to dominate the ethnic other because of a belief in the group's superiority. The Kurds have not been motivated to adopt a strategy of ethnic violence by a belief in the innate superiority of Kurds over Arabs. Even though the Kurds were subject to massive repression and widespread chemical weapons attacks by Saddam Hussein's regime, the extreme forms of intolerance and ethnic hatred that characterized the war in Yugoslavia have not prompted the *Kurds* to adopt a strategy of ethnic cleansing in Kurdistan (although the Kurds claim the Iraqi state subjected them to ethnic cleansing). Until the 2003, the Kurds' battle has been fought with Baghdad, controlled by a series of Sunni-dominated regimes.

Post-2003, however, Iraq resembles a textbook case of an unranked system. The likelihood for violence is thus high, and due to the unranked nature of ethnic relations, the weak status of the new regime, and the attendant risk of U.S. withdrawal, the potential for the more extreme forms of ethnic violence suggested by the Ethnochauvinism Model are possible. Although it is not the most likely scenario, ethnochauvinism looms as a possible source of violence given the level of interethnic tension present as competing groups seek to protect their interests in the new Iraqi state.[2]

THE GROUP SURVIVAL MODEL

The history of the Kurdish experience in Iraq since its creation in 1921 is one of escalating violence by a succession of Iraqi regimes in a persistent effort to undermine, subvert, co-opt, and finally completely destroy a separate Kurdish national identity. As Baghdad's choice of measures to combat the Kurds became increasingly violent, the threat to the Kurds' survival increased proportionately. The Kurds adopted a strategy of ethnic violence based on the widely held belief that their *survival as a distinct ethnic group was threatened* by the policies of a succession of Arab regimes in Baghdad who controlled Iraq from its inception until the collapse of Saddam Hussein's regime in 2003 (Proposition 3).

Arabization, Forced Resettlement, and the Anfal

A succession of Iraqi regimes sought to reduce the number of Kurds in Iraq in absolute terms, and to shift the number of Kurds in relative terms in the contested regions of Iraqi Kurdistan, through Arabization, internal boundary shifts, forced resettlement, and massacre. These policies presented a clear threat not only to the Kurdish ethnic identity, but also to the Kurds' physical survival as a distinct ethnic group in Iraq.

Arabization was first implemented during the mandate period in an effort to create an Iraqi national identity among its inhabitants. Before 1963, Arabization was not as unabashedly violent as it came to be under the Baath. It aimed at a gradual assimilation of Kurds and other minorities in Iraq. When the Baath first seized power in 1963, and again after the second Baath regime came to power in 1968, Arabization came to describe more than forced or induced assimilation. Under the Baath, Arabization became a policy of forced *population transfers*

aimed at shifting the ethnic balance in disputed regions of Kurdistan to undermine the Kurdish claim to the contested region.

Under the Baath, Arabization was employed to resolve the Kurdish threat
once and for all. Large numbers of Kurds were internally displaced in Iraq, and
Arabs from other parts of Iraq and the Middle East were offered financial incentives to move to the homes and farms of Kurds who had been forcibly relocated.[3]
Whole Kurdish villages in the disputed regions of Kirkuk, Aqra, Shaykhan, and
Khaniqin were forcibly evacuated.[4] In their place, Arab settlers from elsewhere in
Iraq and Egypt were imported. In September 1971, Baghdad expelled 40,000 to
50,000 Faili Kurds on the grounds that these Kurds were Iranians, even though
these Shi`a Kurds had settled in Khaniqin and Baghdad during the Ottoman
period.[5] According to the Kurds, Iraq's policies aimed "to depopulate Kurdistan of
its native, historical inhabitants."[6]

In 1975, in the aftermath of the Kurdish collapse, Baghdad accelerated its
efforts to permanently shift the demographic balance in Kurdistan. Kirkuk was
partitioned and reduced in size from eight provinces to three.[7] Portions of Kirkuk
were transferred to the Governorates of Suleimaniya, Diyala, and Tikrit (renamed
Salah ad-Din); an additional portion was used to create the new Governorate of
Irbil, leaving only the oil-rich portion of Kirkuk (renamed At-Tamim, meaning
"nationalization," in 1972, when Iraq nationalized the oil industry). Mosul was
similarly redrawn and the new Governorate of Dohuk, in the far north of Mosul,
was created. The redrawing of governorate boundaries meant that historically
Kurdish regions and population centers were transferred to predominately Arab
governorates. The autonomous region unilaterally imposed by Baghdad in 1974
included only the Kurdish regions of Dohuk, Irbil, and Suleimaniya. Mosul, the
oil-rich region of Kirkuk, and the districts of Mandali and Khaniqin were
excluded, having been administratively transferred to non-Kurdish governorates.
The sum total of these boundary shifts left the Kurds further divided and
restricted the autonomous region to less than half of the territory in which Kurds
formed at least a majority.

In addition to internal boundary shifts, 1 million residents, according to
Kurdish sources, were removed from Khaniqin, Kirkuk, Mandali, Shaykhan,
Zakho, and Sinjar.[8] In 1975 at least 50 Kurdish villages, and perhaps as many as
500, were destroyed in the border regions, and by 1978 that number may have
risen to 1,400 villages, resulting in estimates ranging from 50,000 to 600,000 displaced Kurds who were transferred to the south or deported.[9] In 1987, when the
policy was again resumed, an estimated 3,000 Kurdish villages were destroyed, and
half a million Kurds were deported to detention camps.[10]

It has been estimated that between 500,000 and 1.5 million Kurds were
resettled between 1975 and 1989, and that of that total, 250,000 to 300,000 were
resettled in 1988 alone as part of the *Anfal* campaign.[11] If the estimated population of Kurds in Iraq is 3 million, then an astounding 17 percent—and possibly as
high as 50 percent, based on Kurdish sources—of Iraq's total Kurdish population
was forcibly resettled between 1975 and 1989. Table 7.1 details the cumulative

Table 7.1 Population of the Kirkuk Governorate[1]

Ethnic Identity	1925 (% of Population)	1957 (% of Population)	1977 (% of Population)
Kurds	63	55.0	37.53
Arabs	18	30.8	44.41
Turkomen	19	14.2	16.31

[1.] 1925 figures are from estimates from the League of Nations' records; see Akbar S. Ahmed, 35. The 1957 and 1977 figures are from the official Iraqi government census; see Akbar S. Ahmed, 37 and 41. For more analysis of the 1957 and 1977 census, see Michael M. Gunter and M. Hakan Yavuz, "The Continuing Crisis in Iraqi Kurdistan," *Middle East Policy* 12 (Spring 2005): 127.

impact of these policies on the population of the Kirkuk Governorate. The Kurds declined from 63 percent of the population in 1925 to 37 percent by 1977, while the Arab population increased from 18 to 44 percent in that same period. Although these percentages are based on census figures that are notoriously unreliable, they show a clear downward trend in the Kurdish population as a percentage of the total in Kirkuk, a trend supported by the anecdotal data, and an increase in the percentage of the Arab population.

Although the percentage change in Kirkuk is probably higher than in other areas of Kurdistan due to the significance of Kirkuk's oil, we can assume, given the population transfers and the razing of Kurdish villages, that similar downward trends are apparent elsewhere in Kurdistan. According to Nader Entessar, "it is probably safe to assert that without population transfers, the Kurds would have constituted a slim majority in Mosul and Kirkuk and would have had a strong presence further south in the two districts of Khaniqin and Mandali."[12]

In addition to policies of resettlement and deportation, the Baath regime implemented the *Anfal*—or "spoils of war"—campaign of chemical warfare, mass arrests, torture, and execution of both Kurdish combatants and noncombatants. The Anfal campaign was a deliberate and systematic effort to destroy the Kurdish population in Iraq in absolute terms, in what the Kurds and outside sources have termed genocide.[13] Comprised of eight military offensives, the Anfal campaign began during the final year of the Iran-Iraq War and continued after Iran accepted the UN ceasefire on July 1988.[14]

In the most well-known and deadly incident, Iraq used chemical weapons on the Kurdish town of Halabja, killing 5,000–6,000 inhabitants in March 1988. Similar attacks were aimed at other Kurdish villages suspected of aiding the *peshmergas*[15] or of supporting Iran during the war. Hundreds of thousands of Kurds were arrested, nearly all of whom subsequently disappeared, presumably executed and buried in mass graves in southern Iraq. In other cases, mutilated and tortured bodies were returned to the next of kin. Known as the "lost ones of the Anfal," they included men, women, and children. Estimates of the number of Kurds who perished vary widely, from 150,000 to 200,000, excluding the massacre at Halabja.[16] By July 1989, in what Gareth Stansfield aptly calls "the manipulation of geography,"[17] 45,000 out of 75,000 square miles of Kurdistan had been cleared of its Kurdish inhabitants.[18]

There are no figures available to determine with any degree of accuracy the exact number of Kurds who were resettled, deported, and killed, and even the estimates vary widely. It is reasonable to assume that the cumulative affect of these three policies on the demographic balance in Kurdistan was significant enough to impact both the absolute and relative numbers of Kurds in Kurdistan. Combined with internal boundary shifts, the Kurds now formed the majority only in the three northernmost districts of historic Kurdistan. Clearly the total Kurdish population in Kurdistan suffered a loss in absolute terms (Proposition 3.1), not only in Kirkuk, but throughout Kurdistan. Given the obvious intent of the Iraqi authorities to shift the ethnic balance, it is also likely that the Kurdish population suffered a loss in relative terms (Proposition 3.2). The nature of that decline was dire enough to prompt the Kurds to conclude that their survival as a distinct ethnic group was threatened.

Cultural Autonomy

Ethnic groups are likely to conclude that their survival as a distinct group is threatened when cultural autonomy sufficient to ensure that the group's language, history, and culture can be passed on to members of the group is denied (Proposition 3.3). The lack of cultural autonomy is particularly critical for the Kurds. Their sense of ethnic identity and of Kurdish distinctiveness is derived not so much from a shared religion, language, or link to a specific homeland, but from "a common cultural means of expression and way of life [that] has, more than any other single factor, kept the flames of Kurdish nationalism alive."[19]

Kurdish identity is intimately linked to an almost mystical view of "the Mountain"[20] related in various myths that tell the story of the origins of the Kurds. In one myth, the Kurds are descendants of children hidden in the mountains to escape Zahak, a child-eating giant. Another myth links the Kurds to children of the slave girls of King Solomon, sired by the demon Jasad, and driven by the angry king into the mountains.[21] In each of these myths it is the Mountain that protects and shelters the Kurds. According to Mehrdad Izady, "mountains are the single most important natural phenomenon, and they have shaped the Kurdish history, people, tradition and culture."[22] The Kurds' link with the mountain has shaped a distinct Kurdish cultural identity and protected Kurdish culture from assimilation.[23]

Baghdad's policies of resettlement, deportation, and the destruction of Kurdish villages were not only aimed at reducing the absolute and relative numbers of Kurds in Kurdistan, but also had a more sinister purpose: they aimed to destroy the Kurdish way of life, and thus Kurdish identity. Kurdish villages along the mountainous border zone with Turkey and Iran and in the disputed areas of Kirkuk and Khaniqin were destroyed, and their Kurdish inhabitants were forced to leave the mountain fastness of Kurdistan for the desert south of Iraq. Clan and tribal ties were then further destroyed through resettlement among Arab villages in Nasiriyeh, Diwaniya, al-Mothanna, and al-Ramadi.[24] Other Kurds were reset tled in newly built "cluster villages," in compact, modern homes built to facilitate easy monitoring of their inhabitants' activities and to seal off their residents from the Kurdish peshmergas.[25] Those Kurds who attempted to return were summarily shot. Accustomed to a mountainous terrain and homogeneous culture, the resettled Kurds found themselves isolated in flat desert country among Arab speakers.[26] Indeed, "it is difficult to believe that the regime did not intend to shatter the communities it transferred, and to strip them of their independence and dignity."[27] The extensive repression of Kurdish culture, and the assault on the Kurdish way of life through resettlement, deportation, and the destruction of Kurdish villages, prompted the Kurds to conclude repeatedly that their survival as a distinct ethnic group was threatened (Proposition 3.3).

Lands and Resources at Risk

An ethnic group is likely to conclude that its survival as a distinct ethnic group is threatened when ethnic strangers encroach upon group lands and resources (Proposition 3.4). A succession of Arab regimes in Baghdad abrogated Kurdish property rights, destroyed rural areas in Kurdistan, and followed a policy of deliberate regional neglect, particularly in the oil-rich provinces of Kirkuk and Mosul and in the border regions along the Turkish and Iranian frontiers. These policies had as their aim the destruction of a Kurdish identity in Iraqi Kurdistan.

In the disputed areas of Kirkuk, Khaniqin, and Sinjar, Kurds were barred from purchasing property or obtaining title to new land.[28] In Kirkuk, Kurds were also restricted to selling land to Arabs only.[29] Under the guise of implementing land reform in Kurdistan, the Iraqi authorities confiscated land from Kurdish landowners; they then offered Arab peasants favorable loans and credits, which were unavailable to Kurdish peasants, to purchase the confiscated property.[30]

The encroachment of the state on group lands and resources was further evident in the destruction of Kurdistan's traditional agrarian economy. Iraqi Kurdistan had traditionally been self-sufficient in the production of food grains such that it supplied its surplus to the rest of Iraq. The Anfal campaign devastated the rural areas of Iraqi Kurdistan[31] and destroyed its agricultural economy. Rural Kurds were forced into towns in Kurdistan or in Saddam's "settlements,"[32] which were situated in the lowlands of the Kurdish region outside of Kurdish adminis- tration. The denial of the Kurds' basic land ownership rights, the exclusion of Kurdish villages through new administrative boundaries, and the persistent neglect of Kurdistan presented a *clear threat to the lives and livelihoods of the Kurds*. These measures led the Kurds to conclude that their survival was indeed threatened by the pressure on group lands and resources by the Iraqi state (Proposition 3.4).

Together these four factors—absolute and relative population decline, lack of cultural autonomy, and pressure on group lands and resources—prompted the

Kurds to conclude that their survival as a distinct ethnic group was at risk and to adopt violent means to defend the group against the policies of a series of Arab-controlled regimes in Baghdad (Proposition 3).

THE ETHNIC LEADERSHIP MODEL

A key source of violence in the Kurds' decades-long, violent interethnic war with Baghdad was the Kurdish ethnic leadership's choice of violent means to secure Kurdish autonomy in Iraq. This leadership secured the necessary resources, created and supplied an effective guerrilla army (the peshmergas), and defeated the larger and better-supplied Iraqi forces repeatedly over decades of conflict (Proposition 4). Yet despite repeated success, the Kurdish ethnic leadership failed to secure Kurdish goals. The Kurdish goal of autonomy was repeatedly undermined by endemic factionalism and a persistent struggle for power. As rival Kurdish factions sought to defeat each other, they created opportunities for Baghdad to exploit and repeatedly undermined the very goal for which they been fighting.

Charismatic leadership was able to overcome these divisions, but unification of the Kurds behind a single strategy was fleeting. The case of the Kurds demonstrates both the *charismatic leader scenario* and the *factional leader scenario*. Until the 1975 defeat, the Kurds were largely united behind the single greatest Kurdish leader, Mulla Mustafa Barzani, who was able, unlike his successors, to defeat rival factions and unify the Kurds (Proposition 4.1). Yet critical errors in judgment, including his increasing reliance on external support detailed in the External Support Model below, and Baghdad's effective exploitation of tribal divisions ultimately led to a disastrous defeat in 1975. Thereafter, the Kurds split irrevocably into two factions, and subsequently the choice of violent means was largely driven by the competition for power and preeminence among them (Proposition 4.3).

Mulla Mustafa Barzani and the Battle for Hegemony

The role of the Kurdish ethnic leadership begins with Mulla Mustafa Barzani, a leading member of the Barzani tribe in northern Iraq who became a symbol of Kurdish resistance even during his lifetime. Mulla Mustafa achieved legendary fame for his efforts to unite the Kurds in Iraqi Kurdistan. Mulla Mustafa was a charismatic leader who was able to bridge the gap between the traditional Kurmanji-speaking Kurds of the northwest who remained loyal to the semi-feudal social system dominated by the local aghas and religious sheikhs and the modern, urban, and secular Sorani-speaking Kurds of the southeast.[33] He became prominent in the Kurdish tribal rebellions beginning in the late 1920s and assumed leadership of the Barzani tribe in 1943 until his exile to the United States in 1975.

Mulla Mustafa's leadership was a blend of traditional tribal resistance to the central authority of the Iraqi state and a national movement for Kurdish self-rule. In 1943, Mulla Mustafa assembled a coalition of tribal forces and launched the first national Kurdish uprising against the Iraqi monarchy. In a turn of events characteristic of the sudden shifts in loyalty that would continually plague the Kurdish movement, rival tribes joined the government forces and the rebellion collapsed. Mulla Mustafa fled to Iran, where he began to build a political organization for the Kurds' battle with Baghdad, founding the Kurdish Democratic Party in 1946, renamed the Kurdistan Democratic Party (KDP) in 1960.[34]

Mulla Mustafa renewed the struggle against Baghdad after the 1958 coup d'état against the Iraqi Monarchy. The new government of Abd al-Karim Qasim and members of a military group called the Free Officers invited Mulla Mustafa back to Iraq, and Qasim publicly confirmed him as the leader of the Kurds.[35] Mulla Mustafa quickly took action to secure his position in Kurdistan. Although it suited Mulla Mustafa to cooperate with Qasim, he remained an independent force in Iraq. He had broad support among the Kurds, personally controlled the core of the KDP's forces, and secured vital support from Qasim, who began arming Mulla Mustafa's forces. As Mulla Mustafa defeated rival tribes and became more powerful, his relationship with Qasim worsened.

In a pattern that would repeat itself many times, the Kurds' relationship with Baghdad began to deteriorate as the Kurds increasingly united under Mulla Mustafa's leadership. Sensing the growing threat, Qasim began arming rival tribes. As Baghdad lost its authority over Kurdistan, Mulla Mustafa used the opportunity—not to secure concessions from Baghdad, but to attack the tribes armed by Qasim. By mid-1961, Mulla Mustafa had extended his control over a wide stretch of land from Suleimaniya to Zakho.[36] He had also become a very serious threat to Qasim.

In September 1961 Qasim ordered the widespread bombing of northern Kurdistan, including Barzan, thereby bringing most of the other Kurdish tribes into the war and achieving for Mulla Mustafa what he himself had not yet succeeded in doing. "Qasim had, in effect, brought together two distinct Kurdish tribal groups, the old reactionary chiefs out essentially to protect their landed interests and Mulla Mustafa whose agenda was a blend of tribalism and nationalism."[37] To complete Mulla Mustafa's task for him, Qasim ordered the closure of the KDP on September 24, 1961, thereby driving the KDP, which had thus far remained outside the fray, to join the rebellion. In December 1961 it commenced operations against Qasim as an ally of Mulla Mustafa.[38] Mulla Mustafa had united the Kurds through a blend of traditional tribal politics and national resistance. He effectively resisted Baghdad's efforts to exploit Kurdish divisions and consolidated rival Kurdish groups to sustain a broad-based rebellion against Baghdad's authority over Kurdistan.

Mulla Mustafa used his consolidated authority over Kurdistan to negotiate a ceasefire with the new regime of Abd al-Salam Arif, which announced its commitment to resume talks with the Kurds for "special rights."[39] Poised to negotiate with a new Iraqi regime that seemed willing to offer concessions to eliminate the Kurdish threat, the Kurdish leadership was again rent by division. The KDP leadership, likely motivated by a desire to undermine Mulla Mustafa and assume leadership of the movement as a whole, accused Mulla Mustafa of being a traitor:

Mulla Mustafa had signed a ceasefire agreement, without the knowledge and approval of the KDP, that omitted any mention of Kurdish autonomy, the goal for which they had been fighting, and that used the favored Arab nationalist euphemism, "the northern region," for Kurdistan. Stansfield suggests that Mulla Mustafa engineered the division as part of his plan to seize control of the KDP.[40] Most of the KDP leadership, known as the KDP Politburo, defected, and forces supporting the KDP Politburo clashed with forces loyal to Mulla Mustafa.

Intra-Kurd violence provided Baghdad with the opportunity to resume its traditional policy of exploiting Kurdish divisions. Rather than resolve the Kurdish threat to the new regime through negotiation, Arif began arming Mulla Mustafa and dispatched Iraqi forces into Kurdistan to assist Mulla Mustafa's efforts against his Kurdish opponents.[41] By mid-1964 Mulla Mustafa had secured control over major areas of Iraqi Kurdistan.[42] From 1964 until the collapse of the Kurdish war in 1975, Mulla Mustafa's authority was paramount. He had become the undisputed leader of the Kurds in Iraqi Kurdistan.

Mulla Mustafa could now turn his attention to realizing the very goals the KDP leadership had accused him of betraying. In October 1964 he demanded autonomy for Kurdistan, to include Kirkuk and Khaniqin; the use of Kurdish as the official language in Kurdistan; and a fair share of the oil revenue. The Arif regime, however, had used the intermittent year to consolidate its power and no longer viewed the Kurds as a threat. It refused the Kurds' demands, and Mulla Mustafa was left with little option but to prepare for war.[43] Most of the Kurds supported Mulla Mustafa, and in 1965 Jalal Talabani and Ibrahim Ahmad, as well as many of the KDP dissenters, were allowed back into Kurdistan to support the war.[44]

Cooperation between the two factions was brief. In 1966, when Iraqi Prime Minister Abd Al-Rahman Bazzaz offered the Kurds a 12-point peace plan, Mulla Mustafa accepted it, despite misgivings, in an effort to undermine Talabani, who was trying to negotiate a separate peace agreement with Arif's successors. With the failure of the Bazzaz agreement only a month later, Mulla Mustafa's relations with Ahmad and Talabani dissolved into a bitter feud. In January 1966 Ahmad and Talabani broke away again, accusing Mulla Mustafa of being "tribal," "feudal," and "reactionary."[45] Their forces began fighting alongside the despised pro-government tribes, known derisively as the *jash* ("little donkeys"), and against Mulla Mustafa's forces. In the fall of 1966, the war came to a standstill, and Mulla Mustafa used the respite to consolidate his position in Kurdistan, build up his forces, and attack his rivals.

When the July 1968 coup brought the Baath to power again, Mulla Mustafa used his position to undermine Talabani and Ahmad, who began negotiations with the new regime. Mulla Mustafa attacked Politburo forces; shelled Kirkuk's oil installations, which embarrassed the Baath internationally;[46] and secured support from Iran and Israel. In a series of clashes in the fall of 1968 and the spring of 1969, Mulla Mustafa quickly demonstrated that his forces were a bigger threat to the regime than those of the Ahmad-Talabani faction. The Baathists abandoned Talabani, and both Ahmad and Talabani contritely returned to the KDP.[47]

Mulla Mustafa had triumphed over Ahmad and Talabani, but neither faction had managed to secure an agreement for Kurdish autonomy. Although much of the blame for failing to negotiate an acceptable autonomy arrangement lies with a succession of weak regimes that never intended to share power with the Kurds (a separate, state-level source of violence discussed below), it is hard to avoid the conclusion that rivalry among the Kurdish leadership prevented the Kurds from pushing their advantage against Baghdad on numerous occasions when the regime was weak. Internal divisions also prevented the Kurds from sustaining pressure against the regime and from presenting a united front in negotiations for autonomy with Baghdad. Despite Mulla Mustafa's efforts to unite the Kurds, the consolidation of his leadership was fleeting. Shifting tribal alliances among the Kurdish factions, and between Kurdish factions and Baghdad, achieved nothing for the Kurdish movement as a whole. Ultimately the tensions between the charismatic and factional leader scenarios forced the Kurdish leadership to return repeatedly to a strategy of violence to realize their demands.

Despite Mulla Mustafa's ability to unite the Kurds behind his leadership, he was ultimately unable to prevent Baghdad's continued exploitation of the Kurds' tribal and regional divisions. Beginning in mid-1973, Mulla Mustafa made a number of critical decisions that resulted in the Kurds' defeat. In mid-1973 Saddam Hussein warned Mulla Mustafa that *in extremis* Iraq would abrogate the agreement regarding the Shatt al-Arab waterway in exchange for Iran's abandonment of the Kurds. [48] According to the KDP Preparatory Committee's report on the causes of the Kurds' demise in 1975, Mulla Mustafa's failure to respond to the message constituted a "cardinal error of judgment."[49] Mulla Mustafa had ample historical precedent, however, to argue that Baghdad had no intention of implementing the degree of autonomy being offered. His error in judgment lies not in his failure to trust that Saddam Hussein's offer was genuine, but in his failure to prepare for the eventuality in which Iraq would cede the Shatt al-Arab demarcation, and, in so doing, remove Iran's incentive for continuing to support the Kurds. Mulla Mustafa rejected the 1973 autonomy law, "stak[ing] everything on support promised him by the United States and Iran."[50] On March 15, 1975, the Algiers Agreement was made public, and within hours Iran began withdrawing its forces.[51] The Kurds were abandoned, and 14 years of nearly continuous warfare had secured them neither autonomy nor unity. Although Mulla Mustafa was able, unlike his successors, to unify the Kurds, his leadership was undermined by persistent divisions that Baghdad effectively exploited. Ultimately, his leadership failed to secure the Kurds' goal of autonomy, and the collapse of Mulla Mustafa's strategy left the Kurds deeply divided.

The KDP-PUK Split

After 1975, the Kurdish ethnic leadership's choice of violent means was driven by competition between rival Kurdish factions in a clear demonstration of the factional leader scenario. Despite nearly two decades of warfare against

Baghdad for the shared goal of Kurdish autonomy, the Kurdish movement remained deeply divided. Mulla Mustafa fled to the United States, and the feud between Talabani and the Barzanis quickly reemerged. Both groups clashed violently, further dividing the demoralized and defeated Kurds at a time when they faced their most serious opponent. Internal clashes severely weakened Kurdish resistance well into the Iran-Iraq War, when the Kurds had a tremendous opportunity to exploit Baghdad's vulnerability for their own aims.

Without Mulla Mustafa's leadership, the KDP splintered into several factions. Jalal Talabani united two Iraqi groups—a clandestine Marxist group, and the Socialist Movement of Kurdistan (KSM), led by Ali Askari—to form the PUK in Damascus in June 1975.[52] The KDP's leadership was assumed by Mulla Mustafa's two sons, Idris and Masoud. Together with an associate of their father, Sami (Muhammad Mahmud) Abd al-Rahman, they formed the KDP-Provisional Command (KDP-PL) in November 1975 in Iran.[53]

Until the outbreak of the Iran-Iraq War, violence in Iraqi Kurdistan was largely intra-Kurd. In 1978 tensions came to head with the Hakkari massacre, which was triggered by a battle to fill the vacuum in the Kurdish leadership created by Mulla Mustafa's exile. In April, Talabani ordered Askari, the KSM leader, and his deputy Khalid Said to head an 800-peshmerga force to collect a major quantity of weapons that had been shipped from Syria to Kurdish villages just over the border in Turkey. Talabani gave them written instructions to destroy the KDP-PL bases inside Turkey en route.[54] But Askari, who had developed a working relationship with the KDP, intended to ignore the instructions. A copy of the order reached Sami via his Kurdish informers in Turkey, and Sami chose to preempt the attack, ambushing the PUK forces when Askari and Said marched into Hakkari. The PUK suffered heavy losses, and both Askari and Said were executed on Sami's orders.[55]

The Hakkari massacre deepened the rift between the two Kurdish leaderships, significantly undermined the Kurds' ability to resist Baghdad, and cost the Kurdish effort three skilled commanders and 700 seasoned peshmerga, an important loss given the vastly superior resources of the Kurds' common enemy.[56] Many assumed Talabani had orchestrated the event. Talabani's judgment was called into question, and the PUK splintered.[57] The Hakkari massacre also heightened tensions within the KDP, causing it to splinter when Sami left to form the Kurdistan Popular Democratic Party (KPDP) in 1981.[58] The Kurds were now further divided, with little hope of prevailing against Saddam Hussein. At the outbreak of the Iran-Iraq War in September 1980, divisions among the Kurdish leadership were so severe that Saddam Hussein could boast that the "Kurdish organizations would never be able to achieve anything."[59] Although the various Kurdish groups shared a desire to see Saddam Hussein's government overthrown, their hostility toward each other precluded any unity of action against Baghdad for the first two years of the Iran-Iraq War.[60]

As the Iran-Iraq War escalated, Baghdad exploited the rift to remove the threat of a two-front war against both the Kurds and Iran. Talabani agreed to a ceasefire in November 1983, prompting some 3,000 PUK fighters to defect to the KDP. The immediate beneficiary of the ceasefire, however, was Saddam Hussein, who could now concentrate his forces on defeating the Iranian-KDP offensives in the north. Not surprisingly, the talks failed to produce an agreement, and in 1985 Talabani resumed the war against Baghdad.[61] In the meantime, his efforts had given Baghdad a two-year respite during which Saddam Hussein could concentrate his forces on defeating the KDP and Iran. Talabani's attempt to defeat the KDP undermined the broader goals of the Kurds as a whole (Proposition 4.3).

Internecine Warfare and the KRG

An autonomous Kurdistan finally became a possibility after allied forces created a safe haven in Iraq with a no-fly zone to protect it. Iraqi forces withdrew behind a defensive line, and all contact with the government was cut off. Into this void stepped the Iraqi Kurdistan Front (IKF), an alliance of opposition groups created in 1987, to create an administration for the de facto autonomous region. Despite the formation of the Kurdistan Regional Government (KRG) following elections in May 1992, shifting alliances among the smaller Kurdish parties destroyed the carefully crafted balance of power between the KDP and the PUK. The endemic divisions within the Kurdish movement provided Baghdad and regional powers with the opportunity to intervene, further exacerbating interethnic tension. Within two years a violent civil war threatened to destroy what had been so tenuously created under international protection. Neither the PUK nor the KDP was content with accepting the de facto division of Kurdistan into spheres of influence, as had been the practice between the KDP and the PUK since 1975 and between Mulla Mustafa and the Politburo faction before them. Instead, according to Masoud Barzani, it had become an intra-Kurdish battle for "hegemony"[62] that threatened to destroy the first real chance of Kurdish autonomy (Proposition 4.3).

THE WEAK STATE MODEL

Authoritarian states are a special category of weak states that appear strong through the use of fear, coercion, and force to mask fundamental legitimacy deficits. Iraq is such a weak state. Created by the British in 1921 out of three vilayets (provinces) of Basra, Baghdad, and Mosul, which had been part of the Ottoman Empire for centuries, Iraq was from its inception a weak state. Throughout its brief history, Iraq's rulers have had to contend with persistent violent challenges to their authority and right to rule, the most serious of which, until 2004, was the Kurdish one.

With only two brief exceptions, interrelated authority, capacity, and legitimacy deficits limited Iraq's ability either to offer meaningful concessions to the Kurds or to suppress the Kurdish rebellion on more than a temporary basis (Proposition 5). Instead, a series of Iraqi regimes came to power committed to solving the Kurdish threat to the regime through accommodation (Proposition 5.1), then opted for repression (Proposition 5.2) as the Kurdish threat increased or the regime consolidated its hold on power. The cycle of repression punctuated by brief conciliatory measures prompted the Kurds to repeatedly adopt violent means to secure Kurdish demands. When Baghdad managed to briefly consolidate its power between 1975 and 1980, and again between 1988 and 1990, severe repression prompted the Kurds to conclude that the costs of rebellion were too high. As a result, the Kurds temporarily refrained from adopting a strategy of ethnic violence (Proposition 5.3).

From the outset, the Kurds were satisfied neither with Mosul's inclusion in Iraq nor with the imposition of the Hashemite monarchy by the British. Led by Shaikh Mahmoud of Suleimaniya and later by Mulla Mustafa Barzani, the Kurds mounted a series of tribal revolts that were forcefully repressed, and the Kurdish ethnic leadership was either killed or exiled. Until the overthrow of the Monarchy in 1958, the Kurds did not press their demands in Iraq. The regime's violent repression of their rebellion prompted the Kurds to refrain from adopting a strategy of ethnic violence (Proposition 5.3) until the monarchy was overthrown in a violent coup d'état in 1958.

Qasim's new regime was beset by challenges to its rule from Arab nationalists who sought Iraq's union with the United Arab Republic (UAR); the newly legalized KDP, which sought autonomy for Kurdistan; the Iraqi Communist Party (ICP) that hoped to play a major role in the formation of the Iraqi republic; and the Kurdish aghas who viewed the coup d'état and the potential for major land reform as a catastrophe.[63] Because Qasim had no party structure on which to rely, he was forced to neutralize potential challengers through a traditional policy of divide and rule that temporarily secured the regime but failed to address its underlying authority, capacity, and legitimacy deficits. Qasim first allied himself with the Kurds and Mulla Mustafa, whom he viewed as a potentially powerful counterweight to the Arab nationalists.[64] Between 1958 and 1961, Mulla Mustafa proved invaluable to Qasim, helping to defeat the Arab nationalists, the Baath, the Communists, and rebel Kurdish tribes.

As Mulla Mustafa consolidated his control over Kurdistan, however, he became a serious threat. Qasim could ill afford a war in Kurdistan while troops were needed to buttress the regime's position in Baghdad. Yet his regime was equally incapable of meeting Kurdish demands. Qasim opted to repress the Kurds in a desperate gamble to strengthen his regime. In September 1961 Qasim employed massive air strikes over a wide area of Kurdistan, including Barzan, that, far from suppressing the Kurdish threat, solidified it and ultimately led to his overthrow in a violent coup d'état in February 1963.

The cycle of accommodation and repression continued under Baath rule. The Kurds were seen as a Trojan horse for regional governments seeking to overthrow the regime, and the new leadership was united in its view that the Kurdish threat had to be resolved. The armed forces favored a military solution, but the civilian Baath leaders opted instead to undermine the Kurdish threat through simultaneous accommodation and exploitation of Kurdish divisions. A delegation was sent to begin negotiations with Mulla Mustafa in Kurdistan, but the Kurds' demand for autonomy went beyond what the Baath were willing to accept.

Like its predecessor, interrelated authority, capacity, and legitimacy deficits prompted the weak Baath regime to repress the Kurdish rebellion in a desperate gamble to consolidate its hold on power. The Baath launched a large offensive in Kurdistan that sparked a major war and led to the regime's overthrow after only nine months in power. In a report by the Eighth Party Congress in Damascus in 1965, the Baath acknowledged that their regime had been too weak to withstand the Kurdish threat.[65] The lack of substantive negotiations, as well as the Baath attempt to repress the Kurds, left the Kurds with little alternative but to renew the war. The cycle of accommodation and repression continued after yet another coup d'état, negotiations that fell short of the Kurds' demands, and the resumption of the war in Kurdistan.

In April 1966 Prime Minister Abd al Rahman Bazzaz seized the opportunity created by Arif's sudden death to begin negotiations to resolve the Kurdish threat to the regime. The resulting 12-point autonomy agreement represented the first genuine attempt to resolve the conflict through accommodation. The agreement fulfilled nearly all of the Kurdish demands and was immediately accepted.[66] For the first time since 1961 it seemed that the Kurdish war might finally end. But the second Arif regime proved too weak to withstand pressure from both the Iraqi military and Arab nationalists who continued to oppose any solution to Kurdish demands but a military one. "In the end, the government's weakness destroyed it."[67] Baghdad had been unable to implement the concessions it had promised (Proposition 5.1). Repressive measures had similarly failed to end the conflict (Proposition 5.2), and the Kurds chose to resume the war, adopting violent means to challenge Baghdad's right to rule over Kurdistan (Proposition 5)

The second Baath regime, which seized power in July 1968, rightly recognized the Kurdish threat as the most serious challenge to the new regime's ability to consolidate its authority over Iraq. In an effort to neutralize the threat, the Baath immediately proclaimed their commitment to the Bazzaz declaration, instituted provisions dealing with the Kurdish language and education, recognized the Kurds' right to preserve their nationality, and declared an amnesty for Kurds who had fought in the war.[68] Yet the Baath simultaneously exploited Kurdish divisions to undermine Mulla Mustafa and weaken the Kurdish movement as a whole. Thus, the regime began negotiations with the Ahmad-Talabani faction, which shared the Baath's leftist orientation and, unlike Mulla Mustafa, did not have close ties to Iran.

When Mulla Mustafa's forces began attacking government troops, the Baath shifted their efforts to repression, launching a major military campaign in Kurdistan in August 1969 in a bid to end Mulla Mustafa's independence in the north. But like its predecessors, the attempt quickly reached a stalemate. Baghdad's efforts to consolidate its authority soon escalated to a proxy war with Iran as the Ahmad-Talabani faction, armed by Baghdad, fought against Mulla Mustafa's forces, armed by the Shah, Israel, and the United States.[69] The regime could ill afford a serious war in Kurdistan. It did not have full control over the armed forces that had overthrown the previous Baath government in 1963.[70] In addition, it could not proceed with its economic and social program until the Kurdish problem was resolved.[71] The Baath thus resumed negotiations with the Kurds in December 1969, abandoning Talabani in favor of negotiations with Mulla Mustafa.

The comprehensive March Manifesto went further in granting Kurdish demands than any previous agreement and represented the best autonomy scheme that has been offered by an Iraqi regime. The comprehensive nature of the agreement and the extensive concessions granted to the Kurds reflected both the continuing weakness of the Baath regime and its vulnerability to a renewed Kurdish war in the north. The agreement did produce the much-sought-after respite from the conflict in the north. Between 1970 and 1973, the Kurds refrained from adopting violent means while they still believed that the far-reaching concessions would be implemented (Proposition 5.4).

Yet the cycle of repression punctuated by brief concessions was to resume. During the agreement's four-year implementation period, the Baath steadily resolved divisions within its leadership and began to take steps to end its isolation in the Middle East and internationally, signing a treaty with Moscow in 1972. Combined with the nationalization of the Iraqi oil industry in June 1972, these efforts produced an economic, social, and political framework upon which the Baath hoped to build a stable regime in Iraq.[72] The agreement had bought the regime a much-needed respite. As the Baath strengthened their hold on power, their need for accommodation with the Kurds gradually disappeared.

By 1973, it was clear that the Baath was unwilling to share control. Forced resettlement and Arabization polices aimed to shift the population balance in the region to produce a favorable census upon which any future Kurdish region would be based. Combined with two attempts on Mulla Mustafa's life,[73] the Baath's proclaimed intent to award the Kurds with genuine autonomy was quickly proven to have been a ruse. The Kurds responded with violence, facing a far more dangerous threat now that the regime's hold on power had been consolidated. The Baath were equally committed to resolving the Kurdish threat for the last time. When significantly reduced autonomy schemes offered in 1973 were rejected, the Baath unilaterally amended the planned autonomous region in 1974.[74] Baghdad clearly retained the power to strip the autonomous region of any real autonomy in the new plan, and the Kurds deemed the new arrangement unacceptable. The Kurds concluded that they had little hope of achieving real autonomy in an Iraq ruled by the Baath. Armed with the necessary resources to engage in a major war against the Iraqi army, the Kurds decided to reject the sham autonomy agreement and launched yet another war (Proposition 5).

The 1975 Algiers Agreement represented an important turning point. It signaled that the Baath party had finally managed to consolidate its hold on power. This transformation had fundamental implications for the Kurds, who were to discover this transformation on the battlefield in 1975. The Iraqi army was now strong enough to defeat the Kurds in the field, and the withdrawal of Iranian support led to the Kurds' total defeat. In the aftermath of the Algiers Agreement, the Baath government moved quickly to establish its firm control over Kurdistan. Severe repression prompted the Kurds to suspend violent resistance for nearly five years (Proposition 5.3). Although Iraq's resettlement measures sparked the resumption of a guerrilla movement, the Kurds did not mount a serious effort to challenge the regime until the Iran-Iraq War.

With the outbreak of the war in 1980, Baghdad could no longer devote the resources necessary to continue repressing the Kurdish threat in the north. It rapidly lost its monopoly over the use of force and its control over Iraq's borders. During much of the war, the Kurds were free to rule themselves as Saddam fought for his very existence.[75] Baghdad thus reopened negotiations with the Kurds. In 1983, when negotiations with Masoud proved fruitless, Saddam ordered the execution of 8,000 Barzani males over the age of thirteen. They were taken from the camp in southern Iraq where they had been held since 1975 and paraded in the streets of Baghdad before being executed. According to Saddam Hussein, "they went to hell."[76]

Baghdad continued its repression of the Kurds for the remainder of the war. The success of the combined Kurdish-Iranian operations prompted Saddam to order a massive pacification campaign in Kurdistan and to commit 300,000 troops to the effort. In 1987, Baghdad implemented chemical weapons attacks to deal decisively with the Kurdish threat, targeting the town of Halabja near the Iranian border. After the ceasefire of July 1988, repression only intensified.[77] Iraq was now able to devote all of its resources to a massive cleanup operation in Kurdistan. The Kurdish movement collapsed under the scale of Saddam's campaign of vengeance. The unprecedented violence it employed against the Kurdish population prompted the Kurds to suspend armed resistance for the remainder of the 1980s (Proposition 5.3). Yet repression will only temporarily suppress ethnic grievances, as Baghdad had learned in 1980, until the group reassesses the cost-benefit ratio favorably. In 1990, with Iraq's invasion of Kuwait, the Kurds were suddenly presented with an opportunity to renew their efforts against the Iraqi regime. Despite Baghdad's warning, "if you have forgotten Halabja . . . we are ready to repeat the operation,"[78] the Kurds revolted.

Although Baghdad proved strong enough to put down the revolt despite its losses in the First Gulf War, international intervention served to protect the Kurds from the full extent of Baghdad's wrath. Subsequently, Baghdad was forced to rely on a complete blockade of Kurdistan, including the construction of a fortified line and minefields to isolate Kurdistan from the rest of Iraq, and promises of an expanded autonomy agreement in a desperate attempt to ensure the territorial integrity, if not continued existence, of its regime. The Kurds, however, had concluded that they had little stake in the existing system and began to construct a government for the autonomous region. Decades of repression had also escalated Kurdish demands. By 2003 the Kurdish demand for autonomy resembled independence in everything but name.

THE EXCLUSION MODEL

Iraq is a textbook case of an unranked system. The British decision to create a state in Mesopotamia out of the Ottoman vilayets of Basra, Baghdad, and Mosul meant that Iraq was made up of three separate geographic entities, each with distinct, regionally concentrated ethnic populations. According to Horowitz, unranked systems are produced "by encapsulation within a single territorial unit of groups that formerly had little to do with each other."[79] Although Basra and Baghdad were Arab provinces, the former mostly Shia and the latter Sunni, the province of Mosul, or Southern Kurdistan as it is called by the Kurds, was an ethnically Kurdish province with Turkomen, Christian Assyrian, and other ethnic minorities. Iraq's ethnic groups were thus encapsulated in the new state as parallel or unranked ethnic groups, and Iraq's rulers were faced with the challenge of creating not only the institutions to rule the new state, but also the idea of an *Iraqi* state that would resonate among its multiethnic population. Post-World War II Yugoslavia resolved this challenge by appealing to an inclusive concept of multi-ethnic coexistence, and by codifying its unranked ethnic structure in its federal entities. Iraq's new rulers adopted an exclusive idea of the state founded on its rulers' Arab—and predominately Sunni—identity. Arabization, internal boundary shifts, forced resettlement, and massacre, described in the Group Survival Model above, were employed to create a distinct Iraqi identity that was exclusionary. Iraq's non-Arab minorities were excluded from the idea of the state and from participation in and benefit from the state's institutions and resources.

Because the Kurds were the largest ethnic minority group concentrated in a region with significant natural resources, the Kurdish challenge remained the most serious threat to Baghdad's right to rule. This prompted a succession of Iraqi rulers to repress Kurdish mobilization in an attempt to consolidate Baghdad's authority over Iraq, described in the Weak State Model above, and to exclude Iraq's Kurds not only from participating in and benefiting from the state's institutions and resources, but also from the idea of the state as belonging to all its inhabitants. Under the Baath these measures expanded to secure the Kurds' physical exclusion from the state and the transformation of Iraq from an unranked to a ranked system dominated by Sunni Arabs.

The Kurds rejected the idea of the Iraqi state and their inclusion in it from Iraq's inception. Despite promises of autonomy, once the Kurds were included in the new Iraqi monarchy, none of the measures were implemented and the Kurds rebelled (Proposition 6). After the Iraqi monarchy was overthrown, a cycle of inclusion and exclusion prompted the Kurds to adopt violent means during repeated transitions of rule rather than face what seemed to be, until 2003, perpetual exclusion from the polity (Proposition 6.2).

The Origins of Kurdish Exclusion

The roots of the Kurds' exclusion from Iraq can be traced to the Mandate period. In March 1920, Britain was appointed to exercise a League of Nations

Mandate over Iraq and the vilayet of Mosul, which British forces occupied. Although the final status of Mosul had not yet been resolved, the Kurds were offered the hope of autonomy, if not independence. The Treaty of Sèvres, signed in August 1920, provided for "local autonomy in those regions where the Kurdish element is preponderant" (Article 62) and the possibility that "the Kurds living in that part of Kurdistan at present included in the Vilayet of Mosul" could "become citizens of the newly independent Kurdish state" (Article 64).[80]

Mosul's inclusion was contested by the new Turkish republic, which sought the region and its oil reserves for the Turkish state. In an attempt to gain international recognition for the British claim to Mosul, the British, together with the Iraqi Monarchy, issued the Anglo-Iraqi Joint Declaration to the Council of the League of Nations on December 24, 1922. In it, Britain and the Iraqi Monarchy recognized "the right of the Kurds who live within the frontiers of Iraq to establish a Government within those frontiers [and] . . . to reach some mutual agreement as quickly as possible as to the form they wish this Government to take and as to the boundaries within which they wish to extend its authority."[81]

Despite these promises, the Lausanne Treaty, which replaced the Treaty of Sèvres in 1923, made no mention of the Kurds. In 1925 a commission sent by the Council of the League of Nations to establish the boundary between Turkey and Iraq concluded that the vilayet should be attached to the Iraqi state if certain conditions were met: first, that administrators, magistrates, and teachers in the Kurdish region be drawn from Kurdish ranks; and second, that Kurdish be adopted as the official language in Kurdistan.[82] In response, Baghdad issued the Local Languages Law in 1926, the first time the Iraqi government legally recognized Kurdish cultural rights and a separate Kurdish identity.[83] Although the law met the League of Nations' provisions, it was never carried out.[84] In June 1930, the Anglo-Iraqi Treaty ended the British Mandate and recognized the formal independence of the Iraqi Kingdom, but it made no mention of the Kurds or of their right to autonomous Kurdish administration. The Kurds thus rebelled, adopting a strategy of ethnic violence to force the regime to recognize their demands for inclusion in the Iraqi state (Proposition 6).

Cycles of Inclusion and Exclusion

The proclamation of a Republic by Qasim and the Free Officers in July 1958 gave the Kurds new hope that their demand for inclusion would finally be realized. The provisional constitution promulgated that same month defined the new republic as an inclusive state and acknowledged the Kurds as a distinct ethnic group with national rights. According to Article III, "Iraqi Society is based on complete cooperation between all its citizens, on respect for their rights and liberties. Arabs and Kurds are associates in this nation; the constitution guarantees their national rights within the Iraqi whole."[85]

During the next two years, the Kurds were granted an unprecedented degree of cultural and political freedom in Iraq. Several Kurds were appointed to senior positions in the government, and schools in Kurdish regions were allowed to teach in the Kurdish language.[86] The KDP was legalized, cultural activities flourished, and at least 14 Kurdish journals were published in Iraq.[87]

By 1960, however, Qasim began to retreat from his commitment to Kurdish inclusion in the Iraqi republic. The KDP was banned, the journals closed, and activists in the KDP were arrested. Instead of accepting the Kurds as equal partners in Iraq, they were, in Qasim's words, "an indistinguishable and indivisible part of the Iraqi people."[88] Inclusion was replaced by Arabization. An Arab journal run by an associate of Qasim published a series of editorials calling for "the outright assimilation of the Kurdish people."[89]

The Kurds had briefly enjoyed a heretofore unprecedented degree of cultural and political autonomy, only to have those rights rescinded. The denial of these basic rights and their exclusion from the Iraqi state as equal partners with Iraq's Arab citizens prompted the Kurds to adopt a strategy of violence to protect their new status in Iraq (Proposition 6.1). Despite Qasim's two offers in November 1961 and March 1962 to negotiate a settlement, the Kurds were now committed to ending Qasim's dictatorship and "obtain[ing] the full autonomy of Iraqi Kurdistan within the framework of the Iraqi Republic."[90]

Nearly four decades of exclusion had prompted the Kurds to broaden their demands for inclusion as equal partners in Iraq to extensive territorial autonomy, covering virtually all of the former vilayet of Mosul, as well as legal recognition of the Kurdish armed forces and two-thirds of the national oil revenue for the autonomous region.[91] The new Baath regime countered with a separate offer based on the "recognition of the national rights of the Kurdish people on the basis of self-administration."[92] Because the Baath's hold on power was weak, it offered additional measures to secure the Kurds' agreement, including general amnesty for all Kurdish rebels, the purging of Iraqi officials guilty of misconduct in the north, the lifting of the economic blockade, and the withdrawal of Iraqi military units from Kurdistan.[93] However, the Kurds were alarmed by the regime's negotiations with the Syrian Baath and the UAR, fearing that their exclusion would be permanent in an enlarged state with far greater numbers of Arab nationalists. The Kurds thus increased their demands beyond what they could reasonably hope Baghdad would accept.[94] Shortly before the Baath were overthrown, the regime offered the Kurds "decentralization," rather than autonomy, with Kurdish and Arabic as official languages in a Kurdish province that would exclude Kirkuk.[95]

For the Kurds, inclusion in the Iraqi regime could only be achieved through a substantial autonomy agreement that would secure the Kurds' authority over all of Kurdistan, which they defined to include Kirkuk, Irbil, Suleimaniya, and parts of Mosul, and which they claimed entitled them to a share of the oil revenues. The Kurds were wary of less robust autonomy schemes, and they had ample precedent to argue that only a substantial degree of autonomy would sufficiently protect them. The Baath refused the Kurds' demands, and Mulla Mustafa and the KDP decided to resume the war rather than accept a decentralization scheme that fell far short of securing Kurdish inclusion in the Iraqi state (Proposition 6).

The 1966 Bazzaz Agreement established the full inclusion of the Kurds in Iraq—not only in terms of their participation in the state's institutions and access to the material benefits of the Iraqi state, but also in terms of the recognition of the Kurds as members of the Iraqi state through a robust autonomy scheme. The agreement fully accepted the principle of Kurdish territorial autonomy and called for:

- The use of Kurdish as an official language in the autonomous region
- Nominal control over educational affairs in Kurdistan
- Extensive cultural rights
- General amnesty for those who had fought in the rebellion
- Free elections for a Kurdish legislative assembly, to be established within one year
- Freely elected administrative councils
- Proportional representation for the Kurds in the central government in Baghdad
- Use of Kurdish forces to maintain internal law and order and to provide for the Kurds' security.[96]

However, Arab nationalists opposed the extensive concessions and undermined support for Bazzaz, forcing him to resign. "With his departure the best chance both for the Kurds and a democratic republican Iraq disappeared."[97] The Kurds were once again denied the benefits of inclusion in the Iraqi regime. The Kurds resumed the war to force the regime to meet its demands (Proposition 6.1), and in 1968 the regime collapsed.

Despite the coup d'état, the Kurds continued the war, exploiting the transition of rule to force the new regime to meet its demands (Proposition 6.2). Fearing a repeat of 1963, the Baath began negotiations with the Kurds in December 1969 that quickly deadlocked on the issue of Kirkuk. The Kurds refused to accept an agreement that did not include Kirkuk, and the Iraqi government refused to accept an autonomous region that did. To overcome the impasse, Baghdad suggested granting autonomy to the Kurdish *people* rather than to a specific Kurdish *territory*. The Kurds refused; Baghdad agreed to the principle of territory, but insisted that demarcation of that territory would depend on a proven majority to be decided either by plebiscite or census.[98]

By early February an agreement had been negotiated and was presented to the Kurds for signature. The final form of the agreement, however, reflected none of the compromises reached during the negotiations. To prevent the complete collapse of the negotiations and the resumption of war, the then-Iraqi Vice President Saddam Hussein traveled to Kurdistan and met with Mulla Mustafa, refusing to leave until an agreement had been reached. This meeting culminated in an agreement known as the March Manifesto, published on March 11, 1970.[99]

The 15-point March Manifesto was the most extensive plan that any Iraqi government had endorsed to accommodate Kurdish aspirations until the Transitional Administrative Law (TAL) was promulgated in 2004. The March Manifesto remained, until the collapse of Saddam Hussein's regime, the minimum standard to which the Kurds could agree. Its main elements dealt with autonomy, the structure of the autonomous region's governing bodies, and the relationship between the central government and the local autonomous administration.[100] Baghdad began implementing many of the agreements' provisions immediately. "The March Agreement was the best deal ever offered to the Iraqi Kurds."[101] Had the Manifesto been implemented as written, it is unlikely that *exclusion* would have sparked further Kurdish violence in Iraq.

By early 1971 it became apparent that the agreement had only been a ploy to buy the new government time to consolidate its hold on power. Baghdad refused to accept the Kurdish nominee for vice president (Article 12), the legislative assembly was hand-picked by Baghdad, rather than the result of free elections (Article 15), Kurdish was not recognized as an official language (Article 8), the new provisional constitution did not include the amendments concerning Kurdish national rights (Article 10), Arabization had not stopped (Article 9), and the census (Article 14) had been postponed indefinitely amid charges of forced resettlement and Arabization policies. By the beginning of 1972, Baghdad had twice attempted to assassinate Mulla Mustafa.[102]

In early 1974, there were two more attempts to resolve the stalemate, but neither the Kurds nor the Baath were willing to compromise on the issue of Kirkuk, particularly because Baghdad had nationalized the oil industry. The Kurds refused to accept an autonomous region that did not include Kirkuk as its capital, and Baghdad concluded that additional negotiations would not resolve the deadlock. The Baath leadership unilaterally amended the plan and gave the Kurds 15 days to accept it.[103] The ultimatum caught the Kurds by surprise, and some members of the Kurdish leadership accepted the new law rather than risk another war with Baghdad. Mulla Mustafa and the KDP leadership, however, refused to accept an autonomous region without Kirkuk. For the Kurds, inclusion meant full autonomy, autonomy could only be discussed in territorial terms, and the autonomous region had to include Kirkuk.

The new "Law for the Autonomy in the Area of Kurdistan" had a number of provisions that were unacceptable to the Kurds:

1. Kurdistan was to be determined on the basis of the 1957 census, which the Kurds had repeatedly rejected in negotiations following the March Manifesto, and the regional center was now to be Irbil, rather than Kirkuk (Article 1).
2. Baghdad could appoint and dismiss the executive council, which was to rule the autonomous region (Article 13).
3. Policy, security, and nationality formations would be attached to the Ministry of Interior in Baghdad (Article 17).
4. All decisions adopted by the autonomous region would fall under the judicial oversight of the Supreme Court of Appeal of Iraq.[104]

It was clear that Baghdad retained the power to strip the autonomous region of any meaningful autonomy.[105] In practice, the new law "imposed . . . vastly more central government control over the region than was envisaged by the March Manifesto."[106] The new autonomy law, rather than granting the Kurds participation in the Iraqi state, imposed central control over Kurdistan, effectively excluding the Kurds from the Iraqi state's institutions and material benefits and denying the Kurds inclusion in the idea of the state. The significant degree of authority retained by Baghdad, combined by the subsequent Anfal campaign, suggested that Baghdad's intent was to transform Iraq's unranked ethnic structure into a ranked one.

De Facto Autonomy

Until the outbreak of the 1991 Gulf War, there seemed little chance that the Kurds would be able to successfully challenge the 1974 autonomy law. However, the safe haven and the subsequent Iraqi blockade of the northern part of Kurdistan created the conditions for the Kurds to exist in a legal limbo as a de facto autonomous region, legally part of the Iraqi state, but in practice an independent entity with many of the attributes of a sovereign state, including a government to administer it and armed forces to protect it.

The 2005 constitution of Iraq recognizes "the Kurdish region, along with its established authorities, as a federal region" (Article 114) and stipulates that "laws legislated in Kurdistan since 1992 remain in effect, and decisions made by the government of the Kurdistan region—including contracts and court decisions—are effective unless they are voided or amended according to the laws of the Kurdistan region by the concerned body, as long as they are not against the constitution" (Article 138).[107] The "Kurdish Region" includes all of the Dohuk and Suleimaniya Governorates, most of the Irbil Governorate, and a portion of the Kirkuk Governorate (the area known as Garmain).[108] It does not, however, include all Kurds, nor does it include the remainder of the province of Kirkuk or the city of Kirkuk, which many Kurdish leaders have begun referring to as the "Kurdish Jerusalem."[109] Should the permanent constitution adopt the same or similar provisions in the draft constitution such that the Kurds retain their autonomous status, and should the issue of Kirkuk be resolved favorably, exclusion is unlikely to be a source of Kurdish violence in Iraq.

The inclusion of Kirkuk has been a sine qua non for the Kurds since negotiations for autonomy began under the Qasim regime. If the Kurds insist on a territorial definition of autonomy, as they have since Iraq's creation, or if they come to view Kirkuk as part of a Kurdish ethnonationalist homeland (Model 1), then exclusion of Kirkuk may become a source of violence in the new Iraq. However, Kurdish violence—and, more important, Kurdish secession from Iraq (Proposition 6.3)—are more likely if the Kurds' de facto autonomy is diminished such that the Kurds find themselves once again excluded from the Iraqi state.

THE EXTERNAL SUPPORT MODEL

The violence in Iraqi Kurdistan demonstrates the significant causal relationship between external support and the choice of violent means. Because the Kurds are not confined to Iraq, the Kurds' conflict with Baghdad has had immediate regional and international implications. Unlike the case of Yugoslavia, however, none of the international actors involved in the conflict in Iraq have supported the idea of a Kurdish state, and none of the regional powers have supported the Kurds' goal of *Kurdish* as opposed to *regional* autonomy in Iraq. Whereas Slovenia, Croatia, and Kosovo secured significant support for secession, no one wanted an independent Kurdish state in the Middle East except the Kurds.

External support proved significant in the Kurdish decision to employ violent means against the Iraqi state. Despite the significant risks of undue dependence on third-party support, the involvement of third parties, particularly of Iran and Syria, but also of the United States, Turkey, and Israel, enabled the Kurds to adopt violent means and to challenge a series of Arab rulers in Baghdad for the long-sought-after goal of autonomy (Proposition 7). The External Support Model describes four scenarios whereby groups adopt strategies of ethnic violence, two of which are relevant to the Kurds' choice of violent means.

Escalation

The escalation scenario describes a situation in which external involvement extends the conflict in space, number, intensity, or all three. As one group secures external support, ethnic competitors are forced to offset the perceived advantage by targeting the group through violence or by securing competing sources of external support, thereby triggering escalation (Proposition 7.1). Like the Armenians and the Azerbaijanis, the Kurds secured significant external support, including the direct intervention of third-party forces that led to a significant escalation of violence, widened the war, and protracted the conflict between the Kurds and Baghdad. The case of the Kurds demonstrates both the significant costs and benefits of third-party support. The Kurds' repeated reliance on external support led Baghdad to conclude that the Kurds presented an existential threat to the regime, prompting increasingly violent reprisals, including chemical weapons attacks, massacre, and the destruction of Kurdish villages along Iraq's borders. Yet third-party intervention ultimately secured the Kurds' goal of an autonomous region in Iraq.

Although the Kurds recruited support from among the major regional powers, Iranian support, with only a brief respite between 1975 and 1979, prompted the Kurds to adopt a strategy of ethnic violence against a succession of regimes in Baghdad, leading to a significant escalation and internationalization of ethnic war in Iraq. Iranian support was motivated largely by a desire to weaken a key regional competitor, and Iran used its influence with the Kurds and their dependence on Iranian support to encourage the Kurds to escalate their demands for autonomy and even to believe that Iran supported the Kurds' secession from Iraq.[110] In 1971, as tensions increased between Baghdad and the Kurds over the implementation of the March Manifesto, Mulla Mustafa demanded additional concessions from Baghdad after receiving assurances from the United States, Israel, and Iran of increased support.[111] Baghdad countered with the significantly weakened 1974 Autonomy Law and an ultimatum, but the Kurds continued to believe that they could achieve a better agreement, one that would include Kirkuk.

The Kurds thus rejected the ultimatum and resumed the war, assured that external support would sustain their effort (Proposition 7.1).

In an interview with Edmund Ghareeb after the Kurdish defeat, Mulla Mustafa related that, as the deadline approached in March 1974, he had met with U.S. officials in Iran and handed them a list of arms possessed by the Iraqi forces. Apparently he told U.S. officials, "This is what they have to use against us. If you will give us arms to match those arms, we will fight. Otherwise, we will make peace. We don't want to be massacred."[112] Apparently, U.S. officials responded favorably to his offer.[113] Kurdish concerns over the Shah's commitment to their cause were overcome by the Kurds' belief that the United States would act as a guarantor of the Iranian commitment. Mulla Mustafa later acknowledged the Kurds' error. "We wanted American guarantees. We never trusted the Shah. Without American promises we wouldn't have acted the way we did. We knew Iran could not do it all on its own. We accepted American aid in what we believed was the interest of the Kurdish people."[114]

Not only did Iranian involvement prompt the Kurds to adopt violent means, it also impacted the Kurds' choice of strategy, with disastrous consequences. The Kurds have traditionally followed a guerrilla strategy, necessitated by the severe asymmetry of Kurdish forces relative to Baghdad. Until the Kurds secured extensive support from Iran, Israel, and, to a lesser extent, the United States, the Kurds fought the Iraqi armed forces using a classic strategy of guerrilla warfare.[115] In the 1970s, Israeli and Iranian advisors encouraged Mulla Mustafa to shift to a conventional strategy and to reorganize the peshmergas as a conventional army.[116] When the war resumed in 1974, it was clear that the switch to a conventional strategy was a disastrous choice. The Kurds were rapidly overwhelmed, suffering such extensive losses that within months the Iraqi army held more of Kurdistan than at any time since 1961.[117] As Kurdish losses mounted, regular troops from Iran fought alongside Kurdish peshmergas in Iraq, transforming the war from an internal to an international conflict (Proposition 7.1). Although it remains questionable whether Baghdad ever intended to implement the March Manifesto, third-party support prompted the Kurds to escalate their demands.

Iran's support for the Kurdish movement lasted only as long as its interests dictated. At the 1975 OPEC meeting in Algiers, the Shah agreed to drop his support for the Kurds in exchange for Baghdad's acceptance of the Ottoman-Persian Protocol of 1913, which established a mid-channel line in the disputed Shatt al-Arab waterway, and renunciation of Iraq's claim to Khuzistan. Within hours of the agreement, Iranian forces began to withdraw, and within 48 hours the withdrawal was complete. The Iraqis rapidly defeated the Kurdish forces and began a vicious campaign of reprisals. According to Kerim Yildiz, "the extent to which other regional players dictated the action of Barzani throughout the 1970s should not be understated. Arguably Barzani would not have continued his armed struggle against the seemingly insurmountable Iraqi military had it not been for his belief that the US and Iran genuinely supported Kurdish autonomy."[118]

A decade later, the Kurds were to repeat this mistake. During the Iran-Iraq War, the massive increase in Iranian support prompted the Kurds to abandon their successful guerrilla strategy for a conventional strategy that relied on heavy attacks against military centers in concert with invading Iranian forces.[119] Kurdish forces operated as advance units for the invading Iranian forces and inflicted serious losses on the Iraqi forces. Again, Iranian support had transformed the Kurds' internal conflict with Baghdad to a second front in the Iran-Iraq War (Proposition 7.1). Internationalization of the conflict served to escalate the conflict without securing the Kurds' demands. Iran agreed to a ceasefire in 1988 and the Kurds, unable to continue the war on conventional terms without Iranian backing, suffered another massive defeat. In a near repeat of the disaster in 1975, the shift in strategy produced short-term success, but could not be sustained without external support. The Kurds were again abandoned by a regional power whose interest precluded the realization of Kurdish aspirations.

In the immediate aftermath of the 1991 Gulf War, external support again prompted the Kurds to revolt (Proposition 7.1). Initially the Kurds had refrained from launching an uprising for fear of sparking another chemical weapons campaign in Kurdistan. However, in March 1991, after having been urged to revolt by the Voice of Free Iraq, a CIA-run radio station out of Saudi Arabia, the Kurds responded, believing that they would receive outside assistance and protection.[120] The uprising began on March 4, and by March 13, Dohuk, Irbil, Suleimaniya, Zahko, and even Kirkuk were under peshmerga control.[121]

After crushing the Shia revolt in the south, Baghdad moved the Republican Guard toward Kurdistan and rapidly defeated the Kurdish uprising. The expected support from the U.S. and Coalition forces did not arrive. The United States, fearing the disintegration of Iraq and the risk of an Iranian-inspired Shiite revolution, ruled out intervention. Despite Western appeals for a Kurdish rebellion in the north, it was not in the interest of the international community that Iraq should disintegrate, and the Kurds were again abandoned in favor of the external powers' broader regional interests, resulting in a refugee crisis of tragic proportions as 2.5 million refugees fled toward Turkey and Iran.

Both Jalal Talabani and Masoud Barzani appealed to President Bush, reminding him of his appeal to the Kurdish people. "You personally called upon the Iraqi people to rise up against Saddam Hussein's brutal dictatorship."[122] The international community continued to resist. Finally, Turkey's refusal to admit the refugees inadvertently helped the Kurds' plight, as the specter of a half million Kurds trapped in the mountains finally prompted the UN Security Council to pass Resolution 688 in April 1992, demanding an end to the repression of the Kurds and creating the authority for a safe haven in Kurdistan and a no-fly zone to protect it.[123] Although Iraqi government forces had withdrawn in October 1991, placing the region, in effect, under a double embargo, international actors were hesitant to take any steps that would indicate recognition of the de facto autonomous zone. Unlike the case of Yugoslavia, the international community continued to adhere to the territorial integrity of Iraq. The UN refused to lift the embargo for the Kurdish zones or to monitor elections held in 1992. The Kurds had finally won autonomy, yet their special status was entirely dependent on third-party support.

Division

The division scenario impacts the choice of violent means when third-party support for one group or faction triggers factionalism and within-group conflict (Proposition 7.2). In the case of Iraq, third parties deliberately manipulated Kurdish divisions, exploiting Kurdish factionalism to pursue their own regional interests at the expense of the Kurds' struggle with Baghdad. As third parties extended support to one Kurdish faction, within-group competitors adopted violent means to challenge both their rivals and the ethnic other.

The manipulation of Kurdish divisions was a traditional policy employed to great effect by regional powers after the 1958 coup brought the nationalists to power. As was apparent in the discussion of the Kurdish ethnic leadership above, rival Kurdish groups negotiated third-party support not only for their war with Baghdad, but also for their struggle to assume leadership of the Kurdish movement in Iraq. Third parties were happy to oblige, because support for one faction led to an escalation of intra-Kurd violence that threatened Baghdad but prevented the Kurds from presenting a broader regional threat. Third-party support thus sparked repeated internecine warfare that significantly escalated violence and protracted the Kurds' conflict with Baghdad (Proposition 7.2).

The creation of a de facto Kurdish autonomous region following the 1991 Gulf War again provided regional powers with an opportunity to exploit Kurdish divisions. Fearing the repercussion of an autonomous region for their own Kurdish populations, both Iran and Turkey became actively involved, supporting rival factions in a bid to undermine Kurdish autonomy and triggering a Kurdish civil war from 1994 to 1998 that threatened to undermine the Kurds' hard-won autonomy (Proposition 7.2). U.S. mediation finally ended the war in 1998, but the tenuous power-sharing arrangement negotiated under U.S. auspices suggests that Kurdish divisions remain ripe for exploitation by regional powers. These endemic divisions are likely to remain a significant source of ethnic violence in the new Iraq, particularly if third parties exploit these divisions to undermine the Kurds' significantly expanded role in the new Iraq.

THE RESOURCE MODEL

Unlike the groups operating in the former Yugoslavia and Nagorno-Karabakh, the Kurds have not benefited from ready access to the weapons stockpiles of a disintegrating state. Despite this significant handicap, the Kurds were able to secure the arms and resources necessary to sustain a nearly continuous war with Baghdad (Proposition 8). Indeed, the Kurds have been receiving weapons and financial assistance from outside powers since the aftermath of World War I, when Turkey sought to arm the Kurds in its efforts to reclaim Mosul.[124] It was not, however, until the collapse of the Iraqi monarchy that the Kurds were able to secure substantial resources on the scale necessary to fight a large-scale war.

The Resource Model suggests that crossing the threshold from protest to violence requires arms, ammunition, spare parts, financial resources, and the expertise necessary to sustain violence against ethnic strangers, particularly when the ethnic other controls the state's military forces and resources. The Kurds have not had access to domestic-based supplies on the order of the quantity of weapons available to ethnic contenders in the former Yugoslavia and the Caucasus, in part because the Kurds, unlike the groups in the previous two case studies, were not operating in a failed state until recently. As a result external suppliers, particularly regional powers, were critical to the Kurdish decision to adopt a strategy of ethnic violence. Although the Kurds seized some weapons from the Iraqi forces, particularly during the height of the Iran-Iraq War, most arms were obtained from regional suppliers and financed by third-party resources.

Iran has been the primary source of weapons and financial resources for the Kurds since the early 1960s. After Qasim's overthrow, Iran began supplying funds, arms, and other military equipment to Mulla Mustafa's forces,[125] such that by the late 1960s Mulla Mustafa's forces had grown to more than 20,000 well-equipped peshmergas armed with antiaircraft guns, field guns, and antitank weapons.[126] According to one estimate, by 1966 Iran was supplying at least 20 percent of Mulla Mustafa's requirements.[127]

The steady supply of arms and ammunition, as well as funds to purchase weapons from the region's black market,[128] had a significant impact on the course of the Kurdish-Iraqi war that erupted in 1961. Rapid losses on the battlefield led to Qasim's overthrow, the subsequent overthrow of the Baath regime nine months later, and the collapse of the Arif regime in 1968. Indeed, by 1967 neither the Iraqi government nor the army was in a position to present much of a threat to the Kurds. As a result of Iran's extensive supply, "Baghdad could now only defeat the Kurds if it could seal the border with Iran."[129]

In late August 1969, when the new Baathist government launched a major military campaign against the Kurds, Mulla Mustafa's forces were well prepared. By late 1969, the Kurds had an armory of weapons that included over a hundred light-weight antiaircraft guns, twenty 25-pound field guns, and a number of antitank guns.[130] The attempt rapidly reached a stalemate, prompting the offer of negotiations that led to the 1970 March Manifesto. Again, Iran's financial support and weapons and ammunition supply had given the Kurds the necessary means to escalate the violence and to force Baghdad to the negotiating table (Proposition 8).

In the mid-1970s, Iranian military and financial support was critical to the Kurdish decision to pursue a strategy of violence against Baghdad rather than accept the proffered autonomy law. Iran supplied the Kurds with light and medium field guns (75mm and 130mm) and antitank missiles, and encouraged Mulla Mustafa to continue the war.[131] The Kurds had some 90,000 peshmergas and an equal number of reservists, bolstered by artillery and antitank missiles.[132]

Although the Kurds were also influenced by their belief in a U.S. guarantee, the seemingly reliable supply of both small arms and heavy weapons from Iran was a critical element in the fateful decision to continue the war (Proposition 8).

In addition to being the primary supplier of arms and financial resources, Iran was also the main conduit through which arms from other sources reached the Kurds. Beginning in 1963, Israel initiated a covert program of support for the Kurds in Iraq that included both financial assistance and small amounts of arms and ammunition, all of which reached Kurdistan through SAVAK, Iran's internal security organization. In addition, Israel provided military advisors, who were dispatched to Mulla Mustafa's headquarters in Iraqi Kurdistan and established training camps for Mulla Mustafa's peshmergas in the Kurdish mountains. Israel's Mossad also assisted the Kurds in the creation of Parastin, the Kurdish intelligence unit, in 1966.[133] After the June 1967 War, when Mulla Mustafa provided an invaluable service by engaging Iraqi troops and preventing them from aiding Syrian and Jordanian forces, Israeli military assistance for the Kurds increased dramatically. Mulla Mustafa visited Israel in September 1967, where he was promised 50,000 dollars per month.[134]

Throughout the 1960s Mulla Mustafa appealed to the United States for support, but it was not until the early 1970s, when Moscow and Baghdad signed a Treaty of Friendship and Cooperation, that the United States became interested in the Shah's efforts to undermine the Baath regime. The United States provided some 16 million dollars in aid to the Kurds through SAVAK and reportedly promised sufficient arms and ammunition to match the Iraqi armed forces in the events leading up to the outbreak of the war in 1974.[135]

A second important regional supplier of arms and financial assistance has been Syria. Like Iran, Syria served as an important conduit for outside states to support the Kurds. Syrian support has mostly favored the PUK. In the aftermath of the Algiers defeat, the PUK was formed in Damascus, and its forces were rearmed by Syria and Libya, thereby allowing the PUK to be the first to return peshmergas to Kurdistan. Using its newfound strength, the PUK targeted KDP forces. Syria provided substantial aid to the Kurds during the Iran-Iraq War, and continued to do so in the aftermath of the war, thereby making it possible for the Kurds to continue small-scale, but symbolically critical, resistance even after the Anfal[136] (Proposition 8).

In addition to Iran, Israel, the United States, and Syria, the Soviet Union briefly supplied the Kurds with weaponry and financial assistance in the early 1960s. By 1970, however, Moscow's relations with Iraq had improved, and, after brief attempts to mediate a solution to the Kurdish problem, the Soviet Union began supplying Baghdad with weapons and technical expertise on a large scale.[137]

Turkey also played a minimal role in supplying the Kurds prior to the settlement of the Mosul question, but thereafter Turkey remained hostile to the Kurds, with the one exception of a brief period in the early 1960s when Turkey allowed the Iraqi Kurds to use Turkish territory in their war against Qasim.[138] In the aftermath of the Gulf War, however, Turkey's role changed fundamentally, and Turkey became the Kurds' single-most important source of external support after Baghdad blockaded Kurdistan. Although Turkey does not officially recognize the KRG, it granted the KRG some 13.5 million dollars in aid in 1993.[139]

The Kurdish case demonstrates how access to financial resources and weaponry impact the choice of violent means. Although a group may have a strong sense of identity, a capable leadership, and grievances against ethnic strangers, adopting a strategy of interethnic war is not possible on the scale witnessed in Iraqi Kurdistan without access to the necessary funds and arms and ammunition. Third-party arms and resources repeatedly enabled the Kurds to adopt violent means and to sustain a decades-long war against a series of Arab regimes in Iraq.

CONCLUSION

The case of Iraqi Kurdistan allowed us to apply the multilevel framework of models over decades of violent conflict to explain why the Kurds repeatedly chose to adopt violent means. At the first image, the significant threat to the Kurds' survival by Baghdad's policies of homogenization repeatedly prompted the Kurds to adopt violent means to defend the Kurds' identity and existence in Iraq. Endemic divisions within the Kurdish ethnic leadership triggered not only violence against the ethnic other, but also violent, within-group conflict that undermined the Kurdish effort as a whole and significantly protracted the conflict against Iraq's Arab rulers. These are two significant first image explanations for the Kurds' repeated choice of violent means.

At the second image, we find two additional reasons why the Kurds adopted strategies of violence against Baghdad. First, cycles of accommodation and repression, severe repression, and a genuine offer of autonomy prompted the Kurds to adopt violent means to challenge the state and to resume violent resistance when a series of weak Iraqi regimes failed to accommodate Kurdish demands. A second state-level source of violence describes the choice of violent means as a function of the unranked structure of Iraq's ethnic groups. During repeated transitions of rule, the Kurds adopted violent means in an attempt to overturn the prevailing political-societal order to secure their inclusion.

At the third image, the Kurdish case demonstrates how significant third-party support enabled the Kurds to adopt violent means and to resume fighting after previous efforts failed. It also demonstrates the costs and risks of undue reliance on third-party support, reflected in the significant defeats of 1975 and 1988. Ultimately, as in the case of the Kosovar Albanians, third-party support secured the Kurds' objective. Yet decades of repression, a state-level cause of violence, suggests that the Kurds' willingness to remain in Iraq may be undermined if third parties manipulate Kurdish divisions to secure their interest in the region while Iraq remains weak. Here we see a significant interaction of the second and third image causes of violence, suggesting that the interaction of the models and images requires further discussion. We return to this task in the next chapter.

8

Chapter

Three Interrelated
Images of Ethnic War

INTRODUCTION

Waltz argues that some combination of the three images, rather than any one of them alone, may be required for an accurate understanding of international relations. The application of models at each of the three images in the case studies examined earlier suggests that the same may be argued for interethnic relations. In view of the numerous, yet still unsatisfactory single-level explanations for ethnic conflict, it is time to search not for yet another single cause but for patterns or groups of explanations. This has been the approach adopted in this book. At each level of analysis we have developed models of related propositions that posit the causes of ethnic violence.

The case studies support the argument that groups become violent against the ethnic other—and, often, against the state when it is "owned" by the other—for reasons that have to do with group identity and the competition for power within the group, with the state's response to ethnic mobilization, and with the interjection of third parties in a conflict between groups or between a group and the state. Violent ethnic conflict in Yugoslavia, Nagorno-Karabakh, and Iraqi Kurdistan is explained by models at all three levels of analysis. In none of the cases did the group-level models alone explain the choice of violent means.

Table 8.1 shows the case study results schematically. All the third image models were applicable to each of the case studies examined above. With one exception, both of the second image models explained the state-level causes of ethnic violence. Finally, at least two of the group models were applicable to each case.

In the case of Nagorno-Karabakh, the Exclusion Model did not explain the choice of violent means because Nagorno-Karabakh's Armenians were fighting *for* exclusion. When first the Soviet Union and then Azerbaijan attempted to repress Armenian demands, the Armenians in both Armenia and Nagorno-Karabakh adopted violent means to secede. Exclusion was a motive for violence, not a cause

Table 8.1 Results

Case Studies	First Image: The Group			Second Image: The State		Third Image: The International System	
Yugoslavia	P1	P2	P4	P5	P6	P7	P8
	P1.1	P2.1	P4.1	P5.1	P6.1	P7.1	
	P1.2	P2.2	P4.2	P5.2	P6.3	P7.2	
				P5.3		P7.3	
						P7.4	
						P7.5	
Nagorno-Karabakh	P1	P3	P4	P5		P7	P8
	P1.1	P3.2	P4.2	P5.1		P7.1	
	P1.2	P3.3		P5.2		P7.3	
		P3.4		P5.3			
				P5.4			
Iraqi Kurdistan		P3	P4	P5	P6	P7	P8
		P3.1	P4.1	P5.1	P6.1	P7.1	
		P3.2	P4.3	P5.2	P6.2	P7.2	
		P3.3		P5.3			
		P3.4		P5.4			

of it. In the case of Yugoslavia, the Group Survival Model did not explain either the Serb or the Kosovar Albanian choice of violent means *in Kosovo* despite claims to the contrary (although survival of the Serbs in Kosovo was central to the mobilization of Serbs *outside* Kosovo). Claims to defensive group survival are effective tools of group mobilization and of third-party recruitment. They are also effective in concealing underlying motives for violence—such as dominance over or exclusion of ethnic competitors. Claims to group survival in the case of both groups in Yugoslavia suggest that, despite genuine grievances, fear, and the potential loss of a group homeland, neither group's survival as *a distinct ethnic group* was at risk. Finally, the Ethnochauvinism Model did not explain the choice of violent means in either the Nagorno-Karabakh or Iraqi Kurdistan cases. None of the groups in these two cases justified violence in terms of group superiority, nor did they seek to *dominate* the other.

The case study results demonstrate that the causes of ethnic violence are multilevel in their origins. When we examine how these models interact, we enhance our understanding of why groups adopt violent means. In *Man, the State and War*, Waltz argues that the causes of war can be identified first by a critical consideration of each image, followed by a consideration of the interrelation of the images.[1] The same is true of ethnic violence. We too have critically considered the three images in the chapters on each—the group, the state, and the international system. In this final chapter, we consider how the models are interrelated and how this interrelationship furthers our understanding of ethnic violence.

RELATING THE GROUP TO THE
STATE AND SYSTEM LEVELS

One obvious conclusion from the application of our multilevel framework to the case studies is that the first image may not be sufficient, but it is certainly essential to understanding ethnic violence. The group level will always be relevant because the primary actor in ethnic conflict is not the individual or the state but the ethnic group. The first image is concerned with aspects of ethnic group identity. Some of these aspects are tangible, such as the geographic extent of a homeland or the absolute size of the group, but most are not. The intangible aspects of group identity affect how the group defines itself. These are framed by mythohistoric legacies, myths of ethnic chosenness, a group's distinct culture, or a way of life. They demarcate the boundaries of identity between the group and the other, and they establish a basis for identifying group worth. Although less easy to define, these intangible aspects are vital to understanding an ethnic group's choice of violent means.

A key aspect of group identity is its idea of an ethnic homeland—both the physical, territorial extent of that homeland and the symbolic idea of a homeland. A homeland represents a golden age, a key historical event, the site of past glories and critical battles, an ancient cultural cradle, or the center of a great empire. Possession of that homeland is vital not only to the group's identity, but also to its continued existence as a distinct ethnic group. A second factor is the belief in group superiority. The self-selected markers that define the group not only distinguish it from ethnic competitors, but also justify its superiority and right to dominate the inferior ethnic other. A third factor relates to the expression of group identity. Free expression of a group's culture, language, and way of life protects that identity and ensures that it is passed on to future generations. A final factor relates to the strength of group identity. Ethnicity either transcends competing identities of clan, tribe, or class or competes with them, eroding the primacy of *ethnic* identity and weakening the boundaries of the group with the other. It also prompts power struggles within groups when these crosscutting identities conflict. Each of these aspects of identity, or some combination of them, are integral to the choice of violent means, and four models of related propositions were developed to explain how aspects of group identity prompt groups to adopt violent means.

The first image models offer four persuasive explanations for ethnic war. The interplay of these first image models with those at the second and third images enhances our understanding of why groups adopt violent means. Homeland claims are claims against the ethnic other, but they are also claims against the state. The ethnonational group mobilizes to defend or reclaim a homeland, demanding the right to exclusive ownership of that territory. Both the Kosovar

Albanian claim to Kosovo and the ethnic Armenian claim to Nagorno-Karabakh threatened the dismemberment of the Serbian and the Azerbaijani states, respectively. Because ethnonationalists are rarely willing to settle for autonomy, and because homeland claims are rarely unopposed, a homeland claim challenges all three dimensions of the state arena: the political dimension, which defines the relationship between the state's institutions and its society; the physical dimension of the state, defined by its territorial boundaries; and the idea of the state as belonging to all its inhabitants. When the state is weak, as in the case of Azerbaijan, a homeland challenge may well constitute an existential threat to the state, propelling a violent response aimed at the repression or exclusion of the ethnic group.

Our case studies support the argument that a state's response to ethnic mobilization can either prevent violence or trigger ethnic war. Whereas strong states have the capacity to accommodate ethnic demands, weak states invariably do not. Because of the state-strength dilemma, weak states are likely to respond to group mobilization with repression. The case studies demonstrate that repression greatly increases the likelihood that the ethnonationalist group will rebel. Serbia's repeated, violent repression of Kosovar Albanian demands, culminating in "Operation Horseshoe," prompted Kosovar Albanians to forego their policy of peaceful resistance for one of violent rebellion.

Because ethnonationalists are regionally concentrated, when a state responds to a homeland claim with exclusion, the group is not only more likely to adopt violent means but also to secede. The Serbs first sought to defend homeland ownership through the exclusion of Kosovar Albanians, revoking the province's autonomy and replacing its ethnic Albanian leadership with Serbs. Changes to Yugoslavia's constitution in the 1970s elevated Kosovo to a federal actor. Serbia's exclusion of the Kosovar Albanians meant that they lost not only control of their homeland, but also access to the institutions and resources of the Yugoslav state. When Kosovo was effectively recognized as an integral part of the new Serb state after Dayton, the Kosovar Albanians, who were regionally concentrated in their homeland, perceived that they had little alternative but to secede from Serbia. The likelihood of secession is further enhanced if the ethnonational group is not only regionally concentrated but also unranked. The interaction of the Homeland, Weak State, and Exclusion Models suggests a heightened likelihood of violence and of protracted ethnic war. It also explains why wars fought over homelands are some of the most difficult to resolve.

The Ethnochauvinism Model's explanatory power is similarly enhanced when it works in tandem with models at the second and third images. Ethnochauvinism prompts groups to adopt violent means because the group believes it is superior to the ethnic other and has the right to dominate it. Domination necessarily involves seizing the state or some portion of the state's territory where the other is concentrated. When the chauvinist group is also excluded, it will likely seek to overturn the prevailing political-societal order during transitions of rule, both to ensure its own inclusion and to dominate the inferior other. Thus Serb exclusion in Croatia and Bosnia triggered violent strategies aimed at dismembering those states to secure the Serbs' inclusion in Serbia. When the chauvinist group is also unranked, as the Serbs were in Yugoslavia, it will attempt to transform the system into a ranked one, such that the chauvinist group is superordinate, and the "inferior" other is subordinate. The Ethnochauvinism and Exclusion Models are closely interrelated when dominance can only be achieved through the exclusion of the ethnic other. When these two models operate in tandem, both reinforce the likelihood that violence will escalate to the extremes of ethnic cleansing and even genocide. As the case of Yugoslavia demonstrates, ethnochauvinism erodes the constraints on the killing of innocents and increases the likelihood that exclusion will be achieved not by dominance, but by the removal of strangers through cleansing, expulsion, or extermination.

Chauvinist groups are unlikely to secure overt third-party support for aims that have significant regional and international implications. At the same time, the targeted group has a high likelihood of securing third-party support, arms, or mediation, particularly when chauvinist strategies trigger refugee flows or otherwise threaten regional and international security, as was evident when Kosovar Albanians began fleeing Kosovo for Albania in 1999. The specter of hundreds of thousands of Kosovar refugees prompted NATO intervention in support of the Kosovar Albanians. When third parties enable the targeted group to counter the chauvinist group with violent means, as Albanian arms and resources did for the Kosovar Albanians, the chauvinist group is likely to escalate violence, justifying the use of more extreme measures in terms of its right to dominate the inferior enemy, redress past grievances, and avenge the group against ethnic strangers.

The Ethnic Leadership Model provides a compelling explanation for ethnic violence in each of the three case studies examined above. The interaction of this model with the models at the second and third images enhances our understanding of how and why ethnic leaderships adopt violent means. Ethnic leaderships mobilize group members in support of strategies of ethnic violence. Charismatic leaders are able to build on the charisma and the appeal of the leadership to outmaneuver ethnic competitors, as both Milosevic and Mulla Mustafa Barzani were able to do, whereas militant leaders adopt increasingly hard-line positions to co-opt militant challengers and sideline moderates. The increasingly hard-line position of Azerbaijan's Communist leadership was a direct response to the militancy of the opposition APF. Factional leaders promote violence not only against the ethnic other, but also against ethnic rivals to assume leadership of the group. The PUK and KDP adopted violent means against Iraq's Arab regime and against each other for hegemony. Each of these scenarios is significantly impacted when the state responds by repressing or excluding the group and when third parties extend support and arms for the group's struggle.

When an ethnic group's leadership turns to a strategy of ethnic violence for the realization of group goals, it must mobilize support from among ethnic kin while sidelining and defeating rivals who support more moderate options. State repression effectively completes this task for the ethnic leadership, as was evidenced following Qasim's repression of the Kurdish tribes. State repression undermines support for more moderate strategies, triggers political closure, and widens support for more militant leaders and strategies. A violent state response greatly increases the likelihood that an ethnic leadership will adopt violent means, particularly if the group has the necessary resources to challenge the superior forces of the state.

The interaction of the Ethnic Leadership and Weak State Models also explains why repression makes conflict intractable. Repression creates legacies of mistrust that are likely to persist long after active repression has ended. Even when an ethnic leadership determines that a negotiated settlement is in the group's interest, memories of past failure and repression will impede the leadership's ability to win support for renewed negotiations with the state. Only after Aliyev came to power could the Azerbaijani leadership countenance direct negotiations with the Karabakh Armenians, and then only for a ceasefire, not a settlement. To have acquiesced to the demands of the ethnic Armenians would have undermined the regime. Legacies of mistrust also destroy an ethnic leadership's ability to compromise on group aims. Once repressed, groups are unlikely to support a settlement that falls short of group demands. The legacies of failed accommodation and repression undermine support for settlement and directly contribute to the protraction of conflict.

Exclusion similarly enhances an ethnic leadership's ability to mobilize group members in support of a strategy of violence. Exclusion, unlike repression, aims to redefine the state, its institutions, and its resources without the target group. Exclusion is frequently achieved through violent state homogenization or group-driven cleansing when the group and not the state is the excluding party. When the Exclusion and Leadership Models interact, the likelihood of violence increases. Thus, the KLA was able to mobilize support for violent resistance when Serb exclusion was widely perceived as permanent after Dayton. The interaction of the Ethnic Leadership Model with either the Weak State Model, the Exclusion Model, or both provides a compelling explanation for both a heightened likelihood of ethnic violence as well as protracted ethnic war.

The interaction of the Ethnic Leadership Model with the External Support and Resource Models further enhances our understanding of how and why ethnic leaderships mobilize group members in support of violent means against ethnic competitors. When third parties intervene in support of a group's strategy of ethnic violence, the ethnic leadership may escalate its demands against the state or use the third-party resources to defeat within-group challengers. Thus, Iranian support for the Kurds escalated Kurdish demands against the state. It also triggered within-group violence as the PUK and the KDP battled for hegemony. Both situations—escalated demands outward or score-settling inwards—are likely to escalate and intensify ethnic violence. Third-party mediation that favors within-group competitors will compel the leadership to adopt violent means both against the ethnic other, to derail settlement and force third parties to reengage with the ethnic leadership, and against ethnic kin, so as to secure its position within the group. Mulla Mustafa repeatedly employed this tactic, using violent means to derail negotiations conducted by ethnic rivals. Finally, when third parties recognize the secessionist bid of an ethnic competitor, as in the case of the Kosovar Albanians when Dayton effectively denied their claim to self-determination, an ethnic leadership may promote renewed violence not only to force the international community to recognize the group's bid for independence, but also to preclude ethnic rivals from using the failure to try to unseat it.

The first image suggests that wars fought over aspects of identity are both zero-sum and intractable in nature. Ethnic conflict is zero-sum when the gain for one ethnic group is exactly equal to the loss for the other. The example of a contested homeland is illustrative. When an ethnic group adopts violent means to protect or reclaim a homeland, it demands exclusive ownership of that homeland, rejecting counterclaims of ownership by competing ethnic groups. Homeland ownership brings concrete benefits, yet more important is what homeland ownership means for group identity. Although the concrete benefits of homeland ownership can be offset through alternate schemes of revenue-sharing or minority rights, the identity dimensions of homeland ownership cannot be replaced. Thus Moscow's offer of an aid package for the Karabakh Armenians failed to resolve the underlying issue of homeland ownership. A homeland either belongs to the group or it does not. When conflict centers on aspects relating to ethnic identity, it falls in the category of zero-sum conflicts because of what is at stake. Failure means not only a material loss to the group; it also threatens its very identity.

The first image also explains why ethnic conflict is frequently intractable. Ethnic identity is perceived as nonnegotiable. Group members are unlikely to support a solution that falls short of protecting the identity of the group, and group leaders are unlikely to participate in good faith when negotiations do not fully recognize or protect group identity. Groups are likely to adopt violent means and sustain ethnic war rather than settle for less than their goals and risk the survival of the group. The most intractable ethnic conflicts are the so-called frozen conflicts. Although groups cease fighting, the underlying causes of war are no nearer being resolved than they were at the outset. Groups agree to cease fighting for any number of reasons—exhaustion, severe repression, lack of resources, or loss of external support, among others. In these conflicts, a ceasefire is little more than a respite, a pause between phases of conflict. If ethnic identity issues remain unresolved—a homeland claim, chauvinist bid, or threat to group survival—war will likely resume once conditions improve. When a group's identity is at stake, groups will resume fighting even when the odds of victory are low.

The first image defines a group's choice of violent means as a function of its identity. Our case studies demonstrate that these significant triggers of ethnic violence do not operate in isolation from the state arena and the international system. Although the Homeland, Ethnochauvinism, Ethnic Group Survival, and Ethnic Leadership Models capture the complex reasons why groups adopt violent means at the first image, they are incomplete. The first image models are key pieces of a complex puzzle that can only be completed when we add the state- and system-level causes of violence and examine the interrelationship among each of the models across the three images of ethnic war.

RELATING THE STATE TO THE
GROUP AND SYSTEM LEVELS

At the second image, ethnic violence is understood within the state arena. In Chapter 3 we defined the two primary state arenas in which interethnic war is fought: the multiethnic state and the weak state. These two arenas frequently overlap in practice, as demonstrated by our three case studies. Multiethnic states that are weak, such as Yugoslavia and Iraq, are more likely to face ethnic-based challenges because they lack the authority, capacity, and legitimacy to accommodate ethnic demands. Weak states that have multiethnic populations, such as Croatia, are more likely to face ethnic-based challenges when they seek to strengthen the state in exclusionary ways. Both arenas frame the constraints and opportunities available to states when ethnic groups challenge their rule. Although these arenas overlap, each distinctly shapes an ethnic group's choice of violent means.

The second image explains a group's choice of violent means as a function of how the state responds to ethnic mobilization. The state is thus both an arena and an actor in ethnic conflict. Our case studies demonstrate that three state responses—partial accommodation, repression, and exclusion—have a particularly high likelihood of triggering ethnic war. Partial accommodation prompts groups to adopt violent means when the state offers concessions but fails to implement them. The Kurdish case is replete with examples of partial accommodation that failed to meet Kurdish demands or halt the violence. Repression triggers violence because it destroys trust in resolving ethnic claims in nonviolent ways and, short of severe and successful repression, may leave the group with little choice but to rebel. The ethnic Armenian decision to adopt violent means was triggered by Moscow and Baku's repression of Armenian demands. Exclusion prompts groups to adopt violent means to secure the group's right to participate in and benefit from the state's institutions and resources, either through state ownership or secession. Serbs in Bosnia seized territory for inclusion in a Greater Serbia, whereas Kosovar Albanians adopted violent means to secede. Our case studies demonstrate the interrelationship of the second image causes of ethnic violence with the group and systemic levels. Each of the state responses—partial accommodation, repression, and exclusion—provide an even stronger argument for why groups adopt violent means when the response interacts with the first and third image models.

A weak state's ability to respond to ethnic demands is limited by its authority, capacity, and legitimacy deficits. These deficits constrain the state's ability to implement measures aimed at accommodation and increase the likelihood that a state will respond with repression. An ethnic-based challenge against a weak, multiethnic state is more likely to represent an existential threat, because ethnic challenges threaten the state's territorial integrity, undermine its authority, further weaken its capacity (particularly when the claim threatens a resource-rich region, as in the case of Kurdistan), and erode both its horizontal and vertical legitimacy. Although the emphasis in ethnic conflict is often on group survival, at the second image it is the survival of the state that drives a weak state's response to ethnic mobilization.

One of the most serious threats to state survival is a homeland claim. Homeland claims simultaneously challenge all dimensions of the state—its territory, its ability to control resources in that territory, its authority over that territory, and its legitimacy. The state may attempt to accommodate homeland claims with a range of measures that grant the ethnonationalist group partial or full autonomy, yet, because the state is weak, it may be unable or unwilling to implement them. Ethnonationalists are rarely willing to settle for autonomy, because homeland ownership is vital to the group's identity and continued survival. A weak state is equally unlikely to offer ethnonationalists autonomy in their claimed homeland because the survival of the state depends on keeping the government's authority over its territory intact. Thus, the Soviet Union could not accommodate the Armenian petition for transfer for fear of setting a dangerous precedent. Transfer of the NKAO would also have undermined Soviet rule in Azerbaijan. A weak state is thus more likely to respond to homeland claims with repression. Repression alone has a high likelihood of triggering a violent response. When the state attempts to repress a homeland claim, the likelihood that the group will adopt violent means increases significantly. The interaction of the Weak State and Homeland Models as evidenced in the case of Nagorno-Karabakh provides a more compelling explanation for ethnic violence.

Partial accommodation and repression may also threaten group survival. In this instance, a state-level cause of ethnic group violence triggers a group-level threat to ethnic identity, demonstrating that the Weak State and Group Survival Models are closely related. The case of Iraqi Kurdistan supports this interaction. Iraq's violent repression of the Kurds significantly increased the threat to the Kurds survival in Iraq. Partial accommodation may prompt groups to conclude that the proffered measures provide insufficient protection of the ethnic population in relative and absolute terms, insufficient cultural autonomy to protect the group's distinct culture and way of life, and insufficient measures to ensure that the neglect of group lands and resources will be reversed. The proffered 1974 Autonomy Law met none of these requirements, prompting the Kurds to resume violent resistance both in defense of group survival and to secure self-rule. If the state fails to implement the agreement, either because it lacks the will or the capacity to do so or because the group rejects the agreement in favor of renewed war, the state is likely to repress the serious threat to its regime. Repression will escalate the threat to group survival, prompting groups to adopt violent means to defend the group against the state's violent response.

In the case of severe repression, however, the relationship between these models is reversed. The Weak State Model suggests that severe and successful repression will prompt groups to suspend armed resistance. The Group Survival

Model suggests that severe repression will have the opposite effect: when violence threatens the physical survival of the group, it will mobilize rapidly in self-defense. Our case studies demonstrate that severe repression does prompt a reassessment of the costs and risks of continued rebellion, but that the suspension of violent resistance is only temporary. The Kurds twice suspended their armed resistance following particularly violent state repression, but they resumed conflict once the state had weakened or third-party resources enabled them to resume violent means. Severe repression buys the regime a temporary respite, but it does so at a tremendous cost. Repression destroys the regime's vertical and horizontal legitimacy, undermines its authority, and taxes its capacity, leaving the state further weakened when groups reassess the costs and benefits and resume the war.

This decision to resume fighting is tied to the provision of third-party resources and support. When third parties intervene in ways that enable the group to resume fighting, the group will likely renew its war against the state sooner when group survival is at stake. Again, the case of the Kurds is illustrative. When third-party support and resources are significant, the weak state will face a substantially more capable opponent, and the threat to its own survival increases proportionately. During the Iran-Iraq War, Iranian support for the Kurds forced Baghdad to fight a two-front war and to cede control of Kurdistan to the Kurds for the duration of that war. The interaction of the two third image models with the Weak State Model not only explains the likelihood that groups will resume war, but also explains why a state's response will shift between accommodation when the opponent secures third-party support and repression when the balance of forces favors the state. The case of Iraq demonstrates that when both state *and* group survival are at stake, these cycles of accommodation and repression are likely to be frequent and intense.

The third state response to ethnic mobilization is exclusion. Exclusion offers a more permanent solution to ethnic-based challenges in unranked systems; it removes the offending groups, figuratively or literally, such that the state can proceed unchallenged with building a *nation*-state. The Serbs sought to exclude Kosovar Albanians permanently from Serbia in order to build a Serb nation-state out of the Yugoslav collapse. Exclusion thus has a high likelihood of triggering a violent response. Whereas repression is necessarily violent, exclusion need not be. At one extreme, exclusion is achieved through expulsion, cleansing, or mass extermination of the ethnic other. In these circumstances, exclusion will interact with a threat to group survival in the same way that violent repression triggers rapid group mobilization in defense of group survival. At the other extreme, democratic elections may result in exclusion, as in the case of Bosnia's Serbs. When exclusion occurs through democratic or other legal processes, the threat to group survival is unlikely to be immediate. Over time, however, as the state-owning ethnic group redefines the idea of the state in exclusionary terms, reapportions resources and other material benefits, and either ignores or deliberately neglects group lands and resources, the excluded ethnic group may conclude that its survival is indeed threatened by the cumulative impact of these policies.

Exclusion has a particularly strong impact on homeland claims, because ethnonationalists are regionally concentrated ethnic groups who are frequently also unranked. When the Exclusion and Homeland Models operate alone there is a high likelihood that groups will adopt violent means. When they interact, the likelihood of intense and protracted interethnic war significantly increases, as does the tendency of the targeted group to seek secession. We see this interaction in both the Nagorno-Karabakh and Kosovo homeland wars. A regionally concentrated, unranked ethnonationalist group such as the Kosovar Albanians has little incentive to remain in the state and a strong incentive to secede when the state responds to group mobilization with exclusion. Secession not only protects the homeland, and thus the group's identity, from ethnic strangers, but also secures the benefits of inclusion when the group creates a state of its own. The interaction of the Exclusion and Homeland Models explains the ethnonationalist preference for secession and self-determination in terms of group identity *and* state response.

Exclusion is likely to have immediate regional, if not international, implications. Ethnic groups are rarely confined to state boundaries. When the state responds to ethnic group mobilization with exclusion, as in the case of Bosnia toward the Serbs when it proceeded with the internationally mandated steps for recognition, the state's actions will likely trigger mobilization of regional kin and diaspora communities. These groups will favor secession over autonomy, particularly if these communities are similarly excluded or repressed. The potential to secure a state of their own is likely to raise significant support among ethnic kin and friendly third parties, as well as from regional powers and other systemic actors whose interests are impacted by the potential dismemberment of the targeted state.

Because exclusion has immediate regional if not international implications, it will likely trigger the External Support Model's escalation, mediation, and recognition scenarios. Mediation is itself exclusionary when a third party intervenes to prevent or resolve ethnic violence in a manner that is perceived as favoring one party over others, and recognition, when inconsistently offered to regionally concentrated groups such as a homeland people, is likely to widen the war. Thus, Serbia's exclusion of the Kosovar Albanians and third-party denial of their demand for self-determination combined to prompt the Kosovar Albanians to adopt violent means. Violence served the purpose of resisting Serb rule, but it also drew attention to the Kosovar Albanian plight. Ultimately, a refugee crisis triggered by Serb repression prompted the international community to intervene and recognize Kosovo as an independent state. When an excluded group has access to the arms and resources necessary to sustain violence against the more powerful organs of the state, the likelihood of ethnic war is further increased. Because exclusion has a high likelihood of triggering a secessionist response, the Exclusion Model is closely related to the models at the third image.

The state arena has a significant impact on an ethnic leadership's choice of violent means, suggesting that the Weak State and Exclusion Models are closely related to the first image Ethnic Leadership Model. Partial accommodation that fails to achieve the goals for which the ethnic leadership enters negotiations will undermine moderates and strengthen militant and factional leaders. These more militant rivals will exploit the leadership's failure to secure a favorable settlement to win support for a violent confrontation with the state. The weak state must subsequently contend with a more militant ethnic leadership whose base of support has widened and who will be less likely to resume negotiations. Repression has a similar effect, strengthening more militant leaders and factions within the group and expanding support from among the group for a strategy of ethnic violence. Like repression, exclusion will trigger rapid political closure of the group and enable an ethnic leadership to consolidate its position and win support among group members for a strategy of ethnic violence. When a group is threatened with exclusion, group members may shift support to more militant leaderships who promise a more decisive and violent response to the threat. In the case of Kosovo, the Dayton agreement made Kosovo's exclusion effectively permanent, prompting widespread support for the more militant strategies of the KLA over the moderate policies of Rugova's party. Each state response increases the likelihood that militant leaders will seize control from more moderate rivals and mobilize group members in support of a violent group response. When an ethnic leadership also secures the necessary arms and resources to challenge the state, the likelihood of violence further increases.

The second image allows us to draw an additional conclusion about the nature of ethnic war. Ethnic war is fought in the arena of the state and is shaped by the state's response to group mobilization. The second image suggests that ethnic war is also *about* the state. It is, as Rothschild notes, "the prize to be occupied and exploited by contending ethnic groups."[2] The prize in homeland wars is some portion of state territory; in survival wars it is state policy toward its citizens. When chauvinists seek to dominate the ethnic other, the prize is state ownership, whereas in exclusionary wars that prize is the idea of the state, its institutions, and its resources. In wars following state collapse, the prize is a new state. Ethnic wars are not only about groups. They are also about all the facets of the state—the arena of the state, the state as a contender in conflict, and the state as a prize of ethnic war.

The value of a multilevel approach is that it places the discussion of ethnic violence squarely in the state arena. It recognizes the significant role of the state as arena and actor and acknowledges that ethnic conflict is also about the state. The literature on ethnic conflict has largely ignored the role of the state. A multilevel approach corrects this oversight.

THE THIRD IMAGE CATALYST OF ETHNIC WAR

The third image is the most overlooked dimension of ethnic war because states remain the primary actors in the international system, and ethnic groups are viewed predominantly as substate actors. The sharp rise in the number of violent ethnic-based conflicts worldwide, and the threat these conflicts present to regional and even international stability, suggests that the security environment is evolving in ways that have eroded key systemic constraints on ethnic conflict. This evolving security environment has also created new opportunities for ethnic groups with grievances against ethnic strangers. Ethnic groups are no longer just substate actors. Through instrumental linkages with other states as well as other non-state actors, ethnic groups have in some instances emerged as peer competitors of the state, particularly of weak states. In the extreme, state collapse elevates substate actors to systemic contenders capable of presenting a strategic threat to the international system.

For the purposes of understanding ethnic war, we have defined the third image as that which exists *outside* the state arena. The third image encompasses a myriad of systemic actors—states, international organizations, and non-state actors—that intervene in material and nonmaterial ways to affect an ethnic group's choice of violent means. This interaction between systemic actors and ethnic groups is captured in two models developed in Chapter 4. These models define two categories of systemic impact on ethnic conflict. The first attributes ethnic violence to third-party support or direct intervention, and the second attributes violence to the availability of third-party resources for ethnic war. In each of our case studies, when third parties intervened in material and nonmaterial ways in support of an ethnic group's claim, this support effectively enabled the mobilized ethnic group to cross the threshold from ethnic conflict to interethnic war.

Our findings suggest that the actions of third parties are a catalyst for ethnic violence. A catalyst is an agent that provokes or intensifies change or action. At the third image, the agent is the systemic actor. When systemic actors intervene in support of one or more contending ethnic groups, these actions not only enable groups to adopt violent means, but also provoke or intensify interethnic violence. Our case study findings suggest four distinct systemic catalysts for ethnic war.

The first systemic catalyst is *tangible or political diplomatic support* that materially changes an ethnic group's ability to adopt violent means. When third parties intervene in support of one or more ethnic contenders, the ethnic group beneficiary secures substantial benefits that enable a group with grievances against ethnic strangers or a state controlled by ethnic strangers to adopt violent means. Both tangible and political-diplomatic support change a group's capacity to adopt violent means, particularly when the beneficiary group conflicts with an ethnic group that owns the state. In each of our cases, third-party support for groups such as the Kosovar Albanians, the Armenians, and the Kurds—groups who were fighting a state-owning ethnic other—acted as a catalyst for ethnic violence, enabling these groups to adopt violent means.

The third-party support is also a catalyst for the intensification of interethnic violence. When a third party extends support to one ethnic contender, conflict between the beneficiary group and its competitors is likely to escalate in space, intensity, and number. Additional third parties will intervene in support of rival groups, ethnic competitors will actively recruit third-party support to offset the perceived advantage, and previously quiescent groups may mobilize if their interests are threatened by the enhanced capacity of the mobilized group. The result is to trigger escalatory cycles of third-party involvement that will likely expand the conflict beyond the state arena and, in the event of state collapse, threaten not only regional but also international security. As the conflict escalates, so too does the intensity of ethnic violence.

The second systemic catalyst is *biased or exclusionary third-party mediation* that triggers the adoption of violent means or the resumption of ethnic war. When third-party mediation is perceived as favoring one contending group over others, or deliberately excludes one ethnic group from the settlement process, the disadvantaged or excluded group is left with little option but to resume fighting. For both the Serbs and the Kosovar Albanians, perceived bias and exclusionary mediation were catalysts for violence, creating the perception that both groups had little alternative but to adopt violent means to secure their goals. Inaction will leave the group permanently disadvantaged or worse, whereas the resumption of violence offers the hope of renewed efforts under more favorable auspices. It also buys time for the disadvantaged group to secure new sources of external support or to expand gains on the ground, and, as was true for the Kosovar Albanians, it may force the international community to extend recognition to the rebelling group, particularly if violence threatens regional or international stability. The mediation catalyst not only prompts the adoption or resumption of ethnic war, but also creates an incentive for the disadvantaged or excluded group to escalate violence to force third parties to reopen mediation efforts that fully include the group and address its aims.

As violence intensifies, so too do the efforts of third-party mediators, particularly if violence prompts refugee flows that directly impact neighboring states or threaten regional and even international security. The more intense the violence, the greater the likelihood that rival third parties will compete to control the mediation process and influence the settlement. This competition further intensifies violence when groups undermine the efforts of one mediator, either by further escalation of violence or new gains on the ground, while seeking more favorable terms from the other.

The third systemic catalyst is the *provision of arms and resources by third parties* that enables groups both to launch and to sustain ethnic war. This catalyst enables the adoption and intensification of violence in conflicts that occur short of state collapse. When domestic sources (battlefield capture, government armories, or domestic manufacture) are limited or unavailable, the provision of arms and resources by third parties changes a group's ability to adopt violent means. Although arms need not be sophisticated to launch an ethnic war, advanced armaments become critical when groups challenge the professional forces wielded by the state. The need for sophisticated arms narrows the range of preferable suppliers to states, predominately nearby states. Regardless of the strength of group claims or grievances, the effectiveness of its leadership, the violence of a state's response to group mobilization, or the degree of international support, ethnic groups cannot sustain a strategy of violence against ethnic strangers if they lack the essential resources to do so.

In the rare case of state collapse, however, third-party arms and resources are less likely to act as a catalyst for violence. When states collapse, groups can more easily acquire large numbers of sophisticated weapons from former government stockpiles; recruit former military members, particularly ethnic kin, with the training to use more sophisticated weapons systems; and even absorb entire units with weapons intact, as many successor states did following the Soviet Union's collapse. Under these rare conditions, *state collapse* is a more likely third image catalyst of violence.

The resource catalyst also provokes and intensifies interethnic violence. When one group secures external, third-party arms and resources, ethnic competitors will seek alternate sources to offset the group's advantage, triggering the type of escalatory cycles of violence that marked the war in Bosnia as each group secures the means to escalate the war. As the war intensifies and escalates, additional ethnic groups may be drawn into the conflict, thus widening the war. Third-party resources, particularly when supplied by states, will also intensify violence if the sophistication and number of weapons increase for one or more parties to the conflict. Not only will violence intensify, the war is also likely to become protracted as the availability of third-party arms and resources shifts the cost-benefit calculations in favor of continued war. For both the Armenians and the Azerbaijanis, as well as for the Kurds, third-party resources changed these groups' perceptions in favor of continued violent resistance and significantly protracted the wars.

The final systemic catalyst is the *selective recognition of the right to self-determination* that triggers ethnic war over ownership of the rump state. When third parties offer recognition to one group while denying that right to ethnic competitors, the disadvantaged group is left with two stark alternatives. It must either accept the seemingly permanent loss of nationhood, or else launch a war either to seize all or part of the rump state or to secede, using the reality on the ground to force the international community to proffer recognition. Although a charismatic leadership may persuade the group to delay the dream of statehood, there is a strong incentive for the group to adopt violent means while the institutions and structures of the new state remain in flux.

Selective recognition is a catalyst for new or intensified ethnic conflict. When selective recognition leaves a minority ethnic group in the rump state at the mercy of ethnic competitors, as was evident in the case of Kosovo's Albanian population, it will likely prompt the rapid mobilization of the threatened group, increasing the number of ethnic contenders and widening the war. If recognition is tied to settlement patterns, selective recognition of regionally concentrated groups creates an incentive for dispersed groups to adopt ethnic cleansing and other violent measures to shift the settlement pattern of the contested territory. All three Yugoslav conflicts are replete with examples of selective recognition acting as a catalyst for both new and intensified conflict. Once ethnic strangers are expelled or otherwise removed, the now-dominant group can renew its claim to self-determination, buttressed by referenda that "prove" the now homogenous population's desire for independence. The selective recognition catalyst, although rare, not only enhances the choice of violent means, but also triggers an intensification of violence to the more extreme forms of ethnic cleansing, expulsion, and even genocide.

Prior to the end of the Cold War, the likelihood that a substate actor's claim to self-determination would be recognized was extremely rare. Since the 1990s, however, a number of new states achieved independence following the collapse of the Soviet Union and Yugoslavia. Recognition was selectively granted to federal units (republics) with homogenous populations, but denied to federal subunits (autonomous regions). Dismemberment was limited to the federal state, while federal subunits were kept intact regardless of the desires of their multiethnic populations. Thus, Slovenia, Croatia, and Ukraine were recognized as independent states, while Chechnya, Nagorno-Karabakh, and the Krajina were not. The precedent-setting recognition of Kosovo has created a new dynamic of selective recognition that will likely serve as a catalyst for the further intensification of ethnic violence where such recognition was previously denied. Russia's August 2008 invasion of Georgia cited the Kosovo precedent as justification for its refusal to uphold Georgia's territorial integrity[3] and for its subsequent recognition of both Abkhazia and South Ossetia as independent states. As the selective recognition catalyst becomes more prevalent, the third image will explain not only why conflict is likely to resume where statehood was denied, but also why ethnic violence will escalate as ethnic competitors seek not just to defeat but to destroy the ethnic other.

Each of the third image catalysts interacts with the group and state level causes of ethnic war to enhance our understanding of why groups adopt violent means. One of the most significant interactions occurs in the case of a contested homeland. Because homeland claims are claims against the state, and because ethnonationalists are rarely willing to settle for autonomy, third-party support and arms are critical catalysts of violence. They enable the group to adopt violent means against the superior forces of the state, raise group claims in international fora, legitimize the group's right to self-determination, and ultimately guarantee the viability of the new state. In the Nagorno-Karabakh conflict, both support and arms were catalysts for violence. They enabled ethnic Armenians to adopt violent means to occupy the contested territory and to link it with Armenia proper. Biased mediation and selective recognition are also significant catalysts for violence in homeland wars because the group's identity and survival are at stake. In the case of Kosovo, the Serb perception of Western bias prompted the violent homogenization of Kosovo to secure ownership of the territory by force and in contravention to agreements the Serbs viewed as fundamentally unjust. Both biased mediation and selective recognition create a strong incentive for the disadvantaged group to resume or escalate violence, even when the likelihood of success is low.

In the case of ethnochauvinist claims against ethnic strangers, third-party support and resources enable the group to reorder society and dominate the ethnic other. Because dominance necessarily entails the segregation, deportation, expulsion, or extermination of ethnic aliens, third-party support and resources are critical catalysts of intense ethnic violence that will likely have significant regional implications, particularly if cleansing or mass expulsion trigger refugee flows that threaten the security of neighboring states. Biased mediation or selective recognition that favors the inferior other will further confirm the belief among chauvinist group members that the other are "filthy outsiders and fifth columnists,"[4] and that violence is justified to avenge the group, redress past grievances, and secure the group's rightful dominance over its inferior enemy. The Serb perception of bias on the part of third-party mediators acted as a catalyst for violence to secure the contested homeland and cleanse it of ethnic strangers.

When a group mobilizes to defend its survival against the actions of ethnic strangers, or the state when it is controlled by ethnic strangers, third-party support and resources are critical catalysts of violence. Political-diplomatic support can raise awareness of the group's plight and prompt humanitarian support, including pressure on the state to address group grievances. Tangible support provides aid by way of access or sanctuary that materially enhances the group's ability to defend ethnic kin, as was apparent in the case of Nagorno-Karabakh. Russian support for the Armenians enabled them to seize the strategic Lachin corridor, breaking the blockade of Nagorno-Karabakh. Subsequently, vital supplies and forces from Armenia could reach the enclave and sustain the Armenian war against the Azerbaijanis. Third-party support and intervention also intensify violence. Once the threatened group acquires third-party support and arms, it will mobilize rapidly in self-defense, adopting violence against ethnic strangers or the state. Biased third-party mediation will similarly intensify violence when third-party efforts to resolve conflict fail to protect the group against the threat of ethnic strangers or the state.

Third-party support and arms significantly enhance an ethnic leadership's ability to win support among group members for the adoption of violent means and to sideline or undermine competing ethnic leaderships. These are also critical catalysts of internecine violence when that support favors one faction over others. Rival ethnic leaderships will attempt to secure alternate sources of support, triggering an escalatory cycle of third-party engagement that intensifies violence not only between groups, but also among within-group factions, as was evident in the case of the Kurds. Biased mediation and selective recognition are additional catalysts of ethnic violence when they erode support for moderates who favor compromise, while simultaneously strengthening the position of rival militant leaderships who favor the resumption of ethnic war. Thus, Azerbaijani moderates were sidelined when Russian intervention in support of the Armenians triggered the radicalization of the APF.

Systemic actors are critical catalysts of ethnic violence when a group challenges the state, particularly a weak state. When a weak state responds with partial accommodation, the group's ability to secure tangible and political-diplomatic support—as well as favorable, third-party mediation—is a significant catalyst of violence. They enhance the group's ability to force the state to implement the settlement. Yet third-party support, particularly third-party arms and resources, is also a catalyst for violence when it enables the group to escalate its demands against the state or to believe that a more extensive settlement is within reach. Thus, third-party support for the Kurds prompted Mulla Mustafa to reject the 1973 Autonomy Law and to escalate the Kurds' demands. Once groups reject the proffered settlement, or when the state loses its will or ability to implement the agreement, third-party support and arms enable the group to adopt or resume violence to force the state to meet its demands. When the state counters group mobilization with repression, third-party support and arms enable the group to engage the superior forces of the state, and when mediation favors the state, it enables the group to resume violent means. Although severe repression halts violent resistance, the third-party support that heightens awareness of the group's plight or offers humanitarian support for the besieged group will enable the groups to return to the field sooner. Extreme repression may even trigger direct third-party intervention and recognition when the group is regionally concentrated and third-party interests are served by the weakening of a regional competitor.

When an exclusionary state response involves the expulsion or mass extermination of the ethnic other, the targeted group is likely to secure significant third-party support, as was evident after Serbia's violent repression of the Kosovar Albanians prompted intensified third-party mediation and ultimately NATO intervention. Third-party support and arms are critical catalysts of violence when they enable the excluded group to challenge the state and force either its inclusion, when the group is regionally dispersed, or secession, when the group is regionally concentrated. When a group perceives third-party mediation as biased such that it denies the group's demand for inclusion, or when selective recognition denies the excluded group's right to secede, the group will resume fighting rather than accept its permanent exclusion.

The interaction of the third image with the first and second image causes of ethnic violence allows us to draw some final conclusions about the nature of ethnic war. The first, supported by our case studies, is that the interjection of systemic actors in a conflict both between groups and between groups and the state significantly protracts conflict. Ethnic conflict is inherently asymmetric when it pits a group against the superior resources of the state, or when there is a significant disparity between ethnic contenders. Material support from actors outside the state change the correlation of forces and enable a weaker group to contemplate violent means when it would not otherwise have been able to do so. Intervention, when it encompasses both tangible and political diplomatic support as well as arms and resources, also makes it possible for groups to escalate their goals. In the case of Iraq, third-party support for the Kurds significantly expanded Kurdish demands for autonomy that resembled complete independence in all but name. The escalation of both means and goals significantly protracts conflict; it enables groups to expand the war against a stronger opponent and allows groups to continue resistance in the hope of achieving a more substantial settlement.

We also find an explanation for the more extreme forms of ethnic war at the third image. Ethnic cleansing, expulsion, and mass extermination are increasingly part of the ethnic conflict lexicon in the post-1990 explosion of ethnic war. The erosion of systemic constraints on ethnic conflict offers a partial explanation. The uneven erosion of state sovereignty has created weak or failed states and areas of ungovernability where the state's policing arm no longer reaches. When states collapse, the state arena resembles the international system; each group must secure its own interests and provide for its own security. In these environments, which in places like Somalia resemble a Hobbesian state of nature, little impedes groups from exacting vengeance against ethnic strangers or from violently excluding them from the state arena.

More extreme forms of ethnic violence are also a consequence of incentives unwittingly created by third parties in their efforts to resolve and end ethnic violence. When mediation or recognition is tied to the homogeneity of the contested territory, groups living in multiethnic regions have a strong incentive to overturn prevailing settlement patterns by cleansing or otherwise removing strangers. Although extreme violence is not exclusively the function of systemic intervention in ethnic conflict, when statehood is tied to referenda in complexly settled multiethnic regions, groups have a strong incentive to cleanse ethnic strangers.

The third image catalysts of ethnic violence and their interaction with the first and second images provide the final pieces to the complex puzzle of ethnic violence. Our case studies demonstrate that systemic actors significantly impact a group's choice of violent means. They also demonstrate that violence is a function of the interaction of the first two images with the third. Although the External Support and Resource Models offer compelling explanations for a group's choice of violent means, they rarely operate in isolation from the first and second image triggers of ethnic war.

FINAL THOUGHTS

A multilevel approach corrects the tendency in much of the literature on ethnic conflict to focus exclusively on a single level of analysis. A central argument of this book is that ethnic violence is both complex and multifaceted. Our case studies support the contention that groups adopt violent means for reasons that have to do with ethnic identity and competition for power within the group, with the state's response to ethnic mobilization, and with the interjection of systemic actors between contending groups and between a group and the state. At each image we find distinct reasons why groups adopt violent means. These single-level explanations, captured in eight distinct models, are compelling but incomplete. Ethnic violence is also a function of the interaction of the models across the three images of ethnic war. The myriad reasons why groups adopt violent means can only be understood through a multilevel framework of interrelated models and images.

Waltz argues that every prescription for greater peace in the world is related to one of the three images in international relations, or to some combination of them.[5]

If so, then the three images of ethnic war have some utility for resolving ethnic conflict and perhaps even for preventing it. A multilevel framework is an analytic tool that allows us not only to understand why groups adopt violent means, but also to begin to address the underlying causes of war in a comprehensive way. A viable response to both prevention and resolution must address the causes of ethnic violence at all three images if it is to accomplish either task or have lasting results.

At the first image, resolution must address factors relating to ethnic identity. Resolving the first image triggers of ethnic war requires addressing the intractable nature of these conflicts, as well as the tendency to view these conflicts and their solutions in zero-sum terms. Because issues of identity are claimed to be non-negotiable, resolving violence at the first image must either protect these identities or foster alternate, more inclusive ones. The zero-sum nature of how such conflicts are defined presents one of the most serious challenges. How can a homeland claim be resolved if the much-sought-after gain for one group is an unacceptable loss for the other? A solution that fails to address these issues of identity will have little hope of achieving lasting success.

At the state level, solutions must address the role of the state—as arena, actor, and prize. These solutions involve not only constraints and incentives on the state's response options, but also structural changes that preclude the renewal of exclusionary policies. Because exclusion is in part a function of stratification and settlement patterns, these solutions may involve no less than the restructuring of all three dimensions of the state arena. When conflict is also *about* the state, solutions must address how the distribution of gains—a homeland, autonomous region, or new nation state—is to be equitably divided. How such an equitable distribution is defined is likely to vary greatly among ethnic contenders, adding a further obstacle to settlement. When the fair division of the spoils of war is unrealistic or impossible, incentives for the resumption of war cannot be ignored.

At the third image, the task is complicated by the fact that the solutions themselves can be a catalyst for further violence. Short of exhaustion through war, the greatest chance of successful resolution hinges on third-party mediation. How this mediation unfolds, particularly where self-determination and secessionist claims are at stake, determines to a great extent whether a settlement will be accepted by groups that retain the means to resist.

Given the complexity of causes in ethnic war, resolution is a daunting task even when conditions favor settlement. The number of frozen and ongoing ethnic conflicts worldwide, despite serious and sustained efforts on the part of third-party actors to resolve them, attests to the inherent complexity of conflict resolution. The fact that ethnic conflicts cause more deaths than interstate war behooves continued efforts to create mechanisms to solve these conflicts, as well as greater understanding of why groups adopt violent means against ethnic competitors. A multilevel approach is a blueprint for action. It provides a framework of models that posit why groups adopt violent means, recognizes the significant interaction among them, and charts a course for conflict resolution at all three images of ethnic war.

Notes

CHAPTER 1

1. Marc Champion and Andrew Osborn, "Smoldering Feud, Then War: Tensions at Obscure Border Led to Georgia-Russia Clash," *The Wall Street Journal* (August 18, 2008): A6.

2. August Cole, "Attack on Georgia Gives Boost to Big U.S. Weapons Programs," *The Wall Street Journal* (August 18, 2008): A6.

3. Joseph Rothschild, *Ethnopolitics: A Conceptual Framework* (New York: Columbia University Press, 1981), 196; Milton J. Esman, *Ethnic Politics* (Ithaca, NY: Cornell University Press, 1994), 2.

4. Stanley J. Tambiah, "Ethnic Conflict in the World Today," *American Ethnologist* 16 (May 1, 1989): 338.

5. Samuel P. Huntington, "The Clash of Civilizations?" *Foreign Affairs* 72 (Summer 1993): 22–49.

6. Rothschild, 196; Esman, *Ethnic Politics*, 2.

7. Mary Kaldor, *New and Old Wars: Organized Violence in a Global Era* (Stanford: Stanford University Press, 2001).

8. Rupert Smith, *The Utility of Force: The Art of War in the Modern World* (New York: Alfred A. Knopf, 2007).

9. Monty G. Marshal and Ted Robert Gurr, *Peace and Conflict 2005: A Global Survey of Armed Conflicts, Self-Determination Movements, and Democracy* (College Park, MD: Center for International Development and Conflict Management, 2005), 1.

10. J. Joseph Hewitt, Jonathon Wilkenfeld, and Ted Robert Gurr, *Peace and Conflict 2008: Executive Summary* (College Park, MD: Center for International Development and Conflict Management, 2008), 12. Available at http://www.cidcm.umd.edu/pc/executive_summary/pc_es_20070613.pdf.

11. Roger D. Petersen, *Understanding Ethnic Violence: Fear, Hatred, and Resentment in Twentieth-Century Eastern Europe* (Cambridge: Cambridge University Press, 2002); Stefan Wolff, *Ethnic Conflict: A Global Perspective* (Oxford: Oxford University Press, 2006).

12. Stuart J, Kaufman, *Modern Hatreds: The Symbolic Politics of Ethnic War* (Ithaca, NY: Cornell University Press, 2001).

13. According to Sislin and Pearson, ethnic conflict is the result of grievances seized upon by "heroic, opportunitistic or ruthless leaders." See John Sislin and Frederic Pearson, *Arms and Ethnic Conflict* (Lanham, MD: Rowman and Littlefield Publishers, Inc., 2001), 5.

14. V. P. Gagnon argues that violence in Croatia and Serbia was part of a broad strategy in which images of enemies and violence were used to demobilize certain segments of the population that supported structural changes inimical to the Croat and Serb elites' power bases. See V. P. Gagnon, *The Myth of Ethnic War: Serbia and Croatia in the 1990s* (Ithaca, NY: Cornell University Press, 2004).

15. David Carment, Patrick James, and Zeynep Taydas, *Who Intervenes? Ethnic Conflict and Interstate Crisis* (Columbus: The Ohio State University Press, 2006). See also Raymond C. Taras and Rajat Ganguly, *Understanding Ethnic Conflict: The International Dimension*, 3rd ed. (New York: Longman, 2006).

16. Donald. L. Horowitz, *The Deadly Ethnic Riot* (Berkeley: University of California Press, 2001).

17. Charles Tilly, *The Politics of Collective Violence* (Cambridge: Cambridge University Press, 2003).

18. Heather Rae, *State Identities and the Homogenisation of Peoples* (Cambridge: Cambridge University Press, 2002).

19. Joseph L. Soeters, *Ethnic Conflict and Terrorism: The Origins and Dynamics of Civil Wars* (London: Routledge, 2005).

20. Kenneth N. Waltz, *Man, the State and War: A Theoretical Analysis* (New York: Columbia University Press, 1959).

21. Ibid., 17.

22. Ibid., 39.

23. James Mayall and Mark Simpson, "Ethnicity is Not Enough: Reflections on Protracted Secessionism in the Third World," *International Journal of Comparative Sociology* 33 (1992): 6–7.

24. See Kaldor, *New and Old Wars.*

25. Waltz, *Man, the State and War*, 83.

26. Ibid., 227.

27. Ibid., 189.

28. Wolff, 2.

29. See Andrew Bell-Fialkoff, "A Brief History of Ethnic Cleansing," *Foreign Affairs* 72 (Summer 1993): 110.

30. Rae, 5.

31. Ibid.

32. The United Nations Convention on the Prevention and Punishment of the Crime of Genocide describes genocide as "acts committed with intent to destroy, in whole or in part, a national, ethnical, racial or religious group" (Article 2). See Office of the High Commissioner for Human Rights, *Convention on the Prevention and Punishment of the Crime of Genocide.* http://www.unhchr.ch/html/menu3/b/p_genoci.htm.

33. Waltz, *Man, the State and War*, 146.

CHAPTER 2

1. Monica Duffy Toft, *The Geography of Ethnic Conflict* (Princeton, NJ: Princeton University Press, 2003), 1.

2. Ted Robert Gurr, *Minorities at Risk: A Global View of Ethnopolitical Conflict* (Washington, DC: United States Institute of Peace, 1993), 18.

3. Ibid., 319.

4. Toft, 19.

5. Ibid.

6. Wolff, 45.

7. Paul R. Brass, *Ethnicity and Nationalism: Theory and Comparison* (New Delhi: Sage Publications, 1991), 63.

8. Andreas Wimmer, *Nationalist Exclusion and Ethnic Conflict: Shadows of Modernity* (Cambridge: Cambridge University Press, 2002), 106.

9. Kaufman, *Modern Hatreds*, 16. (Italics in original.)

10. Hannah Arendt, *The Origins of Totalitarianism* (San Diego, CA: Harcourt, Inc., 1968), 227.

11. Anthony D. Smith, "The Ethnic Sources of Nationalism," *Survival* 35 (Spring 1993): 53.

12. Hannah Arendt, "Imperialism, Nationalism, Chauvinism," *The Review of Politics* 7 (October 1945): 457.

13. Akbar S. Ahmed, "Ethnic Cleansing: A Metaphor for Our Time?" *Ethnic and Racial Studies* 18 (January 1995): 8.

14. Arendt, *Origins of Totalitarianism*, 227.

15. Esman, *Ethnic Politics*, 30.

16. Tambiah, 346.

17. Donald L. Horowitz, *Ethnic Groups in Conflict* (Berkeley: University of California Press, 1985), 263.

18. Milton J. Esman, "Political and Psychological Factors in Ethnic Conflict" in *Conflict and Peacemaking in Multiethnic Societies*, Joseph V. Montville, ed. (Lexington, MA: Lexington Books, 1990), 59.

19. Ibid.

20. Gurr, *Minorities at Risk*, 79.

21. Walker Connor, *Ethnonationalism: The Quest for Understanding* (Princeton, NJ: Princeton University Press, 1994), 47.

22. Donald L. Horowitz, "How to Begin Thinking about Soviet Ethnic Problems" in *Thinking Theoretically About Soviet Nationalities: History and Comparison in the Study of the USSR*, Alexander J. Motyl, ed. (New York: Columbia University Press, 1992), 13.

23. Although this book follows the literature and employs the terms "ethnic entrepreneurs" and "cultural entrepreneurs," it is important to note that, despite the term, ethnic entrepreneurs do not create identities out of thin air. They draw upon the group's beliefs and values as well the group's history, symbols, and experiences. Group identity, as articulated by elites, must have resonance within the broader ethnic group if it is to gain any following.

24. Tambiah, 336.

25. Rothschild, 107.

CHAPTER 3

1. For this debate and the supporting data, see Michael Brown, Seam M. Lynn-Jones, and Steven Miller, eds., *Debating the Democratic Peace: An International Security Reader* (Cambridge: The MIT Press, 1996); and Bruce Russett, *Grasping the Democratic Peace: Principles for a Post-Cold War World* (Princeton: Princeton University Press, 1993).

2. Barry Buzan, *People, States and Fear: An Agenda for International Security Studies in the Post-Cold War Era*, 2nd ed. (New York: Harvester Wheatsheaf, 1991), 60.

3. Robert H. Jackson, *Quasi-states: Sovereignty, International Relations and the Third World* (Cambridge: Cambridge University Press, 1990), 21.

4. Buzan, 65.

5. Rothschild, 118.

6. Tofft, 27 and 149–152.

7. *Foreign Policy*, "The Failed State Index 2007" (July/August 2007), http://www.foreignpolicy.com/story/cms.php?story_id=3865. Using 12 social, economic, political, and military indicators, this index ranks 177 states in order of their vulnerability to violent internal conflict and societal dysfunction. A failing state is defined as one where the government does not have control of its territory, is not seen as legitimate by a significant portion of its population, does not provide domestic security or basic public services, and lacks a monopoly of the use of force.

8. See Toft, Appendix 2, for MAR data in an easily accessible format. For the full data set, see Minorities at Risk Project (College Park, MD: Center for International Development and Conflict Management, 2005). http://www.cidcm.umd.edu/mar/data.asp.

9. Multiethnic states are states with two or more ethnic groups, and homogenous states are states with only one ethnic group. Binational indicates states with two ethnic groups. Binational states are rare, and when the groups are both concentrated, as in the case of the former Czechoslovakia, a negotiated settlement leading to secession can resolve group conflict peacefully.

10. Jack Snyder, *From Voting to Violence: Democratization and Nationalist Conflict* (New York: W. W. Norton & Company, Inc., 2000), 24.

11. Ibid., 24–25.

12. See Haldun Gülalp, "Introduction: Citizenship vs. Nationality?" in *Citizenship and Ethnic Conflict: Challenging the Nation-State*, ed. Haldun Gülalp, (New York: Routledge, 2006).

13. Horowitz, *Ethnic Groups in Conflict*, 291.

14. Ibid., 22–36. In a more recent book, Horowitz applies this typology to understanding ethnic riots. See Horowitz, *The Deadly Ethnic Riot*.

15. Horowitz, *Ethnic Groups in Conflict*, 25.

16. Ibid., 30–31.

17. Robert I. Rotberg, "The Failure and Collapse of Nation-States: Breakdown, Prevention, and Repair," in *When States Fail: Causes and Consequences*, ed. Robert I. Rotberg, (Princeton: Princeton University Press, 2004), 9.

18. Rotberg, "The Failure and Collapse of Nation-States," 3.

19. Robert H. Dorff, "Failed States After 9/11: What Did We Know and What Have We Learned?" *International Studies Perspectives* 6 (2005): 22.

20. Kalevi J. Holsti, *The State, War, and the State of War* (Cambridge: Cambridge University Press, 1996), 97.

21. Ibid., 84.

22. Rotberg, "The Failure and Collapse of Nation-States," 5.

23. Holsti, 90.

24. See Alexis Heraclides, "Conflict Resolution, Ethnonationalism, and the Middle East Impasse," *Journal of Peace Research* 26 (May 1989): 198.

25. Gurr, *Minorities at Risk*, 9.

26. Alexis Heraclides, *The Self-Determination of Minorities in International Politics* (London: Frank Cass and Company, Limited, 1991), 198.

27. Ernest Gellner, *Nations and Nationalism* (Ithaca: Cornell University Press, 1983): 1.

28. Horowitz, *Ethnic Groups in Conflict*, 31.

29. Donald L. Horowitz, "Democracy in Divided Societies," in *Nationalism, Ethnic Conflict, and Democracy*, ed. Larry Diamond and Marc F. Plattner (Baltimore: The Johns Hopkins University Press, 1994), 49.

30. Horowitz, *Ethnic Groups in Conflict*, 298.

31. Larry Diamond and Marc F. Plattner, "Introduction," in *Nationalism, Ethnic Conflict, and Democracy*, ed. Larry Diamond and Marc F. Plattner (Baltimore: The Johns Hopkins University Press, 1994), xviii.

32. Horowitz, "Democracy in Divided Societies," 35.

CHAPTER 4

1. Waltz, *Man, the State and War*, 159.

2. John Stack, Jr., "The Ethnic Challenge to International Relations Theory" in *Wars in the Midst of Peace: The International Politics of Ethnic Conflict*, ed. David Carment and Patrick James (Pittsburgh, PA: University of Pittsburgh Press, 1997), 19.

3. Carment, James, and Taydas, *Who Intervenes?*; David Carment and Patrick James, "Ethnic Conflict at the International Level: Theory and Evidence," in *Wars in the Midst of Peace: The International Politics of Ethnic Conflict*, ed. David Carment and Patrick James (Pittsburgh, PA: University of Pittsburgh Press, 1997), 1–10; David A. Lake and Donald Rothchild, "Spreading Fear: The Genesis of Transnational Ethnic Conflict," in *The International Spread of Ethnic Conflict: Fear, Diffusion and Escalation*, ed. David A. Lake and Donald Rothchild (Princeton: Princeton University Press, 1998); Zeev Maoz, "Domestic Political Change and Strategic Response: The Impact of Domestic Conflict on State Behavior, 1816–1986" in *Wars in the Midst of Peace*, ed. Carment and James, 116–147; David R. Davis, Keith Jaggers, and Will H. Moore, "Ethnicity, Minorities, and International Conflict," in *Wars in the Midst of Peace*, ed. Carment and James, 148–163; Stuart Hill and Donald Rothchild, "The Contagion of Political Conflict in Africa and the World," *Journal of Conflict Resolution*, 30 (December 1983): 716–735; John A. Vasquez, "Factors Related to the Contagion and Diffusion of International Violence," in *The Internationalization of Communal Strife*, ed. Manus I. Midlarsky (New York: Routledge, 1993), 149–172; William J. Folz, "External Causes" in *Revolution and Political Change in the Third World*, ed. Barry M. Shultz and Robert O. Slater (Boulder, CO: Lynn Reinner, 1990), 54–64.

4. Stephen Saideman, "Is Pandora's Box Half Empty or Half Full? The Limited Virulence of Secessionism and the Domestic Sources of Integration," in Lake and Rothchild, *The International Spread of Ethnic Conflict*, 127–150; Carment and James, *Wars in the Midst of Peace*; Carment, James, and Taydas, *Who Intervenes?*; Taras and Ganguly, *Understanding Ethnic Conflict*; and Horowitz, *Ethnic Groups in Conflict*, 229–290.

5. Lake and Rothchild, "Spreading Fear," 25.

6. Carment, James, and Taydas, 9.

7. Donald L. Horowitz, "Patterns of Ethnic Separatism," *Comparative Studies in Society and History* 23 (April 1981): 167; Ted Robert Gurr, "The Internationalization of Protracted Communal Conflicts Since 1945: Which Groups, Where, and How," in *The Internationalization of Communal Strife*, ed. Manus I. Midlarsky (New York: Routledge, 1993), 4; Stephen M. Saideman, "Discrimination in International Relations: Analyzing External Support for Ethnic Groups," *Journal of Peace Research* 29 (2002): 27; and Horowitz, *Ethnic Groups in Conflict*, 229–290.

8. Carment, James, and Taydas, 2.

9. I. William Zartman, "Internationalization of Communal Strife: Temptations and Opportunities for Triangulation," in *The Internationalization of Communal Strife*, ed. Manus I. Midlarsky (New York: Routledge, 1993), 37.

10. Querine H. Hanlon, "Globalization and the Transformation of Armed Groups," in *Armed Groups: Studies in National Security, Counterterrorism, and Counterinsurgency*, ed. Jeffrey H. Norwitz (Newport: Naval War College Press, 2008), 116.

11. For a discussion of the proliferation of terms used to describe "new war" see Isabelle Duyvesteyn and Jan Angstrom, eds., *Rethinking the Nature of War* (London: Frank Cass, 2005), 6–7.

12. John Ishiyama, "Does Globalization Breed Ethnic Conflict?" *Nationalism and Ethnic Politics* 9 (2004): 2. See also Arjun Appadurai, "Dead Certainty: Ethnic Violence in an Era of Globalization," *Development and Change* 29 (1998): 905–925.

13. Ishiyama, 2.

14. Ibid., 5.

15. Ibid., 4.

16. Kaldor, *New and Old Wars*. See also Herfried Münkler, *The New Wars*, trans. Patrick Cammiller (Cambridge: Polity Press, 2005).

17. Martin Van Creveld, *The Transformation of War* (New York: The Free Press, 1991), 212.

18. Smith, *The Utility of Force*, 5.

19. Donald L. Horowitz, "Patterns of Ethnic Separatism," *Comparative Studies in Society and History* 23 (April 1981): 167; Ted Robert Gurr, "The Internationalization of Protracted Communal Conflicts Since 1945: Which Groups, Where, and How," in *The Internationalization of Communal Strife*, ed. Manus I. Midlarsky (New York: Routledge, 1993), 4; Stephen M. Saideman, "Discrimination in International Relations: Analyzing External Support for Ethnic Groups," *Journal of Peace Research* 29 (2002): 27; and Horowitz, *Ethnic Groups in Conflict*, 229–290.

20. Heraclides, *Self-Determination of Minorities*, 48–49.

21. Donald Rothchild and David A. Lake, "Containing Fear: The Management of Transnational Ethnic Conflict," in Lake and Rothchild, *The International Spread of Ethnic Conflict*, 214.

22. Ibid., 216.

23. Ibid., 217.

24. Ibid., 222.

25. Robert Cooper and Mats Berdal, "Outside Intervention in Ethnic Conflict," *Survival* 35 (Spring 1993): 134.

26. Horowitz, *Ethnic Groups in Conflict*, 276.

27. Stephen M. Saideman, "Discrimination in International Relations," 40.

28. Myron Weiner, "People and States in a New Ethnic Order?" *Third World Quarterly* 13: 2 (1992): 326.

29. Heraclides, *Self-Determination of Minorities*, 38.

30. Rothschild, 186.

31. Carment, James, and Taydas, 11.

32. Horowitz, *Ethnic Groups in Conflict*, 277.

33. Zartman, "Internationalization of Communal Strife," 31.

34. Joane Nagel and Brad Whorton, "Ethnic Conflict and the World System: International Competition in Iraq (1961–1991) and Angola (1974–1991)" *Journal of Political and Military Sociology* 20 (Summer 1992): 7.

35. Rothschild, 181.

36. Astri Suhrke and Lela Garner Noble, "Introduction" in *Ethnic Conflict and International Relations*, ed. Astri Suhrke and Lela Garner Noble (New York: Praeger, 1977), 6.

37. David Carment and Patrick James, "Secession and Irredentia in World Politics: The Neglected Interstate Dimension" in *Wars in the Midst of Peace*, 212.

38. Lake and Rothchild, "Spreading Fear," 22.

39. Michael T. Klare, "The New Arms Race: Light Weapons and International Security," *Current History* 96 (April 1997): 175.

40. Sislin and Pearson, *Arms and Ethnic Conflict*, 12.

41. Aaron Karp, "Arming Ethnic Conflict," *Arms Control Today* 23 (September 2007): 8–13.

42. Sislin and Pearson, *Arms and Ethnic Conflict*, 20.

43. Ibid., 20.

44. Ibid., 31.

45. Philip Verwimp, "Machetes and Firearms: The Organization of Massacres in Rwanda," *Journal of Peace Research* 43: 1 (2006): 6.

46. See Sislin and Pearson, *Arms and Ethnic Conflict*. See also John Sislin, "Arms and Escalation in Ethnic Conflicts: The Case of Sri Lanka," *International Studies Perspectives* 7 (2006): 137–158.

47. Sislin and Pearson, *Arms and Ethnic Conflict*, 42.

48. Douglas Farah, "The Role of Conflict Diamonds in Al-Qaeda's Financial Structure," (January 4, 2004), http://programs.ssrc.org/gsc/gsc_activities/farah/.

CHAPTER 5

1. V. P. Gagnon, "Ethnic Nationalism and International Conflict: The Case of Serbia," *International Security* 19 (Winter 1994/1995): 141.

2. Vjekoslav Perica, *Balkan Idols: Religion and Nationalism in Yugoslav States* (Oxford: Oxford University Press, 2002), 7.

3. Sabrina Ramet, *Nationalism and Federalism in Yugoslavia: 1962–1991*, 2nd ed., (Bloomington: Indiana University Press, 1992), 243.

4. Tim Judah, *Kosovo: War and Revenge*, 2nd. ed. (New Haven: Yale University Press, 2002), 2.

5. Ibid., 3–4.

6. Ibid., 40.

7. Kosta Mihailovic and Vasilije Krestic, *Memorandum of the Serbian Academy of Sciences and Arts: Answers to Criticisms* (Belgrade: Serbian Academy of Sciences and Arts, 1995), 128. http://www.rastko.org.yu/istorija/iii/memorandum.pdf. See pp 95–140 of the document for the original Memorandum.

8. V. P. Gagnon, "Historical Roots of the Yugoslav Conflict" in *International Organizations and Ethnic Conflict*, Milton J. Esman and Shibley Telhami, eds. (Ithaca: Cornell University Press, 1995), 191.

9. Ivo H. Daalder and Michael E. O'Hanlon, *Winning Ugly: NATO's War to Save Kosovo* (Washington, DC: Brookings Institution Press, 2000), 57–59.

10. Ibid.

11. Judah, *Kosovo*, 240–241.

12. Ibid., 210.

13. Slobodan Milosevic, February 19, 1999, quoted in Judah, *Kosovo*, 211.

14. Quoted in Milan Andrejevich, "Milosevic's Speech at Kosovo Polje," *Radio Free Europe Research, Yugoslav Situation Report* 9 (July 20, 1989): 8. Italics added.

15. Mihailovic and Krestic, *Memorandum of the Serbian Academy of Sciences and Arts,* 128.

16. Ibid., 123.

17. Mihailo Markovic, "Societal Development in Serbia After the Second World War," unpublished manuscript, Belgrade, 1986. Quoted in Alex N. Dragnich, *Yugoslavia's Disintegration and the Struggle for Truth,* East European Monographs CDXXXVI (New York: Columbia University Press, 1995), 14.

18. Ibid., 127.

19. Zdenko Antic, "The Serbian Question," *Radio Free Europe Research,* Yugoslav Situation Report 12 (December 23, 1988): 21.

20. Antic, "The Serbian Question," 3–4.

21. V. P. Gagnon, "Serbia's Road to War," *Journal of Democracy* 5 (Spring 1994): 123.

22. Stan Markotich, "Ethnic Serbs in Tudjman's Croatia," *RFE/RL Research Report* 2 (September 24, 1993): 30.

23. Milan Vego, "The Army of Serbian Krajina," *Jane's Intelligence Review* (October 1993): 438.

24. Italics added. Quoted in Laura Silber and Allan Little, *Yugoslavia: Death of a Nation* (New York: TV Books, Inc., 1996), 131.

25. Mihailo Crnobrnja, *The Yugoslav Drama* (Montreal: McGill-Queen's University Press, 1994), 176.

26. John Zametica, *The Yugoslav Conflict,* Adelphi Paper 270 (London: International Institute for Strategic Studies, Summer 1992), 38–39. See also John R. Schindler, *Unholy Terror: Bosnia, al-Qa'ida, and the Rise of Global Jihad* (St. Paul, MN: Zenith Press, 2007), 48.

27. Gagnon, "Ethnic Nationalism and International Conflict," 162–163.

28. See Ivo H. Daalder and Michael E. O'Hanlon, *Winning Ugly: NATO's War to Save Kosovo* (Washington, DC: Brookings Institution Press, 2000), 58–59.

29. Steve Reiquam, "Emigration and Demography in Kosovo," *Radio Free Europe Research, Yugoslav Background Report* 186 (August 4, 1983): 2.

30. Ramet, *Nationalism and Federalism,* 201.

31. Vuk Draskovic, quoted in Dragnich, 11.

32. Vego, "The Army of Serbian Krajina," 438.

33. Ibid.

34. Ramet, *Nationalism and Federalism,* 227.

35. Ibid.

36. Quoted in Banac, "Post-Communism as Post-Yugoslavism," 177.

37. Ramet, *Nationalism and Federalism,* 227.

38. Christopher Bennett, *Yugoslavia's Bloody Collapse: Causes, Course and Consequences* (New York: New York University Press, 1995), 94.

39. Ramet, *Nationalism and Federalism,* 227–228.

40. Ibid., 228.

41. Gagnon, "Serbia's Road to War," 122.

42. Silber and Little, 63.

43. Sabrina Ramet, "War in the Balkans," *Foreign Affairs* 71 (Fall 1991): 83–84.

44. Ramet, *Nationalism and Federalism,* 235.

45. Gagnon, "Ethnic Nationalism and International Conflict," 150.

46. Ibid., 159.

47. Ibid., 158.

48. Silber and Little, 119–120.

49. Ramet, *Nationalism and Federalism*, 263.

50. Ibid.

51. Zametica, 23–24.

52. Mihajlo Mihajlov, "Can Yugoslavia Survive?" *Journal of Democracy* 2 (Spring 1991): 82.

53. Gagnon, "Historical Roots," 188.

54. Ibid., 187.

55. Ibid., 194.

56. Ibid.

57. Ibid.

58. John B. Allcock, "In Praise of Chauvinism: Rhetorics of Nationalism in Yugoslav Politics," *Third World Quarterly* 10 (October 1989): 215.

59. Ramet, *Nationalism and Federalism*, 20.

60. Suan L. Woodward, *Balkan Tragedy: Chaos and Dissolution After the Cold War* (Washington, DC: The Brookings Institution, 1995), 115–116.

61. Markotich, "Ethnic Serbs in Tudjman's Croatia," 28.

62. Bennett, 141.

63. Markotich, "Ethnic Serbs in Tudjman's Croatia," 28.

64. Stan Markotich, "Croatia's Krajina Serbs," *RFE/RL Research Report* 2 (October 15, 1993): 5.

65. Serbs comprised 67 percent of Croatia's police force. See Markotich, "Croatia's Krajina Serbs," 5.

66. Silber and Little, 108.

67. Lenard J. Cohen, "The Disintegration of Yugoslavia," *Current History* 91 (November 1992): 372.

68. Vego, "The Army of Serbian Krajina," 440.

69. Bennett, 180.

70. Ibid.

71. Woodward, 234.

72. Crnobrnja, 187.

73. Woodward, 131–132.

74. Ibid., 230.

75. Ibid.

76. The Party of Democratic Action (SDA) led by Alija Izetbegovic won 33.8 percent of the vote, the Serbian Democratic Party (SDS) won 29.6 percent, and the Bosnian wing of the Croatian HDZ won 18.3 percent. See Woodward, 122.

77. Gagnon, "Ethnic Nationalism and International Conflict," 163.

78. Bennett, 185.

79. Zametica, 39.

80. Stojan Cerovic, "'Greater Serbia' and Its Discontents," in *Why Bosnia? Writings on the Balkan War*, Rabia Ali and Lawrence Lifshultz, eds. (Stony Creek, CT: The Pamphleteer's Press, Inc., 1993), 263.

81. Judah, *Kosovo*, 44.

82. Ibid., 65.

83. Ibid., 136–137.

84. United Nations Security Council, *Press Release SC/6562*, 3918th Meeting (PM) (24 August 1998), http://www.un.org/News/Press/docs/1998/19980824.sc6562.html.

85. United Nations Security Council, *S/RES/1199*, (September 23, 1998), http://www.un.org/peace/kosovo/98sc1199.htm.

86. Zametica, 15.

87. Lenard Cohen, 373.

88. Woodward, 162.

89. Ibid., 262.

90. Crnobrnja, 179·

91. Gagnon, "Serbia's Road to War," 128.

92. Woodward, 173.

93. Ibid., 198.

94. Zametica, 63.

95. Woodward, 156.

96. Ibid.

97. Zametica, 62.

98. Ibid., 23.

99. Gagnon, "Ethnic Nationalism and International Conflict," 162.

100. Zametica, 24.

101. Woodward, 193.

102. Bennett, 172.

103. Cerovic, 264.

104. Woodward, 164.

105. Ibid., 168.

106. Ibid., 169.

107. Ibid., 146.

108. Bennett, 181.

109. Other requirements included internal democracy; good-faith commitment to peaceful negotiation of their conflicts; respect for the UN Charter, the Helsinki Final Act, the rule of law, human rights, and the rights of ethnic and national minorities; respect for the inviolability of borders and the principle that they may be changed only by peaceful means and common agreement; and, finally, a commitment to peaceful settlement of disputes. See Steven L. Burg, "The International Community and the Yugoslav Crisis," in *International Organizations and Ethnic Conflict*, Milton J. Esman and Shibley Telhami, eds. (Ithaca, NY: Cornell University Press, 1995), 247.

110. Woodward, 242.

111. Ibid., 243.

112. Ramet, *Nationalism and Federalism*, 249.

113. Vego, "The Army of Serbian Krajina," 439.

114. Silber and Little, 142.

115. Ibid., 145.

116. Patrick Moore, "Yugoslavia: Ethnic Tension Erupts into Civil War," *RFE/RL Research Report* 1 (January 3, 1992): 71.

117. Ramet, Nationalism and Federalism, 259.

118. Zametica, 85.

119. Milan Vego, "The Army of Bosnia and Herzegovina," *Jane's Intelligence Review* (February 1993): 63.

120. Woodward, 262.

121. Milan Vego, "The Croatian Army," Jane's Intelligence Review (May 1993): 206.

122. Silber and Little, 107.

123. Richard H. Shultz and Wm. J. Olson, Ethnic and Religious Conflict: Emerging Threat to US Security (Washington, DC: National Strategy Information Center, 1994), 30.

124. Ramet, Nationalism and Federalism, 250, 252; Woodward, 149, 263; Kitty McKinsey, "Croatia Rearms on Black Market," The Gazette (Montreal) (February 5, 1993): A10.

125. Ramet, Nationalism and Federalism, 252.

126. Silber and Little, 111.

127. McKinsey, A11.

128. Tim Judah, The Serbs: History, Myth & Destruction of Yugoslavia, 2nd. edition, (New Haven: Yale University Press, 2000), 295–302.

129. Magnus Ranstorp and Gus Xhudo, "A Threat to Europe? Middle East Ties with the Balkans and Their Impact Upon Terrorist Activity Throughout the Region," Terrorism and Political Violence 6 (Summer 1994): 204.

130. Ibid., 203–204 and 219n51.

131. Vego, "The Army of Bosnia and Herzegovina," 65.

132. Ranstorp and Xhudo, 202–203.

133. Judah, Kosovo, 128–129.

CHAPTER 6

1. Patrick Donabedian, "The History of Karabagh from Antiquity to the Twentieth Century," in Levon Chorbajian, Patrick Donabedian, and Claude Mutafian, eds., The Caucasian Knot: The History and Geo-Politics of Nagorno-Karabagh (London: Zed Books, 1994), 52.

2. Svante E. Cornell, Small Nations and Great Powers: A Study of Ethnopolitical Conflict in the Caucasus (Surrey, England: Curzon Press, 2001), 62–63.

3. Donabedian, "The History of Karabagh from Antiquity to the Twentieth Century," 53.

4. Cornell, 64.

5. Donabedian, "The History of Karabagh from Antiquity to the Twentieth Century," 59–60.

6. Ibid., 62.

7. Ibid., 70.

8. Ibid., 72.

9. Richard Hovannissian, quoted in Shireen T Hunter, The Transcaucasus in Transition: Nation-building and Conflict (Washington, DC: The Center for Strategic and International Studies, 1994), 97.

10. Arie Vaserman and Rami Ginat, "National, Territorial or Religious Conflict? The Case of Nagorno-Karabakh," Studies in Conflict and Terrorism 17 (October-December 1994): 347.

11. A. N. Yamskov, "Ethnic Conflict in the Transcaucasus: The Case of Nagorno-Karabakh," Theory and Society 20 (1991): 651.

12. Audrey L. Altstadt, "Nagorno-Karabakh—'Apple of Discord' in the Azerbaijan SSR," Central Asian Survey 7, no 4 (1988): 210.

13. Ibid., 68.

14. Cornell, 68.

15. Audrey L. Altstadt, *The Azerbaijani Turks: Power and Identity Under Russian Rule* (Stanford: Hoover Institution Press, 1992), 207.

16. Bell-Fialkoff, 113.

17. Nora Dudwick, "Armenia: The Nation Awakens" in *Nations and Politics in the Soviet Successor States*, Ian Bremmer and Ray Taras, eds. (Cambridge: Cambridge University Press, 1993), 265.

18. Richard G. Hovannisian, "Caucasian Armenia Between Imperial and Soviet Rule: The Interlude of National Independence," in *Transcaucasia: Nationalism and Social Change*, Ronald Grigor Suny, ed. (Ann Arbor, MI: University of Michigan Slavic Publications, 1983), 291.

19. "Letter by the Novelist Sero Khanzadian on Mountainous Karabagh Addressed to Leonid E. Brezhnev, General Secretary of the Communist Party of the U.S.S.R.," Document 29, in Gerard F. Libaridian, ed., *The Karabagh File: Documents and Facts on the Region of Mountainous Karabagh, 1918–1988* (Cambridge, MA: The Zoryan Institute for Contemporary Armenian Research & Documentation, March 1988), 50.

20. Ibid.

21. Ronald Grigor Suny, "Nationalist and Ethnic Unrest in the Soviet Union," *World Policy Journal* 6 (Summer 1989): 510.

22. Yamskov, 656.

23. David Rieff, "Nagorno-Karabakh: Case Study in Ethnic Strife," *Foreign Affairs* 76 (March 1997): 127–128.

24. "Memorandum to the Central Committee of the Communist Party of the Soviet Union," quoted in Kevin Devlin, "*L'Unita* on 'Armenian Documents Sent to Kremlin,'" *Radio Free Europe Research,* USSR Background report 39 (March 11, 1988): 3.

25. Ronald Suny, *Looking Toward Ararat: Armenia in Modern History* (Bloomington, IN: Indiana University Press, 1993), 194.

26. "Segments of a Speech by Historian Bagrat Ulubabian, at Yerevan Demonstrations on February 26, 1988. Dr. Prof. Ulubabian was Born in Karabagh and Was Exiled from the Region for His Scholarly and Preservation Work," Document 53b, in Libaridian, *The Karabagh File*, 92.

27. "Memorandum to the Central Committee of the Communist Party of the Soviet Union," quoted in Devlin, "*L'Unita* on 'Armenian Documents Sent to Kremlin,'" 3.

28. The Armenian Center for National and International Studies, *Nagorno-Karabagh: A White Paper,* 2nd ed. (Yerevan, Armenia: The Armenian Center for National and International Studies, 1997): 12–13.

29. Silva Kaputikian, quoted in Kevin Devlin, "Armenian Envoys on Crisis Meeting with Gorbachev," *Radio Free Europe Research*, USSR Background Report 42 (March 15, 1988): 1.

30. Donabedian, "The History of Karabagh from Antiquity to the Twentieth Century," 64.

31. Interview with an Armenian schoolteacher, quoted in Levon Chorbajian, "Introduction to the English Language Edition," in *The Caucasian Knot*, Levon Chorbajian, Patrick Donabedian, and Claude Mutafian, eds. (London: Zed Books, 1994), 7.

32. Cornell, 78–79.

33. Thomas de Waal, *Black Garden: Armenia and Azerbaijan through Peace and War* (New York: New York University Press, 2003), 18.

34. Ibid., 40.

35. Ibid., 62.

36. Ibid. 116–117.

37. Ronald Suny, "The Revenge of the Past: Socialism and Ethnic Conflict in Transcaucasia," *New Left Review* 184 (November/December 1990): 27.

38. "Petition from the Armenians of Mountainous Karabagh to Prime Minister Nikita Krushchev," Document 27, in Libaridian, ed., *The Karabagh File*, 43.

39. Ibid.

40. Ibid., 45.

41. "Population of Nakhijevan and Nagorno-Karabagh, 1914–1979," Table 11.3 in Dudwick, 274.

42. Yamskov, 645.

43. Alexandre Bennigsen and S. Enders Wimbush, *Muslims of the Soviet Empire: A Guide* (Bloomington, IN: Indiana University Press, 1986), 145.

44. Yamskov, 647.

45. Ibid.

46. Claude Mutafian, "Karabagh in the Twentieth Century," in *The Caucasian Knot*, Levon Chorbajian, Patrick Donabedian, and Claude Mutafian, eds. (London: Zed Books, 1994), 143.

47. Yamskov, 645–646.

48. Suny, *Looking Toward Ararat*, 188.

49. Yamskov, 642.

50. Suny, "Revenge of the Past," 7.

51. Ibid.

52. Dudwick, 274.

53. "Petition from the Armenians of Mountainous Karabagh to Prime Minister Nikita Krushchev," in Libaridian, ed., *The Karabagh File*, 46.

54. Mutafian, "Karabagh in the Twentieth Century," 143.

55. "Petition from the Armenians of Mountainous Karabagh to Prime Minister Nikita Krushchev," 45.

56. Dudwick, 269.

57. "Address of His Holiness Vazken I to the Delegates of the Armenian National Movement," November 9, 1989 at Etchmiadzin, Armenian. Quoted in Vigen Guroian, "Faith, Church and Nationalism in Armenia," *Nationalities Papers* 20 (Spring 1992): 48–49. Italics added.

58. Ibid., 49.

59. "Petition from the Armenians of Mountainous Karabagh to Prime Minister Nikita Krushchev," 43.

60. Ibid., 43–45.

61. Ibid.

62. Ibid.

63. Ibid., 45.

64. Arkady Volsky, quoted in Suny, *Looking Toward Ararat*, 209.

65. Arkady Volsky, quoted in Claude Mutafian, "Karabagh in the Twentieth Century," 142.

66. Kaufman, *Modern Hatreds*, 66–67.

67. Ibid., 59–60.

68. Ibid., 60.

69. Ibid.

70. Ibid.

71. Bohdan Nahaylo and Victor Swoboda, *Soviet Disunion: A History of the Nationalities Problem in the USSR* (New York: The Free Press, 1989), 285–286.

72. Cornell, 86.

73. Ibid., 88–89.

74. Ibid.

75. Ibid., 91.

76. David Nissman, "The National Reawakening of Azerbaijan," *The World & I* (February 1992): 80.

77. Altstadt, *The Azerbaijani Turks*, 202.

78. Mark Saroyan, "'The Karabakh Syndrome' in Azerbaijani Politics," *Problems of Communism* 34 (September-October, 1990): 22.

79. Ibid.

80. Elizabeth Fuller, "The Ongoing Political Power Struggle in Azerbaijan," *RFE/RL Research Report* 1 (May 1, 1992): 11.

81. Altstadt, *The Azerbaijani Turks*, 205–206.

82. Mark Saroyan, "'The Karabakh Syndrome' in Azerbaijani Politics," *Problems of Communism* 34 (September-October, 1990): 24.

83. Elizabeth Fuller, "The Ongoing Political Power Struggle in Azerbaijan." *RFE/RL Research Report* 1 (May 1, 1992): 11.

84. Ibid.

85. Ibid., 12.

86. Niall M. Fraser, Keith W. Hipel, John Jaworsky, and Ralph Zuljan, "A Conflict Analysis of the Armenian-Azerbaijani Dispute," *Journal of Conflict Resolution* 34 (December 4, 1990): 669.

87. Vaserman and Ginat, 355.

88. See Ian Bremmer, "Reassessing Soviet Nationalities Theory" in *Nations and Politics in the Soviet Successor States*, Ian Bremmer and Ray Taras, eds (Cambridge: Cambridge University Press, 1993), 22n1.

89. Ibid., 5.

90. quoted in Nahaylo and Swoboda, 289.

91. Ibid.

92. Nahaylo and Swoboda, 284–285.

93. Candidate Politburo member Petr Demichev, quoted in Ibid., 285.

94. Ibid.

95. Mikhail Gorbachev, quoted in Nahaylo and Swoboda, 286.

96. quoted in Nahaylo and Swoboda, 286. See also Vaserman and Ginat, 349.

97. Suny, *Looking Toward Ararat*, 198.

98. Vaserman and Ginat, 349.

99. "Excerpts from a message by Mikhail S. Gorbachev to the Soviet Republics of Armenia and Azerbaijan, as Read in Russian over Yerevan Radio by Politburo Member Vladimir I. Dolghikh," Document 62 in Libaridian, *The Karabagh File*, 102–103.

100. "Resolution of the Presidium of the Supreme Soviet of the USSR Rejecting the Reunification of Mountainous Karabagh with Armenia, March 23, 1988," reproduced in full in *The Caucasian Knot*, Levon Chorbajian, Patrick Donabedian, and Claude Mutafian, eds., 182–183.

101. Nahaylo and Swoboda, 289.

102. Fraser et al., 659.

103. Vaserman and Ginat, 351. See also Kaufman, *Modern Hatreds*, 65.

104. Altstadt, *The Azerbaijani Turks*, 198.

105. Ibid., 204.

106. Saroyan, "The 'Karabakh Syndrome,'" 27.

107. Fraser et al., 669.

108. Vaserman and Ginat, 353.

109. Kaufman, 70.

110. Ibid.

111. Saroyan, "The 'Karabakh Syndrome,'" 29.

112. Vaserman and Ginat, 354.

113. Thomas Goltz, "Letter From Eurasia: The Hidden Russian Hand," *Foreign Policy* 92 (Fall 1993): 101. See also de Waal, 170.

114. Goltz, 101.

115. Vaserman and Ginat, 355. The death toll is debated and numbers range as low as 100 (Armenian sources) to 1,000 (Azerbaijani sources), Human rights organizations estimate the number to be between 200 and 1,000. See Cornell, 95–96. De Waal suggests that a reliable estimate is that of the official Azerbaijani parliamentary investigation, which lists the death toll as 485. See de Waal, 171.

116. De Waal, 195.

117. Goltz., 113–114.

118. Ibid.

119. Ibid., 114.

120. Cornell, 96.

121. Vaserman and Ginat, 360.

122. Fuller, "Russia's Diplomatic Offensive in the Transcaucasus," 32.

123. United Nations Security Council. S/RES/822 (April 30, 1993), http://daccessdds.un.org/doc/UNDOC/GEN/N93/247/71/IMG/N9324771.pdf?OpenElement.

124. Liz Fuller, "Yeltsin, Ter-Petrosian Discuss Bilateral Relations, Karabakh," *RFE/RL News Brief* (May 26, 1993).

125. Liz Fuller, "Yeltsin, Aliev Meet," *RFE/RL Daily Report*, no. 171 (September 7, 1993).

126. Elizabeth Fuller, "The Transcaucasus: War, Turmoil, Economic Collapse," *RFE/RL Research Report* 3 (January 7, 1994): 54.

127. Joseph A Kechichian and Theodore W. Karasik, "The Crisis in Azerbaijan: How Clans Influence the Politics of an Emerging Republic," *Middle East Policy* 4 (September 1995): 64.

128. Ibid.

129. Elizabeth Fuller, "Russia, Turkey, Iran, and the Karabakh Mediation Process," *RFE/RL Research Report* 3 (February 25, 1993): 32.

130. Human Rights Watch/Helsinki, *Azerbaijan: Seven Years of Conflict in Nagorno-Karabakh* (New York: Human Rights Watch, 1994), 44.

131. Tamara Dragadze, "Conflict in the Transcaucasus and the Value of Inventory Control," *Jane's Intelligence Review* (February 1994): 71.

132. Fuller, "Russia, Turkey, Iran, and the Karabakh Mediation Process," 33.

133. Elizabeth Fuller, "The Karabakh Mediation Process: Grachev versus the CSCE?" *RFE/RL Research Report* 3 (June 10, 1994): 15.

134. Quoted in Fuller, "Russia, Turkey, Iran, and the Karabakh Mediation Process," 33.

135. Fuller, "The Karabakh Mediation Process: Grachev versus the CSCE?" 14.

136. Kechichian and Karasik, 63.

137. Ambassador Robert Shugarian of the Embassy of Armenia in Washington, D.C., in a speech at the Fletcher School of Law and Diplomacy, Medford, MA on April 16, 1996.

138. Joseph Masih, "Military Strategy in Nagorno-Karabakh," *Jane's Intelligence Review* (April 1994): 160.

139. Human Rights Watch/Helsinki, 4.
140. Masih, 160.
141. de Waal, 200–203
142. Human Rights Watch/Helsinki, 86–87n310.
143. Goltz, 111.
144. quoted in Ibid.
145. Felix Corley, "Nagorno-Karabakh—An Eyewitness Account," *Jane's Intelligence Review* (April 1994): 164.
146. Corley, 165.
147. de Waal, 199.
148. Ibid.
149. Corley, 165.
150. Ibid.
151. Kechichian and Karasik, 65.

CHAPTER 7

1. Gareth Stansfield and Hasem Ahmadzadeh, "Kurdish or Kurdistanis? Conceptualising Regionalism in the North of Iraq," in *An Iraq of Its Regions: Cornerstones of a Federal Democracy*, ed. Reidar Visser and Gareth Stansfield (New York: Columbia University Press, 2008), 133.

2. International Crisis Group, *Iraq and the Kurds: Resolving the Kirkuk Crisis*, Middle East Report no. 64 (19 April 2007), http://www.crisisgroup.org/library/documents/middle_east___north_africa/iraq_iran_gulf/64_iraq_and_the_kurds_resolving_the_kirkuk_crisis.pdf.

3. Mohammed M. A. Ahmed, "The Political Fallout of Ethnic Cleansing in Iraqi Kurdistan," in *The Kurdish Question and the 2003 Iraqi War*, ed. Mohammed M. A. Ahmed and Michael M. Gunter (Costa Mesa, CA: Mazda Publishers, Inc., 2005), 30–31.

4. David McDowall, *A Modern History of the Kurds* (New York: I.B. Taurus, 1996), 332.

5. Michael Gunter, *The Kurds of Iraq: Tragedy and Hope* (New York: St. Martin's Press, 1992), 17; and Nader Entessar, *Kurdish Ethnonationalism* (Boulder, CO: Lynne Rienner Publishers, Inc., 1992), 123.

6. Interviews with Kurdish sources, quoted in Mordechai Nisan, *Minorities in the Middle East: A History of Struggle and Self-Expression* (Jefferson, NC: McFarland & Company, Inc., 1991), 36–37.

7. Ahmed, "The Political Fallout of Ethnic Cleansing in Iraqi Kurdistan," 38.

8. McDowall notes that these numbers are impossible to verify. See McDowall, 339–340.

9. Entessar, *Kurdish Ethnonationalism*, 127; McDowell, 339; Gareth R. V. Stansfield, *Iraqi Kurdistan: Political Development and Emergent Democracy* (London: RoutledgeCurzon, 2003), 14–15.

10. Michael Collins Dunn, "The Kurdish 'Question': Is There an Answer? A Historical Overview," *Middle East Policy* 4 (September 1995): 81.

11. Robert Olson, "The Kurdish Question in the Aftermath of the Gulf War: Geopolitical and Geostrategic Changes in the Middle East." *Third World Quarterly* 13 (1992): 477. See also Kerim Yildiz, *The Kurds in Iraq: The Past, Present and Future* (London: Pluto Press, 2004), 25.

12. Entessar, *Kurdish Ethnonationalism*, 74.

13. For extensive documentation of the Anfal campaigns see Human Rights Watch/Middle East, *Iraq's Crime of Genocide: The Anfal Campaign Against the Kurds* (New Haven: Yale University Press, 1995).

14. Nader Entessar, "The Kurdish Mosaic of Discord," *Third World Quarterly* 11 (October 1989): 97.

15. Kurdish military forces are referred to as Peshmergas, literally "those who face death."

16. McDowall, 352–353 and 357–360.

17. Stansfield, *Iraqi Kurdistan*, 27.

18. McDowall, 360.

19. Entessar, "The Kurdish Mosaic of Discord," 87.

20. S. Siaband, "Mountains, My Home; an Analysis of the Kurdish Psychological Landscape," quoted in Entessar, "The Kurdish Mosaic of Discord," 87.

21. McDowall, 4.

22. Mehrdad R. Izady, *The Kurds: A Concise Handbook* (Washington, DC: Crane Russak, 1992), 13.

23. Joyce Blau, "The Poetry of Kurdistan: Language Embodies Kurdish National Unity," *The World & I* (August 1991): 624 and Nisan, 27–28.

24. Entessar, *Kurdish Ethnonationalism*, 74.

25. Pesh Merga (March and June 1978), quoted in Entessar, *Kurdish Ethnonationalism*, 8.

26. Olson, "The Kurdish Question in the Aftermath of the Gulf War," 476–477.

27. McDowall, 339.

28. McDowall, 340.

29. Ahmed, 39.

30. Entessar, *Kurdish Ethnonationalism*, 75.

31. Stansfield, *Iraqi Kurdistan*, 41.

32. Yildiz, 67.

33. Dunn, 75, and Michael M. Gunter, "The KDP-PUK Conflict in Northern Iraq," *The Middle East Journal* 50 (Spring 1996): 228.

34. Entessar, "The Kurdish Mosaic of Discord," 91.

35. McDowall, 304.

36. Stansfield, *Iraqi Kurdistan*, 69–70.

37. McDowall, 310.

38. McDowall, 311.

39. Entessar, *Kurdish Ethnonationalism*, 66.

40. Stansfield, *Iraqi Kurdistan*, 72.

41. Entessar, *Kurdish Ethnonationalism*, 66–67.

42. Edmund Ghareeb, *The Kurdish Question in Iraq* (Syracuse: Syracuse University Press, 1981), 41.

43. Entessar, *Kurdish Ethnonationalism*, 67.

44. McDowall, 317.

45. Jalal Talabani, quoted in Gunter, "The KDP-PUK Conflict," 228.

46. McDowall, 326.

47. Gunter, "The KDP-PUK Conflict," 228–229.

48. McDowall, 333.

49. Ibid.

50. Ibid., 336.

51. Ghareeb, 173.

52. McDowall, 343.

53. In 1979 the party resumed its old name.

54. The KDP-PL had three bases in Turkey, which Turkish security forces ignored in an effort to foster intra-Kurdish tensions. See McDowall, 344.

55. McDowall, 344–345.

56. Stansfield, *Iraqi Kurdistan*, 89.

57. The PUK splintered when the bulk of Askari's KSM marched out of Talabani's camp and allied themselves with another faction of the former KDP led by Mahmud Uthman, forming the Kurdistan Socialist Party (KSP).

58. McDowall, 345–346.

59. Quoted in McDowall, 347.

60. Entessar, 130.

61. Gunter, "The KDP-PUK Conflict," 231.

62. Masoud Barzani quoted in Gunter, "The KDP-PUK Conflict," 240.

63. McDowall, 303.

64. Ghareeb, 38.

65. See ibid., 68–69.

66. McDowall, 318.

67. Ibid., 320.

68. Ibid., 325–326.

69. Ibid., 326.

70. Ghareeb, 84.

71. Ibid., 82.

72. Ibid., 132.

73. McDowall, 330.

74. Entessar, *Kurdish Ethnonationalism*, 76.

75. Gunter, "The KDP-PUK Conflict," 230.

76. McDowall, 348–349.

77. Entessar, "The Kurdish Mosaic of Discord," 97.

78. Izzat Ibrahim, Deputy Chairman of the RCC, quoted in Gunter, *The Kurds of Iraq*, 49–50.

79. Horowitz, *Ethnic Groups in Conflict*, 29.

80. *The Treaty of Sèvres*, Section III, Articles 62 and 64, quoted in Kendal, "The Kurds under the Ottoman Empire," in *A People Without a Country: The Kurds and Kurdistan*, ed. Gerard Chaliand (New York: Olive Branch Press, 1993), 34.

81. *Anglo-Iraqi Joint Declaration* (December 24, 1922), quoted in Ismet Sheriff Vanly, "Kurdistan in Iraq," in *A People without a Country: the Kurds and Kurdistan*, ed. Gerard Chaliand, 139–193 (New York: Olive Branch Press, 1993), 146–147.

82. Vanly, "Kurdistan in Iraq," 148.

83. Entessar, *Kurdish Ethnonationalism*, 53.

84. Gunter, *The Kurds of Iraq*, 2.

85. *Article III, Provisional Constitution of the Republic of Iraq*, quoted in Vanly, "Kurdistan in Iraq," 150.

86. Entessar, *Kurdish Ethnonationalism*, 63.

87. Vanly, "Kurdistan in Iraq," 150.

88. Abd al Karim Qasim, quoted in McDowall, 308.

89. Vanly, "Kurdistan in Iraq," 151.

90. Ismet Cheriff Vanly, *The Revolution of Iraki Kurdistan* (Paris: Committee for the Defense of the Kurdish People's Rights, April 1965), 17.

91. McDowall, 314.

92. Agreement of March 7, 1963, quoted in Ghareeb, 59.

93. Ghareeb, 59.

94. Entessar, *Kurdish Ethnonationalism*, 65–66.

95. George S. Harris, "The Kurdish Conflict in Iraq," in *Ethnic Conflict in International Relations*, ed. Astri Suhrke and Lela Garner Noble (New York: Praeger, 1977), 75.

96. Entessar, *Kurdish Ethnonationalism*, 8 and 68; McDowall, 318.

97. McDowall, 319.

98. Ibid., 327.

99. Ibid.

100. Entessar, *Kurdish Ethnonationalism*, 71.

101. Stansfield, *Iraqi Kurdistan*, 75.

102. See Ghareeb, 105–129.

103. Entessar, *Kurdish Ethnonationalism*, 76.

104. McDowall, 336. See also Ghareeb, 157–160.

105. McDowall, 336.

106. Yildiz, 20.

107. Draft Constitution of Iraq. See "Special Bonus: Iraq's draft Constitution in English translation," *Middle East Review of International Affairs* 9 (September 2005), http://meria.idc.ac.il/journal/2005/issue3/Iraqiconstitution/constitution.html.

108. Gareth Stansfield, *Iraqi Kurdistan*, 35.

109. Jalal Talabani has referred to Kirkuk as the "Kurdish Jerusalem." See Luke Harding, "Kurdish Fighters Take Kirkuk," *The Guardian* (April 11. 2003), http://www.guardian. co.uk/world/2003/apr/11/iraq.kurds1. See also Michael M. Gunter and M. Hakan Yavuz, "The Continuing Crisis in Iraqi Kurdistan," *Middle East Policy* 12 (Spring 2005): 127.

110. Mohammad H. Malek, "Kurdistan in the Middle East Conflict," *New Left Review* 175 (May/June 1989): 83.

111. Entessar, *Kurdish Ethnonationalism*, 72.

112. Mulla Mustafa Barzani in an interview with Ghareeb before his death in Washington, D. C. (September 13, 1976). Quoted in Ghareeb, 159.

113. Ibid.

114. Ibid., 140.

115. McDowall, 368.

116. Ghareeb, 162.

117. McDowall, 337.

118. Yildiz, *The Kurds in Iraq*, 22.

119. McDowall, 352.

120. Entessar, *Kurdish Ethnonationalism*, 146. See also McDowall, 372.

121. Yildiz, 35.

122. Gunter, *The Kurds of Iraq*, 53.

123. Ibid., 55. See also Stansfield, *The Kurds in Iraq*, 95–96.

124. Ghareeb, 42.

125. Heraclides, *Self-Determination of Minorities*, 141.

126. Gunter, "The KDP-PUK Conflict," 229.

127. McDowall, 320.

128. Anthony Hyman, *Elusive Kurdistan: The Struggle for Recognition* (London: Centre for Security and Conflict Studies, 1988), 15.

129. McDowall, 320.

130. Ghareeb, 78.

131. Heraclides, *Self-Determination of Minorities*, 141.

132. Yildiz, 23.

133. Entessar, *Kurdish Ethnonationalism*, 118; Ghareeb, 142; and Gunter, *The Kurds of Iraq*, 127n24. Parastin has since been renamed Rechrastini Taybet. See Stansfield, *Iraqi Kurdistan*, 77.

134. Entessar, *Kurdish Ethnonationalism*, 118; Ghareeb, 142.

135. Heraclides, *Self-Determination of Minorities*, 144.

136. Martin van Bruinessen, *Agha, Shaikh and State: The Social and Political Structures of Kurdistan* (New Jersey: Zed Books Ltd., 1992), 42.

137. Heraclides, *Self-Determination of Minorities*, 143.

138. Ibid., 144.

139. McDowall, 384.

CHAPTER 8

1. Waltz, *Man, the State and War*, 15.

2. Rothschild, 118.

3. Russian Foreign Minister Sergei Lavrov noted that the world "can forget any talk about Georgia's territorial integrity." See Champion and Osborn, A6.

4. Akbar Ahmed, 8.

5. Waltz, *Man, the State and War*, 14.

Bibliography

Ahmed, Akbar S. "Ethnic Cleansing: A Metaphor for Our Time?" *Ethnic and Racial Studies* 18 (January 1995): 1–25.

Ahmed, Mohammed M. A., and Michael M. Gunter, eds. *The Kurdish Question and the 2003 Iraq War*. Costa Mesa, CA: Mazda Publishers, 2005.

Allcock, John B. "In Praise of Chauvinism: Rhetorics of Nationalism in Yugoslav Politics." *Third World Quarterly* 10 (October 1989): 208–222.

Altstadt, Audrey L. *The Azerbaijani Turks: Power and Identity Under Russian Rule*. Stanford, CA: Hoover Institution Press, 1992.

———. "Nagorno-Karabakh—'Apple of Discord' in the Azerbaijan SSR." *Central Asian Survey* 7, no. 4 (1988): 63–78.

Andrejevich, Milan. "Croatia Between Stability and Civil War (Part I)." *Report on Eastern Europe* 37 (September 14, 1990): 38–44.

———. "Milosevic's Speech at Kosovo Polje." *Radio Free Europe Research*, Yugoslav Situation Report 9 (July 20, 1989): 7–9.

———. "Reactions to Slovenia's Constitutional Amendments." *Radio Free Europe Research*, Yugoslav Situation Report 12 (October 23, 1989): 7–13.

———. "Resignations and Unrest in Vojvodina." *Radio Free Europe Research*, Yugoslav Situation Report 9 (October 11, 1988): 9–13.

———. "Serbia Accused of Interfering in Bosnian Affairs." *Radio Free Europe Research*, Yugoslav Situation Report 12 (October 23, 1989): 25–29.

———. "The Yugoslav Crisis and the National Question." *Radio Free Europe Research*, Yugoslav Situation Report 10 (August 17, 1989): 3–8.

Antic, Zdenko. "The Danger of Increasing Serbian Nationalism." *Radio Free Europe Research*, Yugoslav Background Report 63 (March 24, 1983): 1–7.

———. "The Serbian Question." *Radio Free Europe Research*, Yugoslav Situation Report 12 (December 23, 1988): 21–25.

———. "Unrest in Montenegro." *Radio Free Europe Research*, Yugoslav Situation Report 9 (October 11, 1988): 3–7.

———. "Yugoslav Government Concerned About Internal Security." *Radio Free Europe Research*, Yugoslav Background Report 150 (November 15, 1983): 1–3.

Appadurai, Arjun. "Dead Certainty: Ethnic Violence in the Era of Globalization." *Development and Change* 29 (1998): 905–925.

Arendt, Hannah. "Imperialism, Nationalism, Chauvinism." *The Review of Politics* 7 (October 1945): 441–463.

———. *The Origins of Totalitarianism*. San Diego, CA: Harcourt, Inc, 1968.

The Armenian Center for National and International Studies. *Nagorno Karabagh: A White Paper*. 2nd ed. Yerevan, Armenia: The Armenian Center for National and International Studies, 1997.

Banac, Ivo. "The Fearful Asymmetry of War: The Causes and Consequences of Yugoslavia's Demise." *Daedalus* 121 (Spring 1992): 141–174.

———. "Post-Communism as Post-Yugoslavism: The Yugoslav Non-Revolutions of 1989–1990." In *Eastern Europe in Revolution*, Ivo Banac, ed., 168–187. Ithaca, NY: Cornell University Press, 1992.

Bell-Fialkoff, Andrew. "A Brief History of Ethnic Cleansing." *Foreign Affairs* 72 (Summer 1993): 110–121.

Bennett, Christopher. *Yugoslavia's Bloody Collapse: Causes, Course and Consequences*. New York: New York University Press, 1995.

Bennigsen, Alexandre, and S. Enders Wimbush. *Muslims of the Soviet Empire: A Guide*. Bloomington: Indiana University Press, 1986.

Blau, Joyce. "The Poetry of Kurdistan Language Embodies Kurdish National Unity." *The World & I* 6 (August 1991): 623–637.

Boutwell, Jeffrey, and Michael T. Klare., eds. *Light Weapons and Civil Conflict: Controlling the Tools of Violence*. Lanhan: Rowman & Littlefield Publishers, Inc. 1999.

Brass, Paul R. *Ethnicity and Nationalism: Theory and Comparison*. New Delhi: Sage Publications, 1991.

Bremmer, Ian. "Reassessing Soviet Nationalities Theory." In *Nations and Politics in the Soviet Successor States*, Ian Bremmer and Ray Taras, eds. 3–26. Cambridge: Cambridge University Press, 1993.

Brock, Peter. "Greater Serbia vs the Greater Western Media." *Mediterranean Quarterly* 6 (Winter 1995): 49–67.

Brown, Cameron S. "Observations form Azerbaijan." *Middle East Review of International Affairs* 6, no. 4 (December 2002): 66–74.

Brown, Gordon. "Armenian Nationalism in a Socialist Century." In *Nationalism and the Breakup of an Empire: Russia and Its Periphery*, Miron Rezun, ed., 97–107. Westport, CT: Praeger, 1992.

Brown, Michael, Sean M. Lynn-Jones, and Steven Miller, eds. *Debating the Democratic Peace: An International Security Reader*. Cambridge, MA: The MIT Press, 1996.

Brzoska, Michael, and Frederic S. Pearson. *Arms and Warfare: Escalation, De-escalation, and Negotiation*. Columbia, SC: University of South Carolina Press, 1994.

Burg, Steven L. "The International Community and the Yugoslav Crisis." In *International Organizations and Ethnic Conflict*, Milton J. Esman and Shibley Telhami, eds., 235–271. Ithaca, NY: Cornell University Press, 1995.

Burg, Steven L., and Paul S. Shoup. *The War in Bosnia-Herzegovina: Ethnic Conflict and International Intervention*. Armonk, NY: M. E. Sharp, 1999.

Buzan, Barry. *People, States and Fear: An Agenda for International Security Studies in the Post–Cold War Era*. 2nd ed. New York: Harvester Wheatsheaf, 1991.

Byman, Daniel L. *Keeping the Peace: Lasting Solutions to Ethnic Conflicts.* Baltimore, MD: The Johns Hopkins University Press, 2002.

Carment, David. "The International Dimensions of Ethnic Conflict: Concepts, Indicators, and Theory." *Journal of Peace Research* 30 (1993): 137–150.

Carment, David, and Patrick James, eds. *Peace in the Midst of Wars: Preventing and Managing International Ethnic Conflicts.* Columbia: University of South Carolina Press, 1998.

Carment, David, and Patrick James. "Ethnic Conflict at the International Level: Theory and Evidence." In *Wars in the Midst of Peace: The International Politics of Ethnic Conflict*, David Carment and Patrick James, eds., 1–10. Pittsburgh, PA: University of Pittsburgh Press, 1997.

———. "Secession and Irredentia in World Politics: The Neglected Interstate Dimension." In *Wars in the Midst of Peace: The International Politics of Ethnic Conflict*, David Carment and Patrick James, eds., 194–231. Pittsburgh, PA: University of Pittsburgh Press, 1997.

———, eds. *Wars in the Midst of Peace: The International Politics of Ethnic Conflict.* Pittsburgh, PA: University of Pittsburgh Press, 1997.

Carment, David, Patrick James, and Zeynep Taydas. *Who Intervenes? Ethnic Conflict and Interstate Crisis.* Columbus: Ohio State University Press, 2006.

Cerovic, Stojan. "'Greater Serbia' and Its Discontents." In *Why Bosnia? Writings on the Balkan War*, Rabia Ali and Lawrence Lifshultz, eds., 259–267. Stony Creek, CT: The Pamphleteer's Press, Inc., 1993.

Champion, Marc, and Andrew Osborn. "Smoldering Feud, Then War: Tensions at Obscure Border Led to Georgia-Russia Clash." *The Wall Street Journal* (August 18, 2008): A1, A6.

Chapman, Malcolm, Maryon McDonald, and Elizabeth Tonkin, eds. *History and Ethnicity.* London: Routledge, 1989.

Chorbajian, Levon. "Introduction to the English Language Edition." In *The Caucasian Knot: The History and Geo-Politics of Nagorno-Karabagh*, Levon Chorbajian, Patrick Donabedian, and Claude Mutafian, eds.,1–50. London: Zed Books, 1994.

Chorbajian, Levon, Patrick Donabedian, and Claude Mutafian, eds. *The Caucasian Knot: The History and Geo-Politics of Nagorno-Karabagh.* London: Zed Books, 1994.

Cohen, Lenard J. "The Disintegration of Yugoslavia." *Current History* 91 (November 1992): 369–375.

Cohen, Philip J. *Serbia's Secret War: Propaganda and the Deceit of History.* College Station, TX: Texas A & M University Press, 1996.

Cole, August. "Attack on Georgia Gives Boost to Big U.S. Weapons Programs." *The Wall Street Journal* (August 18, 2008): A6.

Connor, Walker. *Ethnonationalism: The Quest for Understanding.* Princeton, NJ: Princeton University Press, 1994.

———. "A Nation is a Nation, is a State, is an Ethnic Group, is a . . ." *Ethnic and Racial Studies* 1 (October 1978): 377–400.

———. "Nation-Building or Nation-Destroying?" *World Politics* 24 (April 1972): 319–355.

Cooper, Robert, and Mats Berdal. "Outside Intervention in Ethnic Conflicts." *Survival* 35, no 1 (Spring 1993): 118–142.

Corley, Felix. "Nagorno-Karabakh—An Eyewitness Account." *Jane's Intelligence Review* (April 1994): 164–165.

Cornell, Svante E. *Small Nations and Great Powers: A Study of Ethnopolitical Conflict in the Caucasus.* Surrey, UK: Curzon Press, 2001.

Crnobrnja, Mihailo. *The Yugoslav Drama.* Montreal: McGill-Queen's University Press, 1994.

Daalder, Ivo H., and Michael E. O'Hanlon. *Winnning Ugly: NATO's War to Save Kosovo.* Washington, DC: Brookings Institution Press, 2000.

David, Steven R. "Internal War: Causes and Cures." *World Politics* 49, no 4 (1997): 552–576.

Davis, David R., Keith Jaggers, and Will H. Moore. "Ethnicity, Minorities, and International Conflict." In *Wars in the Midst of Peace: The International Politics of Ethnic Conflict,* David Carment and Patrick James, eds., 148–163. Pittsburgh, PA: University of Pittsburgh Press, 1997.

de Nevers, Renee. "Democratization and Ethnic Conflict." *Survival* 35 (Summer 1993): 31–48.

Denitch, Bogdan. *Ethnic Nationalism: The Tragic Death of Yugoslavia.* Minneapolis: University of Minnesota Press, 1994.

Devlin, Kevin. "Armenian Envoys on Crisis Meeting with Gorbachev." *Radio Free Europe Research,* USSR Background Report 42 (March 15, 1988): 1–5.

———. "*L'Unita* on 'Armenian Documents Sent to Kremlin.'" *Radio Free Europe Research,* USSR Background Report 39 (March 11, 1988): 1–5.

de Waal, Thomas. *Black Garden: Armenia and Azerbaijan through Peace and War.* New York: New York University Press, 2003.

Diamond, Larry, and Marc F. Plattner, eds. *Nationalism, Ethnic Conflict, and Democracy.* Baltimore, MD: The John Hopkins University Press, 1994.

Donabedian, Patrick "The History of Karabagh from Antiquity to the Twentieth Century." In *The Caucasian Knot: The History and Geo-Politics of Nagorno-Karabagh,* Levon Chorbajian, Patrick Donabedian, and Claude Mutafian, eds., 51–108. London: Zed Books, 1994.

Dorff, Robert H. "Failed States after 9/11: What Did We Know and What Have We Learned?" *International Studies Perspectives* 6, no. 1 (February 2005): 20–34.

Douglass, William A. "A Critique of Recent Trends in the Analysis of Ethnonationalism." *Ethnic and Racial Studies* 11 (April 1988): 192–206.

Dragadze, Tamara. "Conflict in the Transcaucasus and the Value of Inventory Control." *Jane's Intelligence Review* (February 1994): 71–73.

Dragnich, Alex N. *Yugoslavia's Disintegration and the Struggle for Truth.* East European Monographs CDXXXVI. New York: Columbia University Press, 1995.

Dudwick, Nora. "Armenia: The Nation Awakens." In *Nations and Politics in the Soviet Successor States,* Ian Bremmer and Ray Taras, eds., 261–287. Cambridge: Cambridge University Press, 1993.

Dunn, Michael Collins. "The Kurdish 'Question': Is There an Answer? A Historical Overview." *Middle East Policy* 4 (September 1995): 72–86.

Duyvesteyn, Isabelle, and Jan Angstrom, eds. *Rethinking the Nature of War.* London: Frank Cass, 2005.

Edmonds, C. J. "Kurdish Nationalism." *Journal of Contemporary History* 6, no 1 (1971): 87–107.

Entessar, Nader. *Kurdish Ethnonationalism.* Boulder, CO: Lynne Rienner Publishers, Inc., 1992.

———. "The Kurdish Mosaic of Discord." *Third World Quarterly* 11 (October 1989): 83–100.

———. "The Kurds in Post-Revolutionary Iran and Iraq." *Third World Quarterly* 6 (October 1984): 911–933.

Esman, Milton J. *Ethnic Politics.* Ithaca, NY: Cornell University Press, 1994.

————. "Political and Psychological Factors in Ethnic Conflict." In *Conflict and Peacemaking in Multiethnic Societies*, Joseph V. Montville, ed., 53–64. Lexington, MA: Lexington Books, 1990.

Esman, Milton J., and Shibley Telhami, eds. *International Organizations and Ethnic Conflict.* Ithaca, NY: Cornell University Press, 1995.

Farah, Douglas. "The Role of Conflict Diamonds in Al-Qaeda's Financial Structure," (January 4, 2004). http://programs.ssrc.org/gsc/gsc_activities/farah/.

Folz, William. "External Causes." In *Revolution and Political Change in the Third World*, Barry M Schutz and Robert O. Slater, eds., 54–64. Boulder, CO: Lynn Reinner, 1990.

Foreign Policy. "The Failed State Index 2007" (July/August 2007), http://www.foreignpolicy. com/story/cms.php?story_id=3865 (accessed January 26, 2008).

Fraser, Niall M., Keith W. Hipel, John Jaworsky, and Ralph Zuljan. "A Conflict Analysis of the Armenian-Azerbaijani Dispute." *Journal of Conflict Resolution* 34 (December 4, 1990): 652–677.

Frelick, Bill. *Faultlines of Nationality Conflict: Refugees and Displaced Persons From Armenia and Azerbaijan.* Immigration and Refugee Services of America, 1994.

Fuller, Elizabeth. "Aliev in Moscow." *RFE/RL Daily Report*, no. 176 (September 6, 1993).

————. "Armenia, Azerbaijan Accept Tripartite Peace Plan." *RFE/RL News Brief* (May 26, 1993).

————. "The Karabakh Mediation Process: Grachev versus the CSCE?" *RFE/RL Research Report* 3 (June 10, 1994): 13–17.

————. "Nagorno-Karabakh: Internal Conflict Becomes International." *RFE/RL Research Report* 1 (March 13, 1992): 1–5.

————. "The Ongoing Political Power Struggle in Azerbaijan." *RFE/RL Research Report* 1 (May 1, 1992): 11–13.

————. "Russia, Turkey, Iran, and the Karabakh Mediation Process." *RFE/RL Research Report* 3 (February 25, 1994): 31–36.

————. "Russia's Diplomatic Offensive in the Transcaucasus." *RFE/RL Research Report* 2 (October 1, 1993): 30–34.

————. "Supreme Soviet Presidium Debates Nagorno-Karabakh." *Radio Liberty Research* RL 314/88 (July 20, 1988): 1–6.

————. "The Transcaucasus: War, Turmoil, Economic Collapse." *RFE/RL Research Report* 3 (January 7, 1994): 51–58.

————. "Yeltsin, Aliev Meet." *RFE/RL Daily Report*, no. 171 (September 7, 1993).

————. "Yeltsin, Ter-Petrosian Discuss Bilateral Relations, Karabakh." *RFE/RL News Brief* (May 26, 1993).

Fuller, Elizabeth, and Philip Hanson. "The Nagorno-Karabakh Package." *Radio Liberty Research* 132/88 (March 29, 1988): 1–3.

Fuller, Graham E. "The Fate of the Kurds." *Foreign Affairs* (Spring 1993): 108–121.

Gagnon, V. P. "Ethnic Nationalism and International Conflict: The Case of Serbia." *International Security* 19 (Winter 1994/1995): 130–166.

————. "Historical Roots of the Yugoslav Conflict." In *International Organizations and Ethnic Conflict*, Milton J. Esman and Shibley Telhami, eds., 179–197. Ithaca, NY: Cornell University Press, 1995.

————. *The Myth of Ethnic War: Serbia and Croatia in the 1990s.* Ithaca, NY: Cornell University Press, 2004.

————. "Serbia's Road to War." *Journal of Democracy* 5 (Spring 1994): 117–131.

Gamaghelyan, Philip. "Nagorno-Karabakh Conflict: Intractable?" *Peace and Conflict Monitor* (July 2005): 3.

Gellner, Ernest. *Nations and Nationalism.* Ithaca, NY: Cornell Unviersity Press, 1983.

Ghareeb, Edmund. *The Kurdish Question in Iraq.* Syracuse: Syracuse University Press, 1981.

Goltz, Thomas. "Letter From Eurasia: The Hidden Russian Hand." *Foreign Policy* 92 (Fall 1993): 92–116.

Goose, Stephen D., and Frank Smyth. "Arming Genocide in Rwanda." *Foreign Affairs* 73 (September/October 1994): 86–96.

Gülalp, Haldun. "Introduction: Citizenship vs. Nationality?" In *Citzenship and Ethnic Conflict: Challenging the Nation-State,* Haldun Gülalp, ed., 1–18. Oxon and New York: Routledge, 2006.

Gunter, Michael M. "A *de facto* Kurdish State in Northern Iraq." *Third World Quarterly* 14, no 3 (1993): 295–319.

———. "The KDP-PUK Conflict in Northern Iraq." *The Middle East Journal* 50 (Spring 1996): 225–241.

———. *The Kurds of Iraq: Tragedy and Hope.* New York: St. Martin's Press, 1992.

Gunter, Michael M., and M. Hakan Yavuz. "The Continuing Crisis in Iraqi Kurdistan." *Middle East Policy* 12 (Spring 2005): 122–133.

Guroian, Vigen. "Faith, Church and Nationalism in Armenia." *Nationalities Papers* 20 (Spring 1992): 31–51.

Gurr, Ted Robert. "The Internationalization of Protracted Communal Conflicts since 1945: Which Groups, Where, and How." In *The Internationalization of Communal Strife,* Manus I. Midlarsky, ed., 3–26. New York: Routledge, 1993.

———. *Minorities at Risk: A Global View of Ethnopolitical Conflicts.* Washington, DC: United States Institute of Peace, 1993.

Hanlon, Querine H. "Globalization and the Transformation of Armed Groups." In *Armed Groups: Studies in National Security, Counterterrorism, and Counterinsurgency,* Jeffrey H. Norwitz, ed., 115–125. Newport: Naval War College Press, 2008.

Harding, Luke. "Kurdish Fighters Take Kirkuk." *The Guardian* (April 11, 2003), http://www.guardian.co.uk/world/2003/apr/11/iraq.kurds1.

Harris, George S. "The Kurdish Conflict in Iraq." In *Ethnic Conflict in International Relations,* Astri Suhrke and Lela Garner Noble, eds., 68–92. New York: Praeger, 1977.

Heraclides, Alexis. "Conflict Resolution, Ethnonationalism and the Middle East Impasse." *Journal of Peace Research* 26 (May 1989): 197–212.

———. *The Self-Determination of Minorities in International Politics.* London: Frank Cass and Company, Limited, 1991.

Hewitt, J. Joseph, Jonathon Wilkenfeld, and Ted Robert Gurr. *Peace and Conflict 2008: Executive Summary.* College Park, MD: Center for International Development and Conflict Management, 2008. http://www.cidcm.umd.edu/pc/executive_summary/pc_es _20070613.pdf.

Hill, Ronald J. "Managing Ethnic Conflict." *The Journal of Communist Studies* 9 (March 1993): 57–74.

Hill, Stuart, and Donald Rothchild. "The Contagion of Political Conflict in Africa and the World." *Journal of Conflict Resolution* 30 (December 1986): 716–735.

Hobsbawm, Eric, and Terence Ranger, eds. *The Invention of Tradition.* Cambridge: Cambridge University Press, 1992.

Holsti, Kalevi J. *The State, War, and the State of War.* Cambridge: Cambrige University Press, 1996.

Horowitz, Donald L. *The Deadly Ethnic Riot*. Berkeley: University of California Press, 2001.
———. "Democracy in Divided Societies." In *Nationalism, Ethnic Conflict, and Democracy*, Larry Diamond and Marc F. Plattner, eds., 35–55. Baltimore, MD: The Johns Hopkins University Press, 1994.
———. *Ethnic Groups in Conflict*. Berkeley, CA: University of California Press, 1985.
———. "How to Begin Thinking Comparatively About Soviet Ethnic Problems." In *Thinking Theoretically About Soviet Nationalities: History and Comparison in the Study of the USSR*, Alexander J. Motyl, ed., 9–21. New York: Columbia University Press, 1992.
———. "Patterns of Ethnic Separatism." *Comparative Study of Society and History* 23 (April 1981): 165–195.
Hovannisian, Raffi K. "Prospects for Peace and Security for Armenia and the Caucasus." Lecture presented at the Fletcher School of Law and Diplomacy, Tufts University, Medford, MA, September 16, 1991.
Hovannisian, Richard G. "Caucasian Armenia Between Imperial and Soviet Rule: The Interlude of National Independence." In *Transcaucasia: Nationalism and Social Change*, Ronald Grigor Suny, ed., 259–292. Ann Arbor: University of Michigan Slavic Publications, 1983.
Human Rights Watch/Helsinki. *Azerbaijan: Seven Years of Conflict in Nagorno-Karabakh*. New York: Human Rights Watch, 1994.
Human Rights Watch/Middle East. *Iraq's Crime of Genocide: The Anfal Campaign Against the Kurds*. New Haven, CT: Yale University Press, 1995.
Hunter, Shireen T. *The Transcaucasus in Transition: Nation-building and Conflict*. Washington, DC: The Center for Strategic and International Studies, 1994.
Huntington, Samuel P. "The Clash of Civilizations?" *Foreign Affairs* 72 (Summer 1993): 22–49.
Hyman, Anthony. *Elusive Kurdistan: The Struggle for Recognition*. London: The Centre for Security and Conflict Studies, 1988.
International Crisis Group. *Iraq and the Kurds: Resolving the Kirkuk Crisis*. Middle East Report no. 64 (April 19, 2007). http://www.crisisgroup.org/library/documents/middle_east___north_africa/iraq_iran_gulf/64_iraq_and_the_kurds_resolving_the_kirkuk_crisis.pdf.
Ishiyama, John. "Does Globalization Breed Ethnic Conflict?" *Nationalism and Ethnic Politics* 9 (2004): 1–23.
Izady, Mehrdad R. *The Kurds: A Concise Handbook*. Washington DC: Crane Russak, 1992.
Jackson, Robert H. *Quasi-States: Sovereignty, International Relations and the Third World*. Cambridge: Cambridge University Press, 1990.
Judah, Tim. *Kosovo: War and Revenge*. 2nd ed. New Haven, CT: Yale University Press, 2002.
———. *The Serbs: History, Myth & Destruction of Yugoslavia*. 2nd. ed. New Haven, CT: Yale University Press, 2000.
Kaldor, Mary. "Elaborating the 'New War' Thesis." In *Rethinking the Nature of War*, Isabelle Duyvesteyn and Jan Angstrom, eds., 210–224. London: Frank Cass, 2005.
———. *New and Old Wars: Organized Violence in a Global Era*. Stanford, CA: Stanford University Press, 2001.
Karp, Aaron. "Arming Ethnic Conflict." *Arms Control Today* 23, no 7 (September 1993): 8–13.
Kasfir, Nelson. "Domestic Anarchy, Security Dilemmas and Violent Predation." In *When States Fail: Causes and Consequences*, Robert I. Rotberg, ed., 53–76. Princeton, NJ: Princeton University Press, 2004.

Kaufman, Stuart J. "An 'International' Theory of Inter-Ethnic War." *Review of International Studies* 22 (1996): 149–171.

———. *Modern Hatreds: The Symbolic Politics of Ethnic War*. Ithaca, NY: Cornell University Press, 2001.

Kazemzadeh, Firuz. *The Struggle for Transcaucasia, 1917–1921*. Oxford: George Ronald, 1951.

Kazimirov, V. "A History of the Karabakh Conflict." *International Affairs* (Moscow) 42, no 3 (1996): 182–195.

Kechichian, Joseph A., and Theodore W. Karasik. "The Crisis in Azerbaijan: How Clans Influence the Politics of an Emerging Republic." *Middle East Policy* 4 (September 1995): 57–71.

Kendal. "The Kurds under the Ottoman Empire." In *A People Without a Country: The Kurds and Kurdistan*, Gerard Chaliand, ed., 11–37. New York: Olive Branch Press, 1993.

Klare, Michael T. "Awash in Armaments." *Harvard International Review* 17 (Winter 1994/1995): 24–28.

———. "The New Arms Race: Light Weapons and International Security." *Current History* 96, no. 609 (April 1997): 173–178.

Lake, David A., and Donald Rothchild, eds. *The International Spread of Ethnic Conflict: Fear, Diffusion and Escalation*. Princeton, NJ: Princeton University Press, 1998.

———. "Spreading Fear: The Genesis of Transnational Ethnic Conflict." In *The International Spread of Ethnic Conflict: Fear, Diffusion and Escalation*, David A. Lake and Donald Rothchild, eds., 3–32. Princeton, NJ: Princeton University Press, 1998.

Lendvai, Paul. "Yugoslavia without Yugoslavs: The Roots of the Crisis." *International Affairs* 67 (April 1981): 251–261.

Libaridian, Gerard J., ed. The *Karabagh File: Documents and Facts on the Question of Mountainous Karabagh 1918–1988*. Cambridge, MS: The Zoryan Institute, 1988.

MacDonald, Charles G. "The Kurds." In *The Ethnic Dimension in International Relations*, Bernard Schechterman and Martin Slann, eds., 123–140. Westport, CT: Praeger, 1993.

Malcolm, Noel. *Kosovo: A Short History*. New York: Harper Perennial, 1999.

Malek, Mohammad H. "Kurdistan in the Middle East Conflict." *New Left Review* 175 (May/June 1989): 79–94.

Maoz, Zeev. "Domestic Political Change and Strategic Response: The Impact of Domestic Conflict on State Behavior, 1816–1986." In *Wars in the Midst of Peace: The International Politics of Ethnic Conflict*, David Carment and Patrick James, eds., 116–147. Pittsburgh, PA: University of Pittsburgh Press, 1997.

Markotich, Stan. "Croatia's Krajina Serbs." *RFE/RL Research Report* 2 (October 15, 1993): 5–10.

———. "Ethnic Serbs in Tudjman's Croatia." *RFE/RL Research Report* 2 (September 24, 1993): 28–33.

Marr, Phebe. *The Modern History of Iraq*. 2nd. ed. Boulder, CO: Westview Press, 2004.

Marshall, Monty G. "States at Risk: Ethnopolitics in the Multinational States of Eastern Europe." In Ted Robert Gurr, *Minorities at Risk: A Global View of Ethnopolitical Conflicts*, 173–216. Washington, DC: United States Institute of Peace, 1993.

Marshall, Monty G., and Ted Robert Gurr. *Peace and Conflict 2005: A Global Survey of Armed Conflicts, Self-Determination Movements, and Democracy*. College Park, MD: Center for International Development and Conflict Management, 2005.

Masih, Joseph. "Military Strategy in Nagorno-Karabakh." *Jane's Intelligence Review* (April 1994): 160–163.

Mayall, James, and Mark Simpson. "Ethnicity is Not Enough: Reflections on Protracted Secessionism in the Third World." *International Journal of Comparative Sociology* 33 (1992): 5–25.

Maynes, Charles William. "Containing Ethnic Conflict." *Foreign Policy* 90 (Spring 1993): 3–21.

McDowall, David. *A Modern History of the Kurds.* New York: I. B. Tauris, 1996.

McMahon, Robert. "Yugoslavia: Belgrade Rejoins UN, Opening Up New Problems." *Radio Free Europe/Radio Liberty* (February 11, 2000). http://www.rferl.org/features/2000/110022220000201812.asp.

Mihailovic, Kosta, and Vasilije Krestic. *Memorandum of the Serbian Academy of Sciences and Arts: Answers to Criticisms.* Belgrade: Serbian Academy of Sciences and Arts, 1995. http://www.rastko.org.yu/istorija/iii/memorandum.pdf.

Mihajlov, Mihajlo. "Can Yugoslavia Survive?" *Journal of Democracy* 2 (Spring 1991): 79–91.

Montville, Joseph V., ed. *Conflict and Peacemaking in Multiethnic Societies.* Lexington, MA: Lexington Books, 1990.

Moore, Patrick. "Yugoslavia: Ethnic Tension Erupts into Civil War." *RFE/RL Research Report* 1 (January 3, 1992): 68–73.

———. "Yugoslavia's 'Serbian Question.'" *Radio Free Europe Research,* Yugoslav Background Report 140 (July 22, 1988): 1–5.

Motyl, Alexander J., ed. *Thinking Theoretically About Soviet Nationalities: History and Comparison in the Study of the USSR.* New York: Columbia University Press, 1992.

Münkler, Herfried. *The New Wars.* Patrick Cammiller, trans. Cambridge: Polity Press, 2005.

Mutafian, Claude. "Karabagh in the Twentieth Century." In *The Caucasian Knot: The History and Geo-Politics of Nagorno-Karabagh,* Levon Chorbajian, Patrick Donabedian, and Claude Mutafian, eds., 109–170. London: Zed Books, 1994.

Nagel, Joane, and Brad Whorton. "Ethnic Conflict and the World System: International Competition in Iraq (1961–1991) and Angola (1974–1991)." *Journal of Political and Military Sociology* 20 (Summer 1992): 1–35.

Nahaylo, Bohdan, and Victor Swoboda. *Soviet Disunion: A History of the Nationalities Problem in the USSR.* New York: The Free Press, 1989.

Nisan, Mordechai. *Minorities in the Middle East: A History of Struggle and Self-Expression.* Jefferson, SC: McFarland & Company, Inc., 1991.

Nissman, David. "The National Reawakening of Azerbaijan." *The World & I* (February 1992): 80–85.

Office of the High Commissioner for Human Rights. *Convention on the Prevention and Punishment of the Crime of Genocide.* http://www.unhchr.ch/html/menu3/b/p_genoci.htm.

Olson, Robert. "The Creation of a Kurdish State in the 1990's?" *Journal of South Asian and Middle Eastern Studies* 15 (Summer 1992): 1–25.

———. "The Kurdish Question in the Aftermath of the Gulf War: Geopolitical and Geostrategic Changes in the Middle East." *Third World Quarterly* 13 (1992): 475–499.

Olson, Wm. J. "The New World Disorder: Governability and Development." In *Gray Area Phenomena: Confronting the New World Disorder,* Max Manwaring, ed., 3–32. Boulder, CO: Westview Press, 1994.

Owen, John M. "Iraq and Democratic Peace." *Foreign Affairs* 84, no 6 (November/December 2005): 122–127.

Perica, Vjekoslav. *Balkan Idols: Religion and Nationalism in Yugoslav States.* Oxford: Oxford University Press, 2002.

Petersen, Roger D. *Understanding Ethnic Violence: Fear, Hatred and Resentment in Twentieth-Century Eastern Europe.* Cambridge: Cambridge University Press, 2002.

"Petition from the Armenians of Mountainous Karabagh to Prime Minister Nikita Krushchev." Document 27. In *The Karabagh File: Documents and Facts on the Question of Mountainous Karabagh 1918–1988*, Gerard J. Libaridian, ed., 42–48. Cambridge, MS: The Zoryan Institute, 1988.

Posen, Barry R. "The Security Dilemma and Ethnic Conflict." *Survival* 35 (Spring 1993): 27–47.

Rae, Heather. *State Identities and the Homogenisation of Peoples.* Cambridge: Cambridge University Press, 2002.

Ramet, Sabrina Petra. *Balkan Babel: The Disintegration of Yugoslavia from the Death of Tito to Ethnic War.* 2nd ed. Boulder, CO: Westview Press, 1996.

———. *Nationalism and Federalism in Yugoslavia: 1962–1991.* 2nd ed. Bloomington: Indiana University Press, 1992.

———. "War in the Balkans." *Foreign Affairs* 71 (Fall 1991): 79–98.

Ranstorp, Magnus, and Gus Xhudo. "A Threat to Europe? Middle East Ties with the Balkans and Their Impact Upon Terrorist Activity throughout the Region." *Terrorism and Political Violence* 6 (Summer 1994): 196–223.

Reiquam, Steve. "Emigration and Demography in Kosovo." *Radio Free Europe Research*, Yugoslav Background Report 186 (August 4, 1983): 1–6.

Rieff, David. "Nagorno-Karabakh: Case Study in Ethnic Strife." *Foreign Affairs* 76 (March 1997): 118–131.

Rotberg, Robert I. "The Failure and Collapse of Nation-States: Breakdown, Prevention, and Repair." In *When States Fail: Causes and Consequences*, Robert I. Rotberg, ed., 1–50. Princeton, NJ: Princeton University Press, 2004.

Rotberg, Robert I., ed. *When States Fail: Causes and Consequences.* Princeton, NJ: Princeton Unversity Press, 2004.

Rothchild, Donald, and David A. Lake. "Containing Fear: The Management of Transnational Ethnic Conflict." In *The International Spread of Ethnic Conflict: Fear, Diffusion and Escalation*, David A. Lake and Donald Rothchild, eds., 203–226. Princeton, NJ: Princeton University Press, 1998.

Rothschild, Joseph. *Ethnopolitics: A Conceptual Framework.* New York: Columbia University Press, 1981.

Russett, Bruce. *Grasping the Democratic Peace: Principles for a Post–Cold War World.* Princeton, NJ: Princeton University Press, 1993.

Saideman, Stephen M. "Discrimination in Interational Relations: Analyzing External Support for Ethnic Groups." *Journal of Peace Research* 39 (2002): 27–50.

———. "Is Pandora's Box Half Empty or Half Full? The Limited Virulence of Secessionism and the Domestic Sources of Integration." In *The International Spread of Ethnic Conflict: Fear, Diffusion and Escalation*, David A. Lake and Donald Rothchild, eds., 127–150. Princeton, NJ: Princeton University Press, 1998.

Saroyan, Mark. "'The Karabakh Syndrome' in Azerbaijani Politics." *Problems of Communism* 34 (September/October, 1990): 14–29.

Schindler, John R. *Unholy Terror: Bosnia, al-Qa'ida, and the Rise of Global Jihad.* St. Paul, MN: Zenith Press, 2007.

Schwandner-Sievers, Stephanie, and Bernd J. Fischer, eds. *Albanian Identities: Myth and History.* Bloomington: Indiana University Press, 2002.

Short, Martin, and Anthony McDermott. *The Kurds.* Rev. ed. London: Minority Rights Group, June 1975.

Shugarian, Rouben. Armenian Ambassador to Washington DC. Lecture at the Fletcher School, Program on Southwest Asia and Islamic Civilization Executive Series, Tufts University, Medford, MA, April 16, 1996.

Shultz, Richard H., and Wm. J. Olson. *Ethnic and Religious Conflict: Emerging Threat to US Security.* Washington, DC: National Strategy Information Center, 1994.

Silber, Laura, and Allan Little. *Yugoslavia: Death of a Nation.* New York: TV Books, Inc., 1996.

Singleton, Fred. *A Short History of the Yugoslav Peoples.* Cambridge: Cambridge University Press, 1985.

Sislin, John. "Arms and Escalation in Ethnic Conflict: The Case of Sri Lanka." *International Studies Perspectives* 7 (2006): 137–158.

———. "Arms as Influence: The Determinants of Successful Influence." *The Journal of Conflict Resolution* 38 (December 1994): 665–689.

Sislin, John, and Frederic S. Pearson. *Arms and Ethnic Conflict.* Lanham, MD: Rowman & Littlefield Publishers, Inc. 2001.

Sislin, John, Frederic S. Pearson, Jocelyn Boryczka, and Jeffrey Weigand. "Patterns in Arms Acquisitions by Ethnic Groups in Conflict." *Security Dialogue* 29, no 4 (1998): 393–408.

Smith, Anthony D. "The Ethnic Sources of Nationalism." *Survival* 35 (Spring 1993): 48–62.

Smith, Rupert. *The Utility of Force: The Art of War in the Modern World.* New York: Alfred A. Knopf, 2007.

Snyder, Jack. *From Voting to Violence: Democratization and Nationalist Conflict.* New York: W. W. Norton & Company, Inc., 2000.

Snyder, Louis L. "Nationalism and the Flawed Concept of Ethnicity." *Canadian Review of Studies in Nationalism* 10 (Fall 1983): 253–265.

Soeters, Joseph L. *Ethnic Conflict and Terrorism: The Origins and Dynamics of Civil Wars.* London: Routledge, 2005.

"Special Bonus: Iraq's Draft Constitution in English Translation." *Middle East Review of International Affairs* 9 (September 2005). http://meria.idc.ac.il/journal/2005/issue3/Iraqiconstitution/constitution.html.

Stack, John, Jr. "The Ethnic Challenge to International Relations Theory." In *Wars in the Midst of Peace: The International Politics of Ethnic Conflict,* David Carment and Patrick James, eds., 11–25. Pittsburgh, PA: University of Pittsburgh Press, 1997.

Stansfield, Gareth R. V. *Iraqi Kurdistan: Political Development and Emergent Democracy.* London: RoutledgeCurzon, 2003.

Stansfield, Gareth R. V., and Hasem Ahmadzadeh. "Kurdish or Kurdistanis? Conceptualising Regionalism in the North of Iraq." In *An Iraq of Its Regions: Cornerstones of a Federal Democracy,* Reidar Visser and Gareth Stansfield, eds., 123–149. New York: Columbia University Press, 2008.

Stofft, William A., and Gary L. Guertner. "Ethnic Conflict: The Perils of Military Intervention." *Parameters* 25 (Spring 1995): 30–42.

Suhrke, Astri, and Lela Garner Noble, eds. *Ethnic Conflict in International Relations.* New York: Praeger, 1977.

Suny, Ronald. *Looking Toward Ararat: Armenia in Modern History.* Bloomington: Indiana University Press, 1993.

———. "Nationalist and Ethnic Unrest in the Soviet Union." *World Policy Journal* 6 (Summer 1989): 503–528.

———. "The Revenge of the Past: Socialism and Ethnic Conflict in Transcaucasia." *New Left Review* 184 (November/December 1990): 5–34.

Swietochowski, Tadeusz. "National Consciousness and Political Orientations in Azerbaijan, 1905–1920." In *Transcaucasia: Nationalism and Social Change*, Ronald Grigor Suny, ed., 209–232. Ann Arbor: University of Michigan Slavic Publications, 1993.

———. *Russian Azerbaijan, 1905–1920: The Shaping of National Identity in a Muslim Community*. Cambridge: Cambridge University Press, 1985.

Tambiah, Stanley J. "Ethnic Conflict in the World Today." *American Ethnologist* 16 (May 1989): 335–349.

Taras, Raymond C., and Rajat Ganguly. *Understanding Ethnic Conflict: The International Dimension*. 3rd. ed. New York: Longman, 2006.

Tilly, Charles. *The Politics of Collective Violence*. Cambridge: Cambridge University Press, 2003.

Toft, Monica Duffy. *The Geography of Ethnic Conflict*. Princeton, NJ: Princeton University Press, 2003.

United Nations Security Council. *S/RES/1199*, (September 23, 1998). http://www.un.org/peace/kosovo/98sc1199.htm.

United Nations Security Council. *Press Release SC/6562*, 3918th Meeting (PM) (August 24, 1998). http://www.un.org/News/Press/docs/1998/19980824.sc6562.html.

United Nations Security Council. S/RES/822 (April 30, 1993). <http://daccessdds.un.org/doc/UNDOC/GEN/N93/247/71/IMG/N9324771.pdf?OpenElement>

van Bruinessen, Martin. *Agha, Shaikh and State: The Social and Political Structures of Kurdistan*. New Jersey: Zed Books, Ltd., 1992.

Van Creveld, Martin. *The Transformation of War*. New York: The Free Press, 1991.

Vanly, Ismet Sheriff. "Kurdistan in Iraq." In *A People Without a Country: The Kurds and Kurdistan*, Gerard Chaliand, ed., 139–193. New York: Olive Branch Press, 1993.

———. *The Revolution of Iraki Kurdistan*. Paris: Committee for the Defense of the Kurdish People's Rights, April 1965.

Vaserman, Arie, and Rami Ginat. "National, Territorial or Religious Conflict? The Case of Nagorno-Karabakh." *Studies in Conflict and Terrorism* 17 (October–December 1994): 345–363.

Vasquez, John A. "Factors Related to the Contagion and Diffusion of International Violence." In *The Internationalization of Communal Strife*, Manus I. Midlarsky, ed., 149–172. New York: Routledge, 1993.

Vego, Milan. "The Army of Bosnia and Herzegovina." *Jane's Intelligence Review* (February 1993): 63–66.

———. "The Army of Serbian Krajina." *Jane's Intelligence Review* (October 1993): 438–443.

Verwimp, Philip. "The Croatian Army." *Jane's Intelligence Review* (May 1993): 203–210.

———. "Machetes and Firearms: The Organization of Massacres in Rwanda." *Journal of Peace Research* 34, no. 5 (2006): 5–22.

Visser, Reidar, and Gareth Stansfield, eds. *An Iraq of Its Regions: Cornerstones of a Federal Democracy*. New York: Columbia University Press, 2008.

Waltz, Kenneth N. *Man, the State and War: A Theoretical Analysis*. New York: Columbia University Press, 1959.

———. *Theory of International Politics*. New York: McGraw Hill, 1979.

Weiner, Myron. "Peoples and States in a New Ethnic Order?" *Third World Quarterly* 13, no 2 (1992): 317–333.

"Will Nagorno-Karabakh Lead to War?" *The Estimate* 4 (January 3–16, 1993): 3.

Wilmer, Franke. *The Social Construction of Man, the State, and War: Identity, Conflict and Violence in the Former Yugoslavia.* London: Routledge, 2002.

Wimmer, Andreas. "Democracy and Ethno-Religious Conflict in Iraq." *Survival* 45, no 4 (December 2003): 111–134.

———. *Nationalist Exclusion and Ethnic Conflict: Shadows of Modernity.* Cambridge: Cambridge University Press, 2002.

Wimmer, Andreas, Richard J. Goldstone, Donald Horowitz, Ulrike Joras, and Conrad Schetter, eds. *Facing Ethnic Conflicts: Toward a New Realism.* Lanham, MD: Rowman & Littlefield Publishers, Inc., 2004.

Wolff, Stefan. *Ethnic Conflict: A Global Perspective.* Oxford: Oxford University Press, 2006.

Woodward, Susan L. *Balkan Tragedy: Chaos and Dissolution After the Cold War.* Washington, DC: The Brookings Institution, 1995.

Yamskov, A. N. "Ethnic Conflict in the Transcaucasus: The Case of Nagorno-Karabakh." *Theory and Society* 20 (1991): 631–660.

Yapp, Malcolm. "'The Mice will Play': Kurds, Turks and the Gulf War." In *The Gulf War: Regional and International Dimensions,* Hanns W. Maull and Otto Pick, eds., 102–118. New York: St. Martin's Press, 1989.

Yildiz, Kerim. *The Kurds in Iraq: The Past, Present and Future.* London: Pluto Press, 2004.

Young, M. Crawford. "The National and Colonial Question and Marxism: A View from the South." In *Thinking Theoretically About Soviet Nationalities: History and Comparison in the Study of the USSR,* Alexander J. Motyl, ed., 67–97. New York: Columbia University Press, 1992.

Zametica, John. *The Yugoslav Conflict.* Adelphi Paper 270. London: International Institute for Strategic Studies, Summer 1992.

Zanga, Louis. "Rise of Tension in Kosovo Due to Migration." *Radio Free Europe Research,* Yugoslav Background Report 149 (June 28, 1983): 1–5.

Zartman, I. William. ed. *Collapsed States: The Disintegration and Restoration of Legitimate Authority.* Boulder, CO: Lynne Rienner Publishers, 1995.

———. "Internationalization of Communal Strife: Temptations and Opportunities of Triangulation." In *The Internationalization of Communal Strife,* Manus I. Midlarsky, ed., 27–42. New York: Routledge, 1993.

Zimmermann, Warren. *Origins of a Catastrophe: Yugoslavia and its Destroyers—America's Last Ambassador Tells What Happened and Why.* New York: Times Books, 1996.

Index

About the Author

QUERINE HANLON is Associate Professor of International Security Studies and Chair of the International Security Studies Department at National Defense University's College of International Security Affairs.